Kingston Frontenac Public Library

39011011420504

Portrait Gallery

EDWARD GREENFIELD

Portrait Gallery

A LIFE IN CLASSICAL MUSIC

First published 2014
by Elliott and Thompson Limited
27 John Street
London WC1N 2BX
www.eandtbooks.com

ISBN: 978-1-90965-358-0

Text © Edward Greenfield 2014

The Author has asserted his right under the Copyright, Designs and Patents Act, 1988, to be identified as Author of this Work.

All rights reserved. No part of this publication may be reproduced, stored in or introduced into a retrieval system, or transmitted, in any form, or by any means (electronic, mechanical, photocopying, recording or otherwise) without the prior written permission of the publisher. Any person who does any unauthorised act in relation to this publication may be liable to criminal prosecution and civil claims for damages.

Every effort has been made to trace copyright holders for extracts used within this book. Where this has not been possible, the publishers will be happy to credit them in future editions.

Plate section image credits:
Two photographs from the archive of Edward Greenfield. All other images are paintings by the artist Jeffrey Spedding.

9 8 7 6 5 4 3 2 1

A CIP catalogue record for this book is available from the British Library.

Typeset by Marie Doherty
Printed in the UK by TJ International

To my friends pictured within.

EG

Contents

Foreword

The relationship between performers and critics must and yet can never be totally harmonious. Sometimes artists can feel (rightly or wrongly) that critics are disparaging just for the sake of being critical, that the comments they make are gratuitous and unfair. Without ever suspending his analytical faculties or denying himself the right to speak his mind, Ted Greenfield has always been rather different from other critics. Yes, Ted can be harsh when he deems it appropriate, but he has always seen it as part of the responsibility of a reviewer – as part of his own, personal mission – to share with his readers the sheer joy that music can bring. This enthusiasm is a very rare commodity and, allied to his longevity, makes him a perfect evangelist for great music and great music-making. This book is full of gems and I am delighted that it should begin with this brief tribute to the kindest and most considerate of critics.

Sir Antonio Pappano

Editor's note

I first learned of Edward Greenfield's name as a scholar at Winchester College, where the pupils followed a time-honoured routine of avid self-improvement and learning from one another, as well as engaging with some of the finest teachers (or 'dons') whom any bright young neophyte might wish to encounter. My best friend at school was Yang Wern Ooi, a fine baritone and now a GP in the Cotswolds, who revered Dietrich Fischer-Dieskau and, when I evinced an interest in classical music, introduced me both to *Gramophone* magazine and to what I think was then termed the *Penguin Guide to Classical Records, Tapes and Compact Discs.* My addiction to the *Guide* was soon almost as compulsive as that to the music itself.

A decade later I was working for Sir Edward Heath, whose eightieth birthday was approaching, an occasion that he inevitably wished to have celebrated with musical events of various kinds. If memory serves, there were five concerts in the spring and summer of 1996, all of which Sir Edward conducted, in whole or in part. I had never thought to chance my arm as an impresario, but in planning this extravaganza I was fortunate to be able to count upon the advice of a long-standing friend and counsellor (and fellow Glyndebourne and Salzburg aficionado) of Sir Edward's – another bachelor Ted, better known to the world as Edward Greenfield OBE.

Throughout my lifetime, Ted has been one of the great characters of musical and journalistic London, in some respects highly modern and in others almost Dickensian in his respect for those traditions in which he perceives merit. As an occasional part-time journalist, I was extremely fortunate to have Ted as a sometime mentor; and he certainly helped me to avoid catastrophe as the combined forces of Ivo Pogorelich, the English Chamber Orchestra and the Philharmonia Chorus descended upon Salisbury Cathedral for a one-off performance on a balmy summer's night in 1996, under the enthusiastic but not always steady beat of an octogenarian former prime minister.

When Ted told me, just a few months ago, that he had prepared a written account of his life, I knew it would contain countless gems, for I had already heard many, but not even most, of the stories within this book, over a glass or six of red wine in Spitalfields. Several of them I had heard twice or more, possibly even in slightly different versions.

Ted's plan then was to publish the work in digital form only, but I knew how much the feel of a real, tangible book, with pages and a spine, would bring both to him and also to all his many friends and admirers. The force of my Luddite argument proved to be irresistible. Fortunately, I also knew the perfect publisher, as I hope the quality of the book that you hold will amply testify. Perhaps less wisely, I volunteered my own services as the first copy editor. I can only hope that the final version of this text comes close to capturing wonderful, colourful, eccentric, irrepressible, mischievous, radical-yet-conservative Ted, with all his maelstrom of tales and moods, travels, quirks and moments of stunning insight and clarity.

The journalist and the reviewer can sometimes appear to be observers – shrewd and discerning observers perhaps – but observers nonetheless, rather than participants, and still less instigators or initiators. One of the great pleasures in this book is the almost child-like delight that Ted takes when he steps out of that frame of non-intervention and changes the path of human (or musical) history in some way. Whether it is a television relay system in Bethlehem or a gender switch in the presentation of a symphony, his satisfaction at making a difference is palpable; and really rather infectious too, I am glad to report.

The somewhat unusual structure of chapters is intended to make life more agreeable, not more difficult, for the reader. I can only cross my fingers and hope it works. For any surviving inaccuracies, I readily apologise. Now, please, relax and enjoy the company of one of the great characters and musical storytellers of our age . . .

Michael McManus, November 2013

Credo

On the day in July 1993 when I retired as chief music critic of the Guardian, *I wrote what I think of as my Credo, setting out my aims in my music criticism. I hope it will help to illuminate the portraits I have included in these memoirs.*

Who needs a music critic? Over forty years on the staff of the *Guardian*, I always counted it a question firmly to keep in mind. Why bother to write about a performance that is dead and gone? How can the experience of listening to music possibly be described adequately? Isn't any writing inevitably going to pale next to the actual experience?

What has long struck me is that the word 'critic' is loaded in the wrong way. In English at least and also, I imagine, in most other languages, the word 'criticism', and with it the word 'critic', suggests adverse comments. Yet in music even more than the other arts the magic of communication depends for the most part on the listener being receptive, and not just negative, let alone hostile. On the face of it a critic, intent above all on picking fault, maybe attending an event reluctantly, not by choice, is one of the last people likely to experience the special magic that music can offer.

Critics after all are expected, even required, to be sour. I would much prefer it, if instead of 'critic' we could find a crisp word meaning 'one who appreciates', but, whatever the semantics, my own consistent belief is that the music critic must aim at appreciation above all, trying never to let the obvious need to analyse in nitpicking detail get in the way of enjoyment. I remember years ago meeting a conductor who said he divided commentators into 'for' critics and 'against' critics. Unashamedly I have always taken an extreme 'for' line.

I have been encouraged by noting how often a knocking notice by a colleague seems to tell me more about his (or her) sleeping pattern or digestive system than about the performance in question. My aim has always been to keep my musical antennae as receptive as I possibly can, whatever the stresses of the occasion might be. My aim always is to go to a concert, or put on a CD, wanting to like.

The jaded response is a boring response. If, of course, the adverse criticism is as lively as George Bernard Shaw's in his days as music critic, then that in itself is proof of a passionate and positive reaction, a love of music. If the composer has been insulted by what a performer has done, then I too will enjoy my attack, but to my mind the music critic's main justification lies in encouraging others to share in enjoyment, in pointing the way towards it – precisely what Shaw was doing. If anyone has been encouraged to go out to listen to music after reading what I have written, that for me is the response I cherish most of all.

In other words, as a critic, I count myself an evangelist. I am a link in the chain between the composer and the listener. Benjamin Britten talked of the 'holy triangle' of the composer, the performer and the listener. I hesitate to talk of a 'holy quadrilateral', but in the role of critic I hope I can count myself as being placed somewhere along the hypotenuse.

My religious analogies are deliberate. Martin Luther said that 'music and theology are heavenly sisters', and I couldn't agree more. The spiritual experience that music gives – not just religious music but secular music too, in whatever area – has the closest relationship with fully religious experience.

Similarly a believer listening to great music and receiving a spiritual experience – as from a late Beethoven quartet or music less elevated – will relate that to feelings experienced in a directly religious context. As an agnostic I can sincerely say that the spiritual dimension music consistently adds to my life is the manifestation of God, something to draw strength from as a believer would.

This is hardly a new idea. What has changed in our society is that church-going and regular religious observance have declined disastrously, and at the same time the availability of music has been expanded enormously by mechanical reproduction, whether on records or through other media. It is no exaggeration to suggest that far more people today find a spiritual dimension in life, something beyond the day-to-day grind, in music – of all kinds – than they do in conventional religious observance. And though arts can similarly convey spiritual qualities, the direct physical impact of music and its essential time element sets it apart.

What is more, with an increasingly wide range of listeners looking specifically for such a quasi-religious dimension, how else to explain the extraordinary popular success of such devotional works as Górecki's Third Symphony or John Tavener's *The Protecting Veil*, which is so different from the regrettably limited impact on a narrow range of listeners of most new music?

In this context the role of the music critic is enhanced. If the composer is the musical prophet, and the performer is the musical seer or minor prophet, the recording can be regarded as the equivalent of a prayer book, albeit one that, as Benjamin Britten complained in his lecture 'On Receiving the First Aspen Award', can be seriously abused, with musical masterpieces treated as wallpaper.

Rightly, Britten wanted listeners to take trouble over their music, but the fact that recordings are regularly used too casually hardly negates their value. It is up to the listener not to devalue the experience, and the highest responses can sometimes come in the most unlikely ways. I remember, when car stereos were new, I went on an hour-long journey and started playing a recording of Beethoven's *Missa solemnis*. To my astonishment, the impact of that massive work was actually enhanced by being heard inside a small travelling box.

I appreciated more than ever before that, almost in contradiction of the work's grandeur, Beethoven in every line was questioning as a thinking individual the meaning of the liturgy, making it an intense personal statement. So in the car I clearly heard Beethoven himself stuttering in excitement, *'Et, et, et resurrexit!'* and was even more moved. The pay-off was that when I reached the end of my journey, the *Agnus Dei* was still continuing, and I felt myself compelled to sit on in the car until the whole work was finished.

The moral is to be ever receptive and I hope that, as a critic and a skilled listener, I can go on pointing the way, not least in the area of music criticism that I count most valuable, reviewing recordings for music-lovers to go out and enjoy, the more unexpectedly the better. Carrying my religious analogy to its conclusion, the critic might be counted as a priest, not I hope a high priest, pronouncing anathema as he pulls his cloak of self-importance round him, but a low priest, an evangelical, an explainer.

One of my greatest joys as a critic and explainer has been to get to know so many of the artists whose music-making I admire, whether as composers or performers. Though the rule is not absolute, it is fascinating to find that, where performers almost invariably are very like their performances in character, particularly singers, composers often belie their music. It took me years after getting to know William Walton – the greatest of my heroes when I was a boy – to relate this quiet, wryly humorous man to the spiky, passionate music of his that I had loved for so long.

Similarly, the painful hypersensitivity of Benjamin Britten as a person, so tellingly and, in my experience, accurately portrayed in Humphrey Carpenter's biography, hardly matches the generosity of so much of his music. One explanation is that, where the performer is an open, direct communicator, the composer is looking inside himself when writing his music, however directly he seeks to communicate.

The idea – very prevalent among American critics – that knowing an artist invalidates criticism seems to me wrong, even if there are obvious dangers. As a 'for' critic I always find it a help knowing artists, making it easier for me to explain their work, and any charge of favouritism is minimised if you know a wide range of composers and performers, not just a few.

Chapter One

Critics and Conductors

During my career I have encountered many talented people, including numerous conductors, whose names have adorned the recordings that caused so many of us to become 'hooked' on record collecting in the first place. Alongside me have also been my own colleagues and rivals – the reviewers, some of whom made sport out of building up the careers of conductors, or else crushing them to dust.

MARTIN BERNHEIMER

The colleague who has most sharply attacked my positive stance as a music critic is Martin Bernheimer of the *Los Angeles Times*, arguably the greatest music critic of his generation in the United States. I first got to know him in 1965, when I spent three months in America funded by the State Department, but our first conflict came in 1973, when we were both attending the opening of the Sydney Opera House.

A seminar was organised on the art of the music critic, with composers and performers taking part as well as critics. In the discussion I outlined my view that the role of the critic should above all be positive, seeking to get readers to listen to music, at which Martin roundly condemned me for being a Pollyanna critic, too pleased with everything and much too soft, a prey to the Establishment. I did my best to counter the accusation, but the jibe rather stuck in my throat, yet then and later Martin and I became good friends, occasionally teasing each other. In fact one year when we were both covering the

Wagner Festival at Bayreuth it was only with the help of Martin that I got my copy through to my paper in London.

The pay-off came when I happened to be in Los Angeles at the time they announced the award of the Pulitzer Prize for criticism to Martin. I was delighted for him, yet I could not resist the temptation to ring him up and ask, 'What price the Establishment now?' In fact he was having a battle with his difficult employers at the time, and such a prestigious award did much to help him in his battle.

ANDREW PORTER

Among my British colleagues, the close contemporary whom I most admire is Andrew Porter. One of his many great gifts is that – to use an expression much used on the *Guardian* – he has always written 'like an angel', able, it seems, to produce the most exquisite prose with infuriating ease. Yet sometimes his gift took him over the top. I shall always remember a piece he wrote about the Shiraz Festival in Iran, when the Shah was still the ruler.

The Shah had masterminded an elaborate arts festival and Andrew, as a distinguished guest, was plainly much moved by the occasion. His piece began in biblical fashion with the phrase, 'We rose at dawn', and I could hear him in my mind using a high-flown voice.

He was particularly taken with a play written by the celebrated poet Ted Hughes, in a newly invented special language, with Andrew supplying examples, of which I remember the phrase 'Boda, boda skrord', which was intended to mean something perfectly ordinary.

I fear I could not resist teasing him, and he proudly informed me when his masterly pieces for the *New Yorker* magazine were published in book form that he had not changed a word. Few critics could subject their regular pieces to such treatment, and present such a polished result.

I also remember teasing Andrew about his brilliant translation of Wagner's *Ring* cycle into English for English National Opera. He was especially proud of using a vernacular tone, and generally he achieved that superbly. Yet, prompted by a fellow critic who was a close friend of us both, I lighted upon the opening phrase in *Siegfried*, with the dwarf Mime working at his forge. The first words of the translation were 'O wearisome labour', which, as I pointed out in an article, was hardly a vernacular expression. What it did was to copy the rhythmic pattern for the German, and it is a tribute to Porter that Germans would sometimes consult the Porter translation when trying to elucidate what Wagner was saying in his often thorny verse.

I was especially grateful to Andrew, when, soon after my little book on Puccini was published, he gave it the most glowing praise, at once perceptive yet generous. When writing the book I had had his responses especially in mind, and I was overwhelmed reading his review. I confess I wept with joy. I valued his review all the more when it was coupled with a review, not quite so glowing, of Mosco Carner's masterly comprehensive survey and analysis of the operas of Puccini.

PHILIP HOPE-WALLACE

Among my *Guardian* colleagues the critic closest to me was Philip Hope-Wallace, who wrote 'like an angel' in quite a different style from Andrew. Philip's great gift was wit, often involving an enormous fund of anecdotes. He remembered reviewing a performance of Bellini's *Norma*, when he wrote that over her dead children Norma was 'like a tigress who has lost her whelps'. Sadly, Philip was then the victim of two sides of *Guardian* correctness. The sub-editors deemed that 'tigress' was a sexist word and changed it to 'tiger', which then involved changing 'her' to 'his', and he was further bugged by the ignorance of one or other compositor, so that Philip's elegant phrase about Norma came out finally as 'like a tiger that has lost his whelks'.

It was the sort of mistake to which we became inured at the *Guardian* in the days when we were geared to writing on a typewriter; and Philip was never the most careful typist in the world, partly because he was brilliant at writing extraordinarily quickly, producing a jewel of a review, not a word too long, that summed up his opinions with sparkling wit. Telephoning reviews to the copytakers at the *Guardian* was also a fraught business, and Philip used to tell of the time when he described the singing of the Schumann song-cycle, *Frauenliebe und -leben* by Irmgard Seefried as 'quite elegant'. That then appeared in print as a 'white elephant performance'.

Philip's reviews almost invariably included memorable phrases, as when he talked of a diva in Mascagni's *Cavalleria rusticana* communing with the birds 'like a jungle locomotive scaring the macaws'. He also wrote about one of Marlene Dietrich's last performances, saying that she sang 'to the nods and becks of many a grey-head old enough to be her daughter'. In his conversation he was even more uninhibited, as when he learned that his drama-critic colleague Ken Tynan had a Chinese mistress: he referred with unashamed lack of concern for political correctness to the 'Chink in Tynan's armoire'; and, when he sent a postcard back from the island of Lesbos, he said he had been watching the locals diving in the sea, 'lesbians to a man'. When he heard that the mother of a South African friend had a hole in her back his wry suggestion was 'gored by a rhino on the veldt'.

He would also fantasise about visits to Sweden, when all they had on at the opera house in Stockholm would be '*Figaros Brollop* and *Fru Butterflog*'. *Figaros Brollop* is an accurate enough translation, but Philip invented *Butterflog* for better effect. He would also suggest that everyone there was called Söderström, and you would have an introduction to Dr Söderström, Mr Söderström, Mrs Söderström, Miss Söderström, Master Söderström and Mme Backside. That last was always part of the package. Of one colleague who wore a gold plastic overcoat, he said she looked just like Nebuchadnezzar, but without the long black beard. Of another hard-drinking colleague in El Vino, the journalists' watering-hole on Fleet Street, he said that it was 'one of those days when G. would simply open his ruby-red eyes a little wider . . .'

Philip's daily pattern was extraordinary. He would go to a pub in Hatton Garden that opened exceptionally early and there consume a pint of Italian Prosecco before wandering down to El Vino. One day on his way there he popped into the surplus store, Headquarters and General, where, amazingly, they had separate matching jackets and trousers at £5 a time. To his delight Philip found jacket and trousers that suited his unique frame, and bore his prize down to El Vino. His drinking friends exclaimed in amazement, 'But it's *yellow!*' Philip told the story against himself with glee.

Philip's wardrobe had been growing shabby over the years, so for the opera at Covent Garden he would sit with his overcoat still on, prompting the general director, John Tooley, to remark that they were used to Philip leaving before the last act, 'But now he doesn't even bother to take his overcoat off!' Even on those occasions when Philip left before the end, the resulting review in the *Guardian* would be masterly in its perception.

Philip lived in grand squalor in a single room in the house in St John's Wood owned by his sister Jacqueline and her partner, Veronica Wedgwood. I loved going over there for Sunday lunch, when I was able to boast that I had had my Sunday lunch cooked by an OM, for it was Veronica not Jacqueline who did the cooking. Veronica always said that in receiving the OM she was a 'little over-parted'. It so happed that the great historian G. M. Trevelyan died just when they wanted another female OM: hence the choice. Sadly, Veronica contracted Alzheimer's tragically early, and Jacqueline loyally looked after her in her last years.

Philip, like many, had a fear of ending up in hospital. He asked that people not go and visit him as it was like seeing someone off at the station: 'Only the bed never goes out!'

NEVILLE CARDUS

My other close music-critic colleague on the *Guardian* was Neville Cardus, who, when I took over as a full-time music critic after my years in the Parliamentary Lobby, was in virtual retirement. I would ring him on a Thursday and ask him what he wanted to do the following week. When I first took over, it was just two concerts a week, which then went down to one, and I like to think that that helped to keep him active into his late seventies. He too wrote 'like an angel' in yet another way, older-fashioned, producing fine Meredithian paragraphs, which flowed from his pen (no typewriter involved) with no correction whatever.

At first I thought of myself as taking the opposite stance to Neville as a critic, seeking to simplify and clarify and analyse. Yet over the years I came to feel we were closer to each other in that his finest reviews, like mine I hope, involved an eagerness to convey the joy of music, something we both wanted to share. Though initially Cardus distrusted me and my generation, he came to regard me as a fitting successor, and our last meeting over lunch sealed his confidence, only a few days before he died suddenly of a stroke. In fact on the very day of his death he rang me first thing and wanted me to join him for lunch again, but sadly I had another engagement.

ANDRÉ PREVIN

The conductor to whom I was closest over many years was André Previn, the most quotable person I have ever known. I was lucky to be invited by his orchestra, the London Symphony Orchestra, on many of their trips abroad, including one in 1971 to Russia and the Far East lasting some five weeks, when I heard Previn's inspired reading of Rachmaninov's Second Symphony on over a dozen occasions, with the 'gulp moment' at a different point each time. Over that period it was convenient for Previn to have someone not in the orchestra with whom to discuss problems, and I became a good confidant.

In due course I wrote a little book about Previn and his many recordings. At the time he was married to Mia Farrow, and it was good to meet, on my trips down to Previn's home at Leigh near Reigate in Surrey, not only Mia but also her mother, the legendary film star Maureen O'Sullivan, the original Jane to Johnny Weissmuller's Tarzan. Mia was not always an easy or undemanding wife to Previn, charming as she was, but Maureen O'Sullivan was in every way a delight, open and sparkling.

Despite her elfin appearance, Mia herself was a much feistier girl than one would expect. She had, after all, had early experience of the Hollywood jungle, having been married to Frank Sinatra before her marriage to Previn. At a concert, someone she knew was having an affair with Previn sat down in front of her. Mia challenged the woman with the accusation that she must be 'the oldest groupie in London'. She then proceeded to kick her in the back throughout the performance.

Both when I was writing my book and at other times Previn was wonderful talking about his life, not least his early years as a prodigy in Hollywood. At the age of fourteen he was already writing and scoring film music. He would take several buses after school and arrive at the MGM lot, there to be given his daily assignment. He would then produce the results the following day, completely scored, and before long he graduated to writing his own scores complete, conducting them himself with the studio orchestra, which consisted of some of the most eminent European musicians, exiled from home as Jews escaping from the Nazis. Previn said he would never have known as a child that he and his family were Jewish, except that when he was still in Nazi Germany, 'they threw rocks at me in the street'.

It was when Previn was still working for MGM that the distinguished violinist Joseph Szigeti heard about the boy being an astonishing sight-reader at the piano, having been taught by his law-yer father always to play *a tempo* when sight-reading something new. Szigeti wanted a pianist to help him prepare works new to him, and this André did brilliantly, sight-reading anything put before him. At the end of one of their sessions Szigeti discovered by chance that the boy did not know the regular chamber-music repertory of Beethoven, Mozart and Schubert. So, from then on, for one evening a week, he insisted that Previn should join him in playing chamber music.

It was a great training for him at a time when precociously he was scoring music for MGM, later writing film music of his own, and then conducting it with the brilliantly talented MGM Orchestra full of expatriate musicians. That gave him the ambition to conduct professionally as a career, rather than just play the piano and compose for films. Initially, it was hard work, when reviews of his concerts with second-line orchestras would regularly refer to 'Hollywood's André Previn'. Yet gradually he was accepted as a conductor in his own right, and became principal conductor of the Houston Symphony Orchestra, in succession to John Barbirolli.

That was the big breakthrough, and it led soon enough to his being invited to be principal conductor of the LSO, an enormous leap. He had greatly impressed the players with his conducting in a series of recording sessions for RCA, including those for the classic version of Walton's First Symphony, which has still not been surpassed.

It was during Previn's long period as principal conductor of the LSO that I got to know him best, and wrote my little book about him. Specially memorable were the LSO tours on which I was invited, notably in 1971 when we travelled together for a whole month, starting with a visit to Moscow and St Petersburg (then Leningrad), accompanied by William Walton and his wife Susana (which was a special thrill for me), plus Peter Pears and Benjamin Britten, who performed with the cellist Mstislav Rostropovich as well as the pianist Sviatoslav Richter. The Soviet Union formed only the first half of the tour, for we then went on to the Far East, visiting in turn Japan, South Korea and Hong Kong. Our principal young soloist was Kyung-Wha Chung, who became a great friend. Previn and I insisted that she should study the Walton Violin Concerto, which in due course she recorded memorably with him and the LSO.

Other tours I went on with Previn and the LSO included visits to Pittsburgh, a city I fell in love with and to which I returned a number of times to give lectures, originally prompted by Previn, who was organising an English-music festival there, with soloists including the young cellist Yo-Yo Ma, who played the Elgar Cello Concerto.

Equally memorable were the LSO tours I went on to the Salzburg Festival, with Previn among the conductors. On the last occasion there were rumblings in the orchestra that the management wanted to replace Previn as conductor – who had handled them through a series of brilliant television programmes – with a conventionally great conductor. I was horrified when Previn rang me after our return from Salzburg to tell me that he was about to sign an agreement resigning his position. I said I would get support from members of the orchestra to oppose the move, but he forbade me from whispering a word.

When I told the *Guardian* office that I wanted extra space the following day because Previn was about to resign, the office understandably said, 'We must have the story today.' I said that I was bound to keep silent so they gave the story to two colleagues who were not my friends, and I remember seeing them like witches over a cauldron getting the story together. When it appeared, it took an anti-Previn line, so it was clear that I was not implicated, and the members of the LSO when they read it immediately set up a movement to prevent Previn from resigning.

Before the day was out the chairman and manager were sacked, to be replaced with those who wanted to keep Previn, a decisive coup that delighted me. It was then that for the first time I was recognised as the *Guardian*'s Chief Music Critic. When I told Previn that it had helped me get my promotion, he responded that I had helped him save his job. Even so, Previn knew that it was time for him to think of moving on, which of course within a couple of years he did. I still kept in touch with him, most of all when he was principal conductor of the Pittsburgh Symphony, and I am sorry that inevitably over the years we have seen less and less of each other. There is no one more amusing to be with than André Previn.

It was at the period when Previn was still regarded primarily as a pianist and film composer that he performed a concerto with Leonard Bernstein and the New York Philharmonic. After they had taken their initial bows and retreated to the wings, Lenny insisted that André should take a bow on his own. When he came off a second time, Lenny was waiting for him and, to his surprise, commanded him, 'Now, drag me on!'

SIR COLIN DAVIS

It was soon after I came down from Manchester to London to be the *Guardian*'s second political correspondent in the Parliamentary Lobby that I had an invitation to go to a rehearsal of the Chelsea Opera Group in a school beyond White City near Wormwood Scrubs. The conductor of Verdi's *Falstaff* was the then unknown Colin Davis. In preparation I played the Toscanini recording, which had just reached me from EMI, and to my astonishment the performance under Davis was in the same league. Only in the new century did he finally record his electrifying interpretation of this final masterpiece of Verdi's old age, an outstanding version taken from a concert in the Barbican, and issued on the LSO Live label. From that moment in the 1950s I nominated Davis in my mind as a great star of the future.

My Cambridge friend Jack Ashley, who was then in the BBC, thought I ought to be broadcasting, so arranged for me to do a test broadcast. The Yorkshire producer involved, the veteran Jack

Singleton, suggested something that could be broadcast, and so I did a script about Colin Davis and *Falstaff*. I spoke to Colin, and I fear he expected a far bigger feature piece, but at least that was my very first broadcast in a London regional news programme.

What disappointed me in Davis's earliest recordings was that they did not convey the high-voltage energy that I detected in his live performances. Then, in a version of Beethoven's Seventh Symphony on an EMI mid-price label, I felt that he had conveyed just the electric intensity I had always hoped for, and happily it was a disc that I had to review for *Gramophone* magazine. For some years it remained a top choice for the Seventh.

Over the years I attended many of the important Colin Davis recording sessions, most strikingly for his unique series of Berlioz performances, not least his pioneering version of the epic opera *Les Troyens*. That was recorded out at the Walthamstow Assembly Rooms, and Davis was masterly in controlling his vast forces, with offstage choruses consigned to side rooms, and the recording engineers for Philips controlling the sound to clarify complex textures. It remains a classic version of this unique opera.

SIR CHARLES MACKERRAS

For many years early in his career Charles Mackerras was in effect a house conductor for the EMI label. He was at the time an assistant conductor of the Sadler's Wells Opera, later English National Opera, and was called in to act as assistant, stepping in when at the last minute the company was let down for important recordings by conductors such as Otto Klemperer or Carlo Maria Giulini – notably Klemperer who was becoming frail and unpredictable.

When the star conductor failed to appear, Mackerras would then record material of his own choice, notably from the Russian and Czech repertory, choosing mostly attractive rarities. Under less stringent control the engineers would experiment more with the sound, and regularly produced spectacular results.

Mackerras had been trained in his native Australia, but soon after arriving in Britain had won a scholarship to Czechoslovakia, and from then on became a specialist in Czech music, notably of Leoš Janáček, a composer barely known in Britain before that. He gave first British performances of Janáček operas at Sadler's Wells, and began to record Janáček less for EMI and more for the emergent Pye Nixa label, some of the recordings being very good indeed.

Thereafter Mackerras's conducting career flourished ceaselessly. He made a historic series of recordings of all the Janáček operas with starry casts, mainly of native Czech singers, for Decca, some with the Vienna Philharmonic, but some with the Czech Philharmonic. They repeatedly won prizes, but Decca was still not satisfied with the sales figures for such expensive productions, though no doubt they will recoup the investment over the years.

ANTAL DORÁTI

It may seem strange now, when Doráti has long been counted a Haydn specialist, that he was generally regarded before that as a specialist in brilliant orchestral showpieces, notably from the Russian school, most strikingly of Stravinsky. I remember the session at Watford Town Hall when he recorded a Haydn symphony for the first time. They had brought in the pianist and harpsichordist Philip Ledger in case Doráti wanted to include a continuo player, and even after Ledger explained the pros and cons he seemed fazed by the idea. Yet within a few years Doráti took on the immense task of recording the complete set of Haydn symphonies with the Philharmonia Hungarica for Decca. Acknowledged as the great Haydn expert, he then also recorded Haydn operas.

I went to the final sessions for the symphonies in the West German town of Mahl where the Philharmonia Hungarica, formed from exiled Hungarian musicians, had its base. It was a great occasion, as indeed were some of the sessions for Haydn operas that Doráti conducted in Switzerland. As I mention later in this book, I have cherished memories from that time, of Jessye Norman going into a room where the hotel clients were having their meal and, with her unique, glorious voice, regaling them with *'Dich, teure Halle'*, from Wagner's *Tannhäuser*. Indeed that hall resounded as never before.

GEORGE SZELL

It came as a surprise when I was told by the *Guardian* office that George Szell had expressed the wish to be interviewed. Szell was the most feared conductor in the music world, and I approached my task with some trepidation. I remember timing my knock on his door at the Savoy at precisely fifteen seconds before ten o'clock, and he was waiting for me. I took with me my very first tape recorder, what was in effect a child's machine. Szell insisted on setting up the reel-to-reel tape, and then, when I was preparing to go ahead, challenged me to test that he had done his work properly.

He then picked up the phone and said to the operator that he was on no account to be disturbed for another hour and a half. I was horrified that I would not have enough questions ready for such a length of time, and it was worse when I found he had the disconcerting habit of answering even the most complex question with a simple 'Yes' or 'No', throwing the ball back into my court.

I had come across that gift of answering monosyllabically only when I was working for the *Guardian* in the Parliamentary Lobby, and the then Leader of the Labour Opposition, Clement Attlee, would have a similarly no-nonsense approach to questioning. Szell was certainly in that league.

Over the following hour I managed to keep my end up, and Szell seemed to enjoy the conversation. I remember asking him a question about his recordings with great pianists of Brahms's First Piano Concerto. I began by pointing out that at that time he had recorded the work twice, with Clifford Curzon and Rudolf Serkin. He swiftly corrected me, reminding me that, in the days of short-playing 78 rpm discs, he had also recorded it with Artur Schnabel.

I pointed out to him that in his conducting of the long opening *tutti* for the orchestra his approach was quite different between his Curzon version and his Serkin one. He promptly attacked me, asking the rhetorical question, 'And don't you think a conductor should respond to his soloist?' The answer of course was yes, but Szell might have been thought so positive a conductor that he would not behave so flexibly.

LEOPOLD STOKOWSKI

When at the age of thirteen I saw the Disney film *Fantasia*, little did I realise that one day I would get to know the legendary conductor behind the project, Leopold Stokowski, who notoriously had had an affair with Greta Garbo, and had appeared in the film *A Hundred Men and a Girl* with Deanna Durbin. The prominence Stokowski achieved as a populariser too often tended to detract from his very positive musical achievements. From before the First World War when, still very young, he became the principal conductor of the Philadelphia Orchestra, Stokowski not only welded that unique band to produce the rich 'Philadelphia Sound', he was at the forefront in promoting new music.

Stokowski was responsible for conducting the first American performances of many important works, such as Schoenberg's massive *Gurrelieder*. He was also exceptionally adventurous as a pioneer of recording. *Gurrelieder* was one of the works of which he made the first recording, and his programme in the film *Fantasia* broke unexpected ground in including a section from Stravinsky's *Rite of Spring*, still regarded in the 1930s as a difficult work.

I remember walking home from the cinema, drunk with the experience of hearing the *Rite*, or at least the sections of the work that Stokowski chose in illustrating the emergence of life on Earth, including the rise and demise of the dinosaurs. Stravinsky himself did not approve of that butchering of his score, but it certainly brought his music to a vastly bigger audience. I myself promptly went out and bought Stokowski's own studio recording of the complete work and, from then on, became devoted to everything Stravinsky wrote, even though at the time his work after the first three big ballets tended to be dismissed by writers on music.

When, thanks to the help of the Stokowski scholar Edward Johnson, I first met Stokowski in the first of several long interviews, I had just had the privilege of attending several rehearsals with the great maestro. When this frail old man waved his hands in front of the players, the orchestra immediately made a totally different sound. It was an astonishing phenomenon. I asked him whether he could explain it, and he promptly fixed me with his ice-blue eyes, and said, 'It is the eye!'

CARLO MARIA GIULINI

I first got to know this most dedicated of conductors when an old friend of mine, Robert Leslie, became manager to Carlo Maria Giulini. As Placido Domingo has revealed, here was an exceptionally quiet and gentle man, who in the middle of the *Dies irae* of Verdi's *Requiem* (a work with which he was specially associated) would blaze like a demon, utterly transformed by the music. He was quietly spoken, which is rare in an Italian conductor, and directed his rehearsals by sheer magnetism and never by shouting, as I witnessed many times when I attended recording sessions with him.

He came from a rural background, growing up on the estate owned by his parents, and I remember a lunch with a number of colleagues, when before our meal the subject of conversation turned to wine, and Italian wine in particular. One of my colleagues prided himself on his knowledge of wine and was quickly talking in terms totally incomprehensible to the rest of us. He then turned to Giulini, and asked for his opinion.

Giulini quietly explained that on the family estate they grew vines and harvested the grapes as a matter of course. 'We made the wine and we drank it,' he concluded, and we were rather pleased to see our wine expert totally defeated. Giulini was the opposite of a wine snob, and he would disconcert his hosts in the record company he worked for, Deutsche Grammophon, when they would buy an expensive claret and he would promptly top it up with water.

KARL BÖHM

One of the most memorable rehearsals I ever attended came in August 1973 in the Grosses Festspielhaus in Salzburg, when the London Symphony Orchestra was giving its first concert in a series of five. The conductor was Karl Böhm, notorious as a disciplinarian, and everyone was on tenterhooks wondering how he would get on with the LSO, always regarded as an arrogant orchestra. The work he chose to start with was Brahms's Second Symphony, and he conducted the first movement straight through, not bothering to stop the players.

Towards the end of the first movement, there is an important horn solo. The LSO's principal horn at the time was Jeff Bryant and, after a few bars, Böhm commented with some surprise (always regarding Viennese horns as the finest in the world), 'Good!' A few phrases later he commented, 'Very good!' and, as the solo ended, 'Very, very good!' It was the beginning of a love affair that culminated some years later when Böhm was appointed to the honorary post of president of the orchestra. Böhm was indeed a tough taskmaster but his admiration for the orchestra and the players' admiration for him carried them on.

As principal conductor of the Dresden Staatskapelle in the 1930s Böhm was a favourite conductor in Germany over the Nazi period. Like any artist under a totalitarian regime, Böhm had to work with the Nazi hierarchy, and though he went further than most, he was never a member of the Nazi Party. Yet it is said that at the end of a rehearsal with the Vienna Philharmonic he would announce to the players, 'I must now go and telephone my Führer.'

After the Second World War the process of denazification brought a British official to Böhm's home in his native city of Linz. The official was married to a leading orchestral harpist, Renata Scheffel-Stein, and he had warm admiration for Böhm. He was horrified to see prominently displayed in the conductor's living room a whole gallery of signed portraits of the Nazi leaders. The official told Böhm quickly to destroy the photos before anyone else less sympathetic saw them. It suggests a curious naivety on Böhm's part that he did not think to destroy them earlier, before he was tackled by any official.

My last memory of Böhm came a year before he died. He was conducting Strauss's *Ariadne auf Naxos*, and for once, invited by Decca, I was sitting just behind the conductor's podium in the Kleines Festspielhaus at Salzburg. I was transfixed, for this was the most dedicated performance imaginable, if slower than usual. The following morning I was walking outside the Deutsche Grammophon *Treffpunkt* (meeting area) when I saw Böhm's amanuensis. I said what a wonderful experience it had been at *Ariadne* the night before. The amanuensis immediately dragged me to a telephone to speak to the maestro, who felt he had given a bad performance. How extraordinary it was to find myself reassuring such a veteran maestro.

EUGEN JOCHUM

One of the conductors to whom I felt very close over his last years
was the German Eugen Jochum. That was largely because his artistic
agent was my friend Robert Leslie, who masterminded the expansion
of his conducting career to take in countries where he was hardly
known, except though his recordings. That was so in Britain, and
Robert organised a visit that involved a series of concerts across the
so-called 'provinces'. Robert reported to me that Maria, Jochum's
strong-willed wife, had paid him a compliment, possibly uncon-
sciously echoing a famous line from Wagner's opera *Die Meistersinger
von Nürnberg*: 'Before we met you, Robert, we were just childs.' From
then on Robert called them 'Father and Mother Child'.

That series of concerts across such a wide variety of towns and
cities gave them the opportunity of doing more than merely going to a
concert hall in each city. Naturally, they went to Stratford-upon-Avon
and then to Oxford, where they visited Christ Church Cathedral.
There they heard the magnificent cathedral (and college) choir singing a Byrd Mass. It was of course sung in Latin, and Eugen and
Maria, devout Catholics from the Rhineland, were thrilled to hear the
Mass in Latin. They had been much distressed by Vatican II and the
abandonment of Latin in the Mass in favour of the vernacular. The
experience of coming to a Protestant country and hearing the Latin
text moved them deeply, and they both cried with joy.

HERBERT VON KARAJAN

The only time I had a substantial conversation with Herbert von
Karajan was in Berlin during the recording sessions for Puccini's
Tosca at the Philharmonie. The officials of Deutsche Grammophon
first of all demanded that I should provide a list of questions to be
submitted, but I explained that I never worked that way, and would

not bother to come to Berlin if they insisted. At that they gave in, and as I suspected, there was no problem in starting my conversation with this surprisingly shy man.

I began by pointing out that I was an old friend of the great recording producer Walter Legge, who masterminded the early EMI recordings that first made Karajan a globally famous figure. That readily broke the ice, and very soon I dared to ask him a question that might well have angered him. I told him about Stokowski suggesting that his magic lay 'in the eye', but, as was well known, Karajan regularly conducted with his eyes closed.

Happily, he laughed at my daring, and explained very clearly that if he conducted with his eyes closed he had no visual distractions, and he could much better separate the different strands of sound from the different players, knowing exactly where they all were. That, I feel, is not just a clear explanation, but also a totally convincing one.

He went on to suggest that he felt it his gift to raise the level of any orchestra new to him at least two notches in quality. He then started to laugh, as he told me about an orchestra specially assembled for him on one occasion in Seattle, a festival orchestra. He remembered starting to conduct Beethoven's *Coriolan* Overture, and bringing his baton down on the first *fortissimo* chord. Instead of delivering a *fortissimo* the players made a sort of whinnying sound, not at all what Karajan wanted. His conclusion was that though it was a good orchestra with many excellent players, 'they just couldn't play loud'. The idea plainly amused him, and it was good to appreciate that the great man had a sense of humour about himself.

SIR GEORG SOLTI

The first time I met Georg Solti he was in his room at Covent Garden soon after his recording of Wagner's *Götterdämmerung* had appeared, the third instalment of his pioneering recording of the *Ring* cycle for Decca (Solti recorded the cycle out of its usual sequence, ending with *Die Walküre,* which is actually the second opera). He seemed pleased when I said I felt that there was an extra warmth in the interpretation, compared with what had gone before, and in explanation he said, with a misty look in his eye, 'Sometimes in your life events affect your music-making.' It was only later that I discovered that it had been during those sessions in Vienna that, for the first time, he was able to be with his wife-to-be, Valerie, full time.

As Valerie Solti has explained to me, it had been a real *coup de foudre*, love at first sight. Then a television reporter, Valerie had gone to meet Solti in his hotel room. The first thing he had asked her was whether she could help him to find his socks, surely a unique start to a love affair.

Solti had managed to escape from Budapest immediately after the *Anschluss* had brought Hitler's troops into Austria. Despite anti-Semitism in Hungary, he had as a *répétiteur* in the opera house been given his first chance to conduct a single performance – of Mozart's *Figaro* on the very night of the *Anschluss* – but when later he fled to Switzerland it was very much as a pianist. He won an important piano competition, and his then first wife-to-be, older than him, had taken him under her wing and promoted his career.

That was how his earliest recordings for Decca were as a pianist, accompanying the great German violinist Georg Kulenkampff, whose previous partner on disc had been Wilhelm Kempff. That quickly led to Solti's first recordings as a conductor. I asked him about that change of direction and how it had come about, and he said with charming modesty that it was because, after the war, 'there was a shortage'. That was how against the odds he became music director of the Opera in Munich, and conducted performances of Strauss's *Der Rosenkavalier* with the composer present. He also had the great honour of conducting at Strauss's memorial service.

At my first meeting with Solti I asked him about his plans for the future, and he mentioned his strong desire to record Elgar's First

Symphony. I pointed out to him that the composer's own 1930 recording, an electrifying performance, departed in some details from the score, something that surprised him. An LP version of the original 78s was just appearing, and I arranged for him to be sent a copy, which helped him make a recording of his own that still stands the test of time.

At that first meeting too he made the unforgettable remark, seemingly intended to be taken seriously: 'I'm glad you think I am improved.' Then, having been terribly proud of fathering his first two children in his fifties, he admitted a hint of disappointment that they were not boys, when he had long had the ambition to have a model railway. He even asked me about the possibilities, knowing I was an enthusiast too.

It was well known that Karajan prevented Solti from appearing at the Salzburg Festival, of which Karajan was the music director. Yet when Karajan was ailing in what turned out to be his last months of life and there was a possibility that he would not be able to conduct the new production of Verdi's *Ballo in maschera* as planned, Solti was approached, and indeed he did take over. As Solti said to me with a hint of glee in his voice that he could not suppress, 'He died!'

The recording sessions in Kingsway Hall for Elgar's First Symphony took place during a crisis period of the Edward Heath government, with power cuts threatened every day. In the lovely slow movement, which justifiably Solti took much more slowly than Elgar himself, we all held our breath, hoping against hope that a power cut would not break the spell. It remains a magical performance. 'What beautiful music!' commented Solti.

When a year or so later Solti was awarded a knighthood, he was still a German citizen. He promptly pulled every string he could to arrange for his naturalisation as quickly as possible, so that as a British citizen he could use the title, an endearing sign of vanity. That was how he became Sir Georg Solti, and I remember meeting his solicitor, who wondered whether Solti realised how much the change of nationality was going to mean in extra tax.

LORIN MAAZEL

The most extraordinary conducting prodigy of the twentieth century must have been Lorin Maazel. At the age of nine he was invited by Arturo Toscanini to conduct the maestro's own orchestra, the NBC Symphony, and it seems he already knew his own mind, and didn't just wag a stick before the players. His parents had moved from Los Angeles to Pittsburgh so that their precocious son could continue to study with the same teacher.

Maazel was shy about commenting on his boyhood experiences, but I persuaded him that there would be no question of my making fun of the idea, as others had. What I remember most clearly from his comments were the problems he encountered when after his conducting period he had to knuckle down to working in high school. He was then a marked person, hardly likely to be popular with his contemporaries, and the masters would equally taunt him, saying, 'Why can't you remember French verbs when you can conduct an orchestra?' The most illogical of comments. Happily the boy was a good student in almost all his subjects, thanks largely to his phenomenal memory.

I interviewed Maazel on many occasions, but the most memorable took place in the first-class section of an Air France plane between London Heathrow and Paris. He had the night before conducted the last of a series of performances of Verdi's *Luisa Miller* at Covent Garden, yet in the middle of the night he had been woken up by his then wife, the pianist Israela Margalit, calling from Israel to ask him what to do about one of their children who had mumps. He somehow managed to solve the problem, and arrived at the airport looking grey.

Yet he gave the most articulate interview and, when we arrived in Paris, he asked whether I would like to come with him in his car and pick up his parents from their hotel. I was delighted to meet this charming couple, the father, Lincoln Maazel, an actor, looking rather like Colonel Sanders of Kentucky Fried Chicken fame, and his typically Jewish mum. They plainly worshipped their genius son, and I greatly enjoyed their company at the recording sessions that followed during the day, for Mozart's *Don Giovanni*, planned to be used as the soundtrack for the Joseph Losey film.

BERNARD HAITINK

Just as Maazel was reluctant to talk about his boyhood experiences as a conductor, so Bernard Haitink at first refused to talk about his boyhood in Amsterdam at the time of the Nazi Occupation of Holland. I persuaded him that the last thing I wanted to do was to turn it into a sensational story. That is how in a long talk I had with him on the eve of his fiftieth birthday he did talk about those wartime years, and the trials they created. Haitink's father was in charge of providing the electricity for the City of Amsterdam, which involved him in split loyalty. If he efficiently provided electricity he could be accused of being a collaborator, yet if he fell short the Nazi occupiers might accuse him of sabotage.

So it was that, living within a stone's throw of the Concertgebouw, the young Haitink was able to attend the orchestra's concerts under the collaborator Willem Mengelberg, even though many Dutch music-lovers boycotted them. The audience generally consisted of Nazi officers, who made rather a fuss of the boy in the stalls. Even so, it was the danger to his father that mainly exercised him. He remembers taking a walk one afternoon with his father, and on returning they saw an SS officer knocking on the door of their house. They then continued their walk for an hour or so, until they were confident the immediate danger was past. Even so, Haitink senior was imprisoned for six months, and on his release his family could barely recognise him.

That experience of attending so many concerts led Bernard towards wanting to be a conductor, but he first had to become a professional violinist, only later graduating to the role of conductor thanks to the perception of the Music Director Eduard van Beinum.

He was then fortunate to follow van Beinum as principal conductor of the Concertgebouw at a phenomenally early age, thanks to the older conductor's premature death. Incidentally, the tape I recorded of Haitink to celebrate his fiftieth birthday was so flawless that there was not a single sentence I could miss out, an astonishing tribute not only to his clarity of thought but to his command of English, not his native language.

RICCARDO MUTI

Riccardo Muti is one of the few conductors who tend to go against the latter-day fashion of conductors acting as persuaders, using psychology, instead of dominating as a dictator, like George Szell or Karl Böhm. He is not so much a dictator as they were, but he has always known his own mind and is determined to get his way. I used regularly to see him over breakfast in his hotel in Anif during the Salzburg Festival, but the interview I cherish most was in Barcelona, when the New Philharmonia, of which he was music director, was making a weekend visit.

He described one of his first concerts in Britain, when he was contracted to conduct the LSO in a performance of the Verdi *Requiem* in Bristol, in June 1973. His eyes flashed with Neapolitan anger, still remembering his fury at the treatment he received, for he believed the LSO players, realising his English was limited, had tried to take advantage of him. They had mistaken their man. His comment in Barcelona, for which he bent down towards my cassette recorder, was simply, 'I hate the LSO.' Neapolitans don't readily forget a slight and, to the best of my knowledge, that remains his one and only engagement with that orchestra.

In the Barcelona rehearsals he was unsparing of the orchestra, until he got precisely what he wanted, and at one point he made the second violins play an admittedly tricky passage on their own, quite an indignity for a major section of the orchestra. At each rehearsal the players were warned that he was about to arrive, and greeted him in something like silence, quite rare with London orchestras.

DANIEL BARENBOIM

The exceptional versatility of Daniel Barenboim as a musician is perfectly illustrated by the fact that, although he made his reputation as an outstanding pianist, making his first commercial recording before he reached his teens (a version of Kabalevsky's delightful *Sonatina*), he has become even more important in his role as conductor, occupying major posts on both sides of the Atlantic and conducting Wagner regularly at Bayreuth, the ultimate compliment for a Jewish conductor.

Barenboim was born in Argentina, and his early musical training was in Israel, to where his parents had emigrated. From a very early age his international career developed rapidly, and it was he who gave the first recitals when the Queen Elizabeth Hall was opened, a complete cycle of Beethoven sonatas, which he also recorded for EMI.

His recording contract was a crucial factor in developing his career, for he was naturally spontaneous-sounding in the studio, and recording sessions often involved one take only, which was then accepted as the finished version by his regular recording manager, Suvi Raj Grubb, who became a close friend. Walter Legge was Grubb's mentor and trusted him implicitly. It was Grubb who, against the odds, convinced the bosses at EMI to allow Daniel Barenboim to record a full set of the thirty-two Beethoven piano sonatas, a feat that only Artur Schnabel had accomplished for the company until that time. Their faith was repaid and numerous other wonderful, musically enriching, projects followed, not least among which was Barenboim's complete cycle of the Mozart piano concertos, with the English Chamber Orchestra.

Barenboim's first important recordings in the dual role of conductor and pianist came when with the Mozart piano concertos, directing the orchestra from the keyboard. That led to EMI recording him conducting Mozart symphonies, and his career as a conductor was very positively launched, for he displayed the same magnetic qualities on the podium as he did at the keyboard. There were those who accused EMI of being foolish in their many projects with Barenboim, but over the years their confidence has been amply justified.

MARISS JANSONS

It was when I received a request from *Gramophone* to review a new version of Tchaikovsky's Fifth Symphony that I was alerted to the arrival of another major conductor, Mariss Jansons. My first reaction was to wonder why an independent label, Chandos, would bother to issue a new account from the Oslo Philharmonic and a then unknown conductor, when only a month or so before Karajan had recorded it in a new version with the Vienna Philharmonic.

Very quickly after starting my direct comparisons I realised that the Jansons was in every way finer than the Karajan, not only as an interpretation, but also in the quality of the playing as well as the sound. I wrote my review accordingly, and I learned later that the Oslo orchestra had been so impressed by their dynamic young conductor that they had offered their services to make this recording as a speculative project. How right they were, and Jansons and the Oslo Philharmonic went on to record a complete cycle of the Tchaikovsky symphonies plus the *Manfred* Symphony, a set that still stands the test of time many years later.

It was only when Jansons and the Oslo orchestra moved to EMI that I first got to know him personally, and it was fascinating to see this quiet, seemingly unassertive character rehearsing an orchestra, always crisp and to the point, getting exactly the effect he wanted with the minimum of words. His perception was extraordinary and I remember when I arrived in the control room of the Oslo studio where the recording was made, high above the hall, he had spotted my arrival straight away.

I remember too the concert when Jansons and the Oslo Philharmonic appeared for the first time at the Salzburg Festival. The rich and pampered Salzburg audience was obviously wondering why a Scandinavian orchestra was appearing at this most prestigious festival with its astronomical prices. It took very little time for Jansons and the orchestra to make their mark, and by the end of the concert the enthusiasm bubbled up, and Jansons and the Oslo orchestra have been welcome visitors ever since. It is noticeable too that Jansons has over the years developed the art of wooing an audience, not least in his choice of encores, some of them very original. For example he has often played as an encore the movement *Wild Bears*, from Elgar's *Wand of Youth* music, which in his hands sounds remarkably Russian.

I remember having coffee with Mariss in Salzburg during one festival, and suggesting to him that if he weren't so modest he might match the dominance of his great hero, Karajan. So it is that latterly he has become music director simultaneously of two of Europe's finest orchestras, the Concertgebouw in Amsterdam and the Bavarian Radio Symphony Orchestra in Munich, an extraordinary achievement. No conductor is more beloved by orchestral players than Jansons.

SIR SIMON RATTLE

Doing a public interview with two conductors in duet has its hazards. I realised that when I started my conversation with the young up-and-coming Simon Rattle on the one hand and the veteran Charles Groves on the other. I need not have worried. It was Sir Charles who, as principal conductor of the Royal Liverpool Philharmonic, spotted the talents of this precocious young percussionist, and subsequently did all he could to support his career as a conductor.

Groves also maintained a strong connection with the Bournemouth orchestras and Simon duly worked a great deal with them, making a number of his earliest recordings with the Bournemouth Symphony Orchestra, including his excellent first version of Mahler's Tenth Symphony in the Deryck Cooke completion.

By the time of our conversation Rattle had already developed an association with the Los Angeles Philharmonic, and was beginning his spectacular career as principal conductor of the City of Birmingham Symphony Orchestra, making it one of the most admired orchestras in the country in defiance of the London orientation that tends to dominate in Britain.

What has always been striking about Simon, despite becoming one of the world's leading conductors as music director of the Berlin Philharmonic, is absence of self-importance. I remember going to interview him at his home in Islington, North London, and his cleaner greeted me at the door explaining that the maestro had just gone round the corner for some milk in case I wanted it in my tea. Then in a bistro in New York once when I was having a meal with fellow jurors on the International Record Award, Simon came over from his table to greet me, much to their surprise, when plainly I should have taken the initiative to greet him and his then wife.

CHARLES DUTOIT

Charles Dutoit is the conductor who turned the Montreal Symphony into a great international orchestra. I was fortunate to receive for review from *Gramophone* the first international recording made by Dutoit and the orchestra. It was of Ravel's *Daphnis et Chloé*, the complete ballet, and I was instantly bowled over, even though already there were outstanding versions from Pierre Monteux, Charles Munch and others.

Knowing Canada, and the way that the francophone Canadians had a chip on their shoulder not only in relation to the anglophone Canadians, but also to the French in Paris, I phrased my first sentence to take care of those feelings: I gave my view that this was 'the greatest French orchestra in the world, whatever they may think in Paris'. At the time Montreal had suffered a serious blow, not just financially, by the failure of the Montreal Olympics. I confess that I was disappointed when I heard nothing in response to my review.

It was only four or five months later that I learned that it had a resounding impact in the city. In response to this review in an international magazine the city had responded by feting Dutoit and the orchestra as belonging among the great glories of Montreal, and Dutoit in a poll was counted one of the two most popular Montreal citizens, something no one would ever have expected of a classical conductor.

SIR ANTONIO PAPPANO

The emergence of Tony Pappano as an important conductor pinpoints a career that is the opposite of conventional. Unlike almost any other leading conductor, Pappano never went to a music college, but grew into the role of conductor via being a *répétiteur* for singers. The son of Italian parents, he was born in Epping on the outskirts of London, and from his early boyhood played the piano, accompanying the singing students that his father had as his pupils.

The family moved from Epping to a flat in central London near Victoria, and the boy's earliest tuition was at a local school. A few years later the family moved yet again to a city in upstate New York, and there Pappano in his early teens developed as an accompanist, notably as a *répétiteur* working with singers, understanding their needs. In due course he was poached by scouts from the Metropolitan Opera House in New York, and a little later still he came to Europe to continue his career.

The crucial development came when Pappano was contracted to accompany a singer in an audition with Daniel Barenboim in Bayreuth. It was not the singer who impressed Barenboim but her accompanist. Barenboim made Pappano one of his assistants, and his career as conductor was on its way. In due course he became music director at the La Monnaie opera house in Brussels and, from there, it was an easy step to his arrival as music director of the Royal Opera House, Covent Garden. Since then he has established himself as one of the leading conductors of the day, a maestro who at Covent Garden is regularly praised over the widest repertory. I like to think that my first review of him in *Gramophone*, of a version of *La bohème* that had otherwise received indifferent reviews, was a breakthrough. I instantly knew that here was a great Puccini conductor.

RICHARD HICKOX

To my everlasting embarrassment the first review I ever wrote about Richard Hickox poked fun at the fact that Richard Hickox was conducting the Richard Hickox Singers and the Richard Hickox Orchestra, implying that he was a mere cipher. I could not have been more wrong, and very soon the Richard Hickox Orchestra became the City of London Sinfonia; Hickox had managed to secure sponsorship from city businesses, partly as a response to the festival he founded. The Spitalfields Festival was dedicated to helping to restore Nicholas Hawksmoor's masterpiece, the great church of Christ Church Spitalfields.

Over the years Hickox emerged as one of the most natural talents among contemporary conductors, brilliant overall for creating in recordings the sense of a live performance full of electricity and not merely of a studio run-through. He recorded for many different labels, but in recent years he developed a special relationship with the Chandos label, for which he made an enormous list of outstanding recordings, including a great deal of English music and much choral music.

Performing baroque music prompted him to found his own period instrument orchestra, Collegium Musicum 90, an excellent counterpart to the City of London Sinfonia. His work schedule was phenomenal both in the recording studio and in the concert hall and then the opera house, when for half the year he was working in Australia as the music director of Australian Opera, an unexpected development, but one that he grasped eagerly. Sadly, in 2009 he died suddenly and quite unexpectedly during sessions in Cardiff with the BBC National Orchestra of Wales, the saddest of losses.

RICHARD BONYNGE

Richard Bonynge's career as a conductor initially centred round conducting operas in which his wife Joan Sutherland starred. As she said, she found it much more comforting to have a conductor who, having been her mentor, understood her every phrase, so she didn't have to explain what she wanted. At that period he was often attacked for riding on the back of his wife's success, but increasingly he demonstrated that he was a fine conductor in his own right, and his career, far from contracting when Sutherland officially retired from singing, expanded still further.

It was in the recording studio above all that he came to shine, not just in operas in which his wife did not star but also in ballet music, often in scores that had been largely forgotten. He himself is a musical scholar, and has made a vast collection of scores over the years, specialising in nineteenth-century opera but also extending to ballet scores, above all those of French composers. As in Donizetti and Bellini, his gift for lifting rhythms seductively was a great asset in conducting any ballet score, and his knowledge of the recording process made him a very welcome conductor with recording managers and engineers. The results were often spectacular, particularly with Decca.

His conducting career also flourished in opera generally, and for some years he was music director of Australian Opera in Sydney, initially while his wife was still appearing, but also later after she had retired. Unfortunately, Australian musical politics ensured that, before too long, he withdrew from that tricky post, but not before he had masterminded many successful performances, some of which have appeared on video and DVD. In his eighties he remains very active, and plainly will continue in his career as long as he can.

SIR JOHN ELIOT GARDINER

John Eliot Gardiner is to my mind the most inspired of the new generation of conductors who concentrate on using period instruments, mainly in baroque music. Gardiner in fact took some time to change over from modern instruments with his Monteverdi Choir. Yet, when he did, the results were phenomenal. I remember seeing him over a lunch organised by his record company, and said that in a piece I had just written I had described him as the 'Karajan of period performance'. His immediate response was to ask, 'Why not the Toscanini?'

That was the sort of remark that gave him the reputation of being arrogant, but I always insisted that he had a lot to be arrogant about. Certainly, his command of scholarship was phenomenal, not just in his original baroque area. I remember an hour-long talk he gave without notes on the Schumann symphonies, which he had just recorded in newly edited versions, including both the original version of No. 4 and the composer's radical revision.

It was a revelation, making one eager to hear the results, using the second period-performance orchestra he had founded, the Orchestre Révolutionnaire et Romantique, to distinguish it from his regular English Baroque Soloists.

Gardiner had long been hyperactive, and when at Cambridge, studying not music but a science subject, he had formed a choir with which he conducted the 1610 *Vespers* of Monteverdi in the chapel of King's College. That was a work which in those days was all too rarely performed, and I made a special trip to Cambridge to hear it. I wrote it up in a glowing review in the *Guardian*, one of the first reviews in a national newspaper that Gardiner had ever had. It was something he never forgot, giving me the credit for helping him to emerge as a conductor.

Over the years he has developed the work of his Monteverdi Choir, the group of professional singers that he brought together alongside the Monteverdi Orchestra. His hesitance to switch to period instruments was partly due to the excellence of the Monteverdi Orchestra, some of whose players were reluctant to change their playing techniques.

SIR ROGER NORRINGTON

The careers of Roger Norrington and John Eliot Gardiner have a striking number of parallels. Both trained as singers, and early in their careers founded small choirs of professional singers, specialising in tackling and recording difficult *a capella* works. Their conducting expanded in similar directions, only Norrington adopted period performance rather earlier than Gardiner, and later still they began to conduct full symphony orchestras in general repertory, Norrington becoming principal conductor of the Stuttgart Radio Symphony Orchestra.

Both Norrington and Gardiner in their pursuit of period performance took note of authentic practice, notably in the reduction or elimination of vibrato in the strings, Norrington with the London Classical Players (later disbanded) and Gardiner with the English Baroque Soloists and later the Orchestre Révolutionnaire et Romantique. In their interpretations of Beethoven they both took note of the composer's metronome markings, thought for genera-tions to have been impossibly fast, possibly the result of using a faulty metronome.

JOSÉ SEREBRIER

José Serebrier, born in Uruguay but very much a cosmopolitan figure at home in many different countries, is among the most active of conductors. I first met him when he was a judge for the Van Cliburn Piano Competition in Fort Worth, Texas, and I was reporting on it, but on that occasion we barely exchanged words. Only later, when José approached me about the work of Leopold Stokowski, did we become friends.

Serebrier was the chosen assistant to Stokowski for some years, and Stokowski gave the first performance of Serebrier's First Symphony, a recording of which has now appeared on CD, for Serebrier is not just a conductor but a composer too, and in recent years he has managed to record a number of his works including sym-phonies. I was able to introduce him to my friend Edward Johnson, one of the principal experts on that great conductor and for years the editor of the journal *Toccata*, of the now sadly defunct Stokowski Society.

Through help from Johnson, Serebrier has been able to make a series of superb recordings of the orchestral arrangements that Stokowski made of many different works, notably of Bach's organ music, which was for many years out of fashion, but has now been restored to popularity. Serebrier never merely copies what Stokowski himself did in conducting his own arrangements, but brings out the richness of the sound and the originality of the orchestral effects that Stokowski conceived.

With the benefit of modern digital recording of the highest quality – usually for the budget label Naxos – he has recorded a wide range of Stokowski arrangements, not just of Bach originals, but of examples such as his symphonic syntheses of Wagner and of arrangements of Mussorgsky, which are far from conventional. For his Naxos recordings, Serebrier has usually worked with the Bournemouth Symphony Orchestra, which in his hands, when recorded in the excellent acoustic of a hall in Poole, Dorset, is revealed as a band of world class.

Interlude 1: Family

My father was the eldest son of a railway worker, Harry Greenfield, who was a signalman on the Midland Railway and a lifelong member of the Labour Party. To everyone's wonderment, in 1917 he was made a Justice of the Peace, an extraordinary honour for a working man at the time. I am named Harry (my second name) after him, even though he had died in 1927, the year before I was born. I also have a wonderful illuminated address, given to him by his trade union colleagues to mark his becoming a JP.

My father's career started when he became a solicitor's clerk straight from school. He took a course in Pitman's shorthand, and won prizes for his exceptional speed. That brought him to the attention of Frank Wild, Ernest Shackleton's deputy on his Antarctic expeditions. As a very fast speaker he was delighted with my father's abilities, and it so happened he had been asked by Lloyd George to make recommendations for candidates to become managers of the newly founded labour exchanges. That is how, in his early twenties, my father became manager of a small exchange at Armley, in the suburbs of Leeds.

He also joined the Freemasons, which became one of his principal focuses for the rest of his life. He was Master of the St Philip Lodge in Southend-on-Sea in the year when I was born, 1928. Neither I nor my brother was interested in becoming a Mason, and much later I suggested that it was like 'a glorified League of Ovalteenies'. So from then on my father's lodge became 'Dad's Ovalteenies'. He didn't like that but still laughed.

In due course, from Armley he was promoted to be manager at the exchange in Loughborough, Leicestershire, during the First World War. Although he tried to join the army, he was counted to be more valuable in his job. My father was never a ladies' man, but, standing out among the female clerks, was my mother; he proposed and they married in 1920.

My brother Peter was born in 1922, and I followed in 1928, but through our early years my brother loathed the new intruder, calling me 'Face-ache' and 'Sisifus', among other things. Then, on 2 June 1940, when our school was evacuated to Belper in Derbyshire, we suddenly became the firmest of allies, and so it remained for the rest of his life, which was sadly cut short by throat cancer even though he had never smoked. Despite the best efforts of the Royal Marsden he had to have a laryngectomy, so that only his devoted wife, Jean, was able to hear his words whispered on the breath.

While I had my career at the *Guardian* newspaper, Peter in due course had become one of the three general managers of the Guardian Royal Exchange. Amusingly, my father on one occasion asked his secretary to ring the *Guardian* and, although she got the wrong Guardian, he was able to talk to my brother, who knew where I was (in Aldeburgh) whereas my employers did not.

My father had a wicked sense of humour, which came out when he was talking to friends who came to stay, immediately asking them, 'So, when are you going back?' He would also come out impromptu with odd phrases from melodramas such as, 'No wedding bells for 'er!' or, 'Dead and never called me mother!' Or he would imitate the voice of a parson on the radio with such phrases as, 'all power and might'.

Meanwhile my mother led a largely independent existence, with tennis one of her main interests. Although they very rarely went out together, Father and Mother remained devoted, and never ever looked for any other partners. For the last two years or so of his life, my father always seemed to be at death's door, liable to perish at any moment. Death came unannounced one morning, just when my mother had brought my father's breakfast, and he simply fell back in bed, lifeless.

My mother was then left with no pension, scandalously so when my father had been an Executive Officer in the Ministry of Labour for over fifty years, but my brother and I were fortunately able to supply the necessary funds. It meant so much to me when, some twenty years later, my mother said she thought the years since had been the happiest of her life. I had made it abundantly clear that I was never going to marry, telling her that she 'didn't know how lucky she was', while squeezing her hand, making it clear that she would never be supplanted by anyone else. Sadly, for the last six years of her life she had to go into a rest home, which she loathed, until at the age of eighty-seven she had a stroke and died two weeks later without recovering consciousness; a mercy really. It was not a bad record: at eighty-one she had still been bicycling around Leigh-on-Sea.

Over the years, as close as any brother has been my dear cousin Bill Hall, the son of my mother's brother Ernest. Our lives have run on similar but never parallel lines. Whereas in the army I was stationed in four or five different places, Bill was always within reach of his home in Loughborough, enabling him to live at home. Where I acquired a dozen of my closest friends for life in the army, he did not. When I was at Cambridge University, Bill studied at Nottingham, again living at home in Loughborough. Since the army we have continued to have parallel lives, for Bill acquired his first car within months of my getting my first car.

On graduating, Bill became a schoolmaster, devoted to his job until taking early retirement. He has been the most dedicated of theatre-goers, almost always going on his own, which he prefers. Always he has been an indispensable friend and confidant. He remains a pillar of help in my life, not least when we listen to recordings I have to review for *Gramophone*: he has become 'my other pair of ears', often more acute than me. Long may it be so.

Chapter Two

Bernstein and the Magic of Music

Even in his later years, Leonard Bernstein was an inexpressibly dominant and charismatic figure. He touched lives in a manner that remains uniquely wonderful and enriching in my experience. Indeed I believe he enriched us all. Even his manifest flaws served only to add charm, to remind us that even he, genius that he was, was still flesh and blood, a contingent human being not a demigod. He was a force of nature and a freak of nature; and he fully deserves his special status here, with a chapter all to himself.

What, I asked Leonard Bernstein on one occasion, was his first musical memory? He seemed nonplussed. As neither of his parents was musical, he thought it might be something on the radio. He then had an inspiration. It was, he said, when his aunt Clara taught him at the age of six to play the ukulele. Young as he was, he appreciated that the sounds he was making involved more than wood and catgut.

That, it seems to me, is one of the most revealing comments on the magic of music you could get. He emphasised that he was not joking, and when another aunt left her piano in the Bernsteins' hallway, when the future conductor was eleven, it was the ukulele writ large. Lenny claimed that, far from being precocious, he was in many ways a late developer. He certainly made up for any delay and, within a year or so, had begun to display the musical genius that made him unique.

My conversation with Lenny took place in Vienna in March 1986 when his full-length opera, *A Quiet Place*, was being given its premiere. Before that I had interviewed Lenny over meals, in the recording studio and even in a taxi, but never had had the chance for a fully fledged interview with a tape-recorder and ample time. Lenny's assistant, Margaret Carson, was told to limit the interview to an hour, but she was fascinated herself, and Lenny was so obviously enjoying himself, as we replenished our glasses from time to time, that she let it run on for ninety minutes or more.

In that interview he outlined the whole development of his career. His father, realising that there was no question of persuading his son to join the family cosmetic business, did ensure that he had the best musical training possible. He first went to Harvard, before graduating to the Curtis Institute in Philadelphia, one of the leading training colleges in music.

There he was spotted by the conductor Dmitri Mitropoulos, who became a mentor to him, and later he was befriended by Serge Koussevitzky, music director of the Boston Symphony Orchestra, to whom Lenny acted as an assistant, not least during the Tanglewood Festival, the summer event sponsored by the orchestra. There his experience rapidly expanded. It was not just as a classical pianist and composer that he excelled but in the popular field as well, making him multifaceted to an astonishing degree.

Here was someone with an astonishing charismatic element in his make-up, and I asked him whether he himself was aware of possessing special qualities of magnetism. He told me of the day in 1937 when the premature death of the composer George Gershwin was announced. As an impecunious student, he was acting as a helper in a summer camp for teenagers, and he was faced with a noisy audience of teenagers and their visiting parents.

He told them of the death of Gershwin as a great composer, and said he would play a short piece as an elegy for him. He sat down, and played one of Gershwin's preludes, a quiet piece: to his amazement the rowdy audience kept perfectly silent while he played, intent on listening although they were not at all an especially musical group. That, he felt, had something to do with his own magnetism. It quickly became apparent then – and more so later – that Lenny was so multi-talented that it was difficult to tell which role he should follow – conductor, composer or pianist in many different fields, classical and jazz. This was brilliantly summed up for Lenny's seventieth birthday by his collaborator on *West Side Story*, Stephen Sondheim, who produced witty new lyrics for Kurt Weill's celebrated *Saga of Jenny*, beginning with the line: 'Poor Lenny – Ten gifts too many – The curse of being versatile . . .'

It was during the war, in 1943, that Bernstein's year of marvels took place. He had to take the place of Bruno Walter at the last minute in a New York concert, and his performance was so remarkable that it was reported on the front page of the *New York Times*. It was also that year that his first ballet was performed on Broadway, while his First Symphony, *Jeremiah*, was played with great success by the New York Philharmonic. Plainly Bernstein was a young man to watch.

Mitropoulos was not his only mentor. Aaron Copland also advised him, after hearing him play his difficult *Piano Variations* at a party. Copland never gave him anything like a composition lesson, but he advised him on what course to take in developing his career. Many years later I asked Lenny which conductors had most influenced him, and to my surprise he said Fritz Reiner, who had given him some instruction at the Curtis Institute.

As is well known, Reiner was the least demonstrative of conductors, barely moving the end of his baton more than a few inches. It is even said that a double-bass player in his Chicago Symphony Orchestra once brought a pair of binoculars to see his beat, but Reiner did not see the funny side of that, and dismissed him on the spot, something that could be done in those days when conductors were autocrats.

Lenny by contrast was one of the most acrobatic of conductors, even leaping into the air on occasion. He explained to me that what he had learned from Reiner was to know exactly what you meant by every gesture, however slight: I can believe that even Lenny's most extravagant acrobatics were completely controlled.

One of the most memorable of Lenny's recording sessions that I attended was with the LSO at the EMI studios in St John's Wood. He had just performed Stravinsky's *Rite of Spring* at the English Bach Festival, organised by Lina Lalandi, and came to the studio to put his reading on disc. Over two sessions he patiently put every section together, a task that was made the more difficult as at the time Sony/CBS was determined to record in quadraphonic 'surround sound'.

Lenny stood in the middle of the orchestra conducting to all four points of the compass, and over the two sessions had everything covered. He then said that he wanted to extend the session to do a complete performance, now that everything was in the can. Fortunately the musicians were available, and so in an extended recording session Lenny conducted a complete performance of Stravinsky's masterpiece. And that is what appears on the finished disc. It was this experience more than anything that subsequently, in his recordings for Deutsche Grammophon, led to Lenny preferring to record live performances rather than slogging away at regular studio recordings.

He always scheduled a tidying-up session after such live recordings, and I remember when I was in Vienna to interview the great Wagnerian soprano Birgit Nilsson that the window of her hotel room looked out over the back of the Wiener Musikverein. She knew that Lenny was scheduled to record Beethoven's Ninth Symphony in concert, yet, as she pointed out, much of the performance was in fact recorded afterwards in 'patching takes'.

In the same Musikverein, home of the Vienna Philharmonic, I remember an occasion when Lenny recorded not just Brahms's First Piano Concerto but Haydn's Symphony No. 88. The Haydn went very well, but he decided to demonstrate the virtuosity of the orchestra – which had just awarded him the orchestra's Ring, a prized honour – by not using his arms. He simply sat in front of them, and occasionally moved his shoulders, yet the Vienna Philharmonic amazingly was able to negotiate all the stuttering entries in the finale without a fault – an amazing feat.

It was in one of the Brahms Concertos with Krystian Zimerman that Lenny was for once thwarted in one of his suggestions for the interpretation. 'Can't you expand that phrase?' he suggested to Krystian, who responded with a curt, 'Everyone does that,' insisting on taking his own course. What was remarkable about the performance was the extraordinary slowness, perfectly sustained without loss of tension by either the soloist or the orchestra.

It was on Lenny's last visit to London in 1989, when he came to record the latest version of his musical *Candide*, that a press conference was called at the last minute. It was mid-morning at the Savoy, and relatively few of us were there. Yet when Lenny came into the large reception room, he looked round for someone he knew, and came loping over to say hello to a friendly figure, me. He began by saying he had seen an excellent piece I had written in the *Guardian* (he always claimed to be a *Guardian* reader). I know myself, if I chance to meet a *Guardian* colleague, I will say how much I enjoyed a piece of theirs, but I can rarely if ever remember what it was.

Lenny amazingly did remember. It was about Vladimir Ashkenazy, who was returning to Moscow for the first time since his defection. I had expanded the piece as much as I could, as my *Guardian* bosses were irritated that I had not accepted the invitation made by the RPO for me to join the party to Russia. I was determined to show that, by following the visit on television, I could do an even better, fuller piece than if I had actually been present, with all the Soviet restrictions that I knew would be imposed.

How right I was. The cameras followed Ashkenazy in his car from the airport to his hotel, and at one moment he pointed to what he described as his favourite building in Moscow, the Spartak Stadium. The cameras also followed Ashkenazy when, as a final contribution, he conducted Tchaikovsky's Fourth Symphony. I remember outrageously using the phrase, 'Blinking back a tear as he began the coda', to demonstrate what detail the television coverage provided.

When Lenny complimented me, I explained that I had not

actually been in Moscow, but had written my piece on the basis of
the television programme. He was astounded, and questioned me
further. Cameras were snapping us both, as the television men were
wondering to whom Lenny was talking so warmly. Fortunately, I was
able to get copies of the photos, both black and white and colour, and
that is how I have a portrait of Lenny and me taken from the photos,
painted by my favourite portrait painter, who specialises in musical
subjects, Jeffrey Spedding.

On that London visit the recording of *Candide* was bedevilled by
the fact that, one after another, the cast went down with the influenza
that was reaching epidemic proportions in London. Lenny himself
was suffering but he refused to give up, and persisted in continuing with the recording, though plainly, with watering eyes and every
sign of 'flu, he should certainly have been in bed. He dignified the
complaint as 'the royal 'flu', a rare and rarefied ailment of which no
one else had ever heard.

It was several months later in Vienna that I saw Lenny for the
last time. It was now February 1990 and he was due to sign a new
contract with DG, one that included exciting items such as Britten's
opera *Peter Grimes*, a work whose American premiere he had given
many years before. When he saw me there, he asked why I was present and, provocatively, I said, 'Because I love you, Lenny,' much
to the surprise of my companion, the then editor of *Gramophone,*
Chris Pollard.

The purpose of his Vienna visit was to make a live recording of
Bruckner's Ninth Symphony that very evening. In the event it was a
disappointing performance with little of the high-voltage electricity
one always associates with Bernstein performances. He was sub-
jected to a supper with the assembled company afterwards, dozens
of people, just when he obviously wanted to get back to his hotel and
rest. Knowing that I was one of the people who might have revived
Lenny's spirits, the press lady of DG had me sitting directly opposite
him, joined by another friend likely to draw him out.

Yet nothing we did could rouse him from his obvious depression and, as soon as he could, he pleaded tiredness and left. Happily, the repeat performance recorded the following day was quite different, as the finished discs clearly demonstrate, and so DG had its last Bernstein Bruckner's Ninth after all.

I was especially admiring of the two works he wrote to celebrate the Bicentenary of the United States in 1976. The first was *Songfest*, a work of which Lenny was rightly proud. It is an extended song-cycle with orchestra, using an inspired sequence of poems, including one by Walt Whitman, which brought out the poet's homosexuality, movingly so, 'To What You Said'. Particularly touching is Lenny's setting of some lines in the middle: 'I am that rough and simple person. I am he who kisses his comrade lightly on the lips at parting, and I am one who is kissed in return.' In the varied sequence of settings Lenny included one by Gertrude Stein, and a moving address to her husband by the early American poet Anne Bradstreet.

The other Bicentenary offering by Bernstein was a Broadway musical outlining the sequence of presidents from George Washington onwards, *1600 Pennsylvania Avenue*, taking its name from the address of the White House in Washington, where much of the action was set. It was predicted to be a flop, even though all the contributors, not just Lenny, were most distinguished. I happened to be in Washington on the LSO's Bicentennial tour when it was given a preview in Washington, and I managed to attend a matinee performance.

I was thrilled by the first half, in which you followed a black servant, Lud, from his boyhood through a period when blacks in Washington were in danger of being enslaved, until he became a senior assistant in the White House. It used a haunting song, vintage Bernstein by any comparison, 'Take Care of This House'. In the second half the piece rather lost its way in a sequence of unrelated numbers. I wrote a letter, suggesting to Lenny that he might rescue the first half, and use it as a cantata. I knew Lenny was staying at the

Watergate Hotel, and so I walked all the way from my hotel to the Watergate to deliver my letter.

Unfortunately, he did not receive it at the time for some reason; it was six months later that I received a delightful letter from him promising to consider my idea, as *1600 Pennsylvania Avenue* had indeed proved to be a total flop on Broadway. Sadly, he never got round to doing it himself but, since his death, other sympathetic hands have produced a cantata based as I suggested, and I was glad to be given the chance of introducing it on its world premiere at the Barbican in London.

The other work by Bernstein that in a way I might have influenced was his Third Symphony, *Kaddish*, a symphony of mourning. I had the first recording to review for *Gramophone*, and I gave it a rather dusty reception. I objected to the idea of a woman narrator reciting the words of God. 'Why not a man?' I asked. I did not realise that the reciter was Lenny's beloved wife, Felicia Montealegre, who died sadly young in 1978. I made a number of more detailed suggestions for amendments too. I did not think about my review until much later, when Lenny was making a definitive recording of his revised version for DG. To my embarrassment, but in a way to my gratification, he had made all the alterations I had suggested.

Over the years I have been privileged to know many musicians with charismatic qualities. Yet Lenny stands out above them all, even such figures as Yehudi Menuhin or Mstislav Rostropovich, with his supreme charisma. I hope that what I have written about these great characters here will bring out their warm human qualities and the affection I have had for them all.

Interlude 2: Southend-on-Sea

At Leigh North Street Junior School in the 1930s, the big event of each year came on 24 May, Empire Day, originally marking Queen Victoria's birthday, when the school would perform a pageant celebrating the glories of the British Empire. We would assemble in the big hall, while in the centre of the stage, representing Britannia, was Pamela Jay, a tall gawky girl with blonde hair. They would borrow a fireman's helmet from the fire station round the corner for Pamela to wear, and, sitting proudly, she would display a round shield emblazoned with the Union flag.

Pamela, sweet as she was, was not the sharpest knife in the drawer. Nor was Betty Joslin, my companion one year in the pageant, when together we represented Canada. We were told to enter and move to centre stage and bow to the central figure. Betty was so overcome with wonder at what she saw that she forgot to bow, and I, ever concerned for getting things right, jabbed her sharply in the ribs with my elbow, saying in a stage whisper, 'Bow!' I did not understand why everyone roared with laughter.

I remember the opening of the little jingle we had to deliver to Britannia:

Our home is in Canada, land of the west.
Of all the earth's places we love it the best,
Its mountains and prairies, di-daa di-di-daaa . . .

Which is where my memory, perhaps mercifully, gives out.

One Saturday morning in September 1934, when I was just six years old, profoundly altered the rest of my life. At the end of our road in Leigh-on-Sea was a large house called The Gables. This housed a branch of the Metropolitan Academy of Music, a private academy for teaching all kinds of musical subjects, including singing, piano, violin and cello, as well as drama. Consequently, when one entered, one would regularly be assailed by a cacophony of competing sounds of music teachers giving lessons.

On that Saturday morning I first went to an elocution class conducted by an inspired teacher, Clare Angel, and I followed that by going to another part of the Academy for a percussion-band class conducted by a wonderfully patient teacher, Doris Mingay. My mother wanted me to go to the elocution class, because she was determined that 'Our Teddy' should not speak Essex. By that she meant what has now been dubbed 'Estuary English', the product even then of Southend-on-Sea, on the estuary of the Thames.

Very soon I graduated from the class to private lessons with Clare Angel, and was meticulously guided to speak with a received pronunciation. I was caught young enough for the process to be completely natural, and for many years – but no longer – it was a great benefit in my broadcasting career in the BBC. Clare also taught me how to produce my speaking voice, so that I have always had a loud voice, using all my sinuses. She was the most handsome, square-jawed woman, then still in her late twenties, a pillar of the Girl Guide movement, who attracted much admiration from her teenage girl students. I had no idea about lesbianism, but I listened intently to the girls who appeared with me in the plays that Clare presented, saying how 'frightfully keen' they were on Clare.

Miss Mingay's percussion-band class marked my first serious entry into the joys of music. I had already shown signs of being musical, and soon enough I graduated from the percussion-band class, which taught me the rudiments of music, to singing lessons with my great mentor, Freda Parry, and piano lessons with Doris Mingay. It was a halcyon period of discovery for me, for though I was never a good pianist, I was just beginning to discover music seriously, and I drank in every experience eagerly. I was also starting to write my own music, encouraged in my mind by Freda Parry's message that music is about enjoyment.

Freda was a great character, a centre of music in the then phil-istine Southend-on-Sea. She was the great-niece of the composer Hubert Parry, so in her Junior Choir we sang not only 'Jerusalem' but also Parry's parallel setting of John of Gaunt's speech from Shakespeare's *Richard II*: 'This royal throne of Kings, this sceptr'd isle', ending with 'this Earth, this realm, this England'. It is a marvel-lous song, a counterpart to 'Jerusalem' that deserves to be far better known. Freda Parry's Junior Choir even appeared on BBC *Children's Hour*, which was very important before the days of television, and I have a vivid memory of Broadcasting House in 1938, and remember being delighted to get the autograph of Val Gielgud, then the head of BBC Drama.

My greatest moments of glory came a little later, at the beginning of the Second World War, when in the early days charity concerts for a time took the place of curtailed professional performances. 'Little Teddy Greenfield' had quite a success reciting poems that gener-ally cast me as a naughty boy, very much against character I fear (or perhaps I should be proud). I went on to do some of the mono-logues of Marriott Edgar, made popular by Stanley Holloway, such as *The Lion and Albert*. My Lancashire accent was counted quite authentic.

Many of the concerts where I performed – generally in church halls – were reviewed in the local weekly paper, the *Southend Standard*. Most of them appeared over the initials RTP, whose reviews were regularly enthusiastic about my performances. Rhoda Tuck Pook ('RTP'), as we discovered, was a great character. She was the daugh-ter of the paper's proprietor, and by the measure of Southend-on-Sea she was an exotic figure, always wearing black with dark glasses hid-ing her identity. She was a good, knowledgeable critic, and she had a secondary claim to fame in that she was a frequent winner in the very popular competitions that lightened the final pages of the *New Statesman*, then at its peak under Kingsley Martin. I remember that, at Cambridge some years later, friends were fascinated that I knew

Rhoda Tuck Pook personally. They had always assumed it was a pseudonym!

We were fortunate as the 1930s progressed in that, in addition to Empire Day, we had two major national events, the Silver Jubilee of King George V in 1935 and the Coronation of King George VI in 1937. At Leigh North Street these were both the excuse for major celebrations. We were all given little presents by the local Council, a commemorative spoon in 1935 and a Coronation book in 1937. We had a celebratory tea on each occasion with a disgusting 'lemonade' beverage made with powder, plus sandwiches, sausage rolls and the like.

It is also a sign of the period that, when the new liner, the *Queen Mary*, was launched from the John Brown shipyard on the Clyde, the whole school was taken to the big hall to hear the occasion reported on the radio. It might have been because the launch was a major national event, signalling the end of the period of recession and slump three or four years earlier. It was expected that the Queen would name the vessel 'Britannia', a name apt for Cunard, the names of whose vessels regularly ended in '–ia', and it came as quite a surprise when she announced the name of *Queen Mary*. At the time I had a Dinky Toy model of the ship made before the launch when it was called simply the '534', its number in the John Brown shipyard.

The other great event came in 1938, at the time of the Munich crisis, when the prime minister, Neville Chamberlain, had been to see Hitler. Such was the optimism in the air that we were all issued with gasmasks, a major operation. I remember the school caretaker, Mr Wells, shepherding the queues of people waiting for their gasmasks, uttering the not especially reassuring mantra, 'All in good time.' Soon enough, at the outbreak of war in 1939, we would be urged to carry them everywhere we went, even though the danger of a gas attack was minimal.

Chapter Three

The Originals

Throughout my life I have had the fortune to know a wide variety of individuals, some of them personal friends, others major public figures. What they all have in common is how little they have in common, with one another or with anyone else; but each made a deep impression on my life.

WALTER LEGGE

As the recording manager of EMI Walter Legge brought about a revolution in the way that recordings are regarded. His idea was that, far from being a mere 'photograph' in sound of an artist's live performance, a recording should be crafted to bring out special qualities, making the recording a work of art in itself. Not only that, Legge in 1945 founded an orchestra of hand-picked players that quickly achieved standards of performance never achieved in Britain before, the Philharmonia.

It was more than just a recording orchestra; it was one that helped to transform the recording careers of such artists as Herbert von Karajan in his early years and later Otto Klemperer, giving them a status beyond what they had achieved before. Walter also enticed Arturo Toscanini to London for one famous visit in the autumn of 1952, during which the aged maestro conducted all four Brahms symphonies, plus two lesser pieces. The recording of those concerts at the Royal Festival Hall, made under the supervision of Legge himself, were at last released, by Testament, in the year 2000, after decades of contractual wrangling. It is nothing short of a revelation: this was indeed a wonderful ensemble, possessed of some of the greatest soloists of their day. On top of all this Legge married one of the greatest singers of the century, Elisabeth Schwarzkopf, whose career from then on he masterminded, even though as a very positive artist in her own right she did not always follow his instructions.

Legge's career in EMI started in the 1920s, but it was in the early 1930s that he had the brilliant idea of founding the Society movement. This involved making recordings with specialist appeal, asking for subscriptions for them, instead of making them available in a shop. His first project was to record the *Lieder* of Hugo Wolf with such great artists as Elena Gerhardt and Gerhard Hüsch. Legge was a devotee not just of the *Lieder* of Wolf but of *Lieder* generally, which helped him to guide Schwarzkopf towards expanding her mastery of that art form.

In his early years as recording producer his greatest coup was to persuade EMI to record Mozart's *Die Zauberflöte* in Berlin with Thomas Beecham conducting, rather than at Glyndebourne, where EMI's pioneering recordings of the Mozart–da Ponte operas had been made. It was at the height of the Nazi period in Germany, yet Legge overcame all problems, and over the summers of 1938 and 1939 he secured an inspired performance under Beecham, very well cast, including Erna Berger as Queen of Night, Tiana Lemnitz as Pamina, Gerhard Hüsch as Papageno and Helge Rosvaenge as Tamino. In the small professional choir that took part was the young Elisabeth Schwarzkopf, but Legge failed to notice her. 'I must have been blind,' as he said later.

I first got to know Walter when he was at the height of his powers as EMI recording manager, masterminding in particular a whole series of opera recordings that have never been surpassed, not least those conducted by Herbert von Karajan in his early years. Outstanding were the recordings of Humperdinck's *Hänsel und Gretel* and Strauss's *Der Rosenkavalier*, both with Schwarzkopf. Part of Legge's genius lay in assembling casts that were as near ideal as possible, using such singers as Irmgard Seefried, Christa Ludwig and Dietrich Fischer-Dieskau.

Some of my happiest memories of the period came in the extended listening sessions at the house in Hampstead that he and Schwarzkopf owned. They would go on until three or even four in the morning, with Walter delighting in playing me some of the recordings made by his favourite singers of the past such as Titta Ruffo. He would also reminisce about his memories of such artists, and I only wish I had a recording of all the many stories he told me.

When I went to Legge's Hampstead home, he would regularly keep me waiting for quite a time, a delay made the more congenial by the strong Martinis prepared by his secretary. On one occasion when I was very pressed for time, I deliberately arrived late, only to find Walter drumming his fingers in impatience. 'You're late, my boy,' he said, and it soon emerged just why he was impatient. I had just settled down with my first Martini, and the phone rang. His secretary picked it up, and said, 'It's Bayreuth for you.'

At that Walter visibly expanded, and said in his grandest voice, 'Ach Wieland!', referring to the brilliant grandson of Richard Wagner who more than anyone established the new post-war tradition at Bayreuth, simplifying the staging in the interests of clarity. It was Walter's joy that I had been there to witness the telephonic encounter, and I was touched that afterwards he said how wonderful it was to be rung up by Wagner's grandson, a response that I never expected from someone who had achieved so much himself as a leading figure in the music industry. By nature he was not a modest man, but on this occasion he came near to displaying that quality.

In expansive mood Walter would say, 'I modelled my wife's voice on six singers.' He would then list them – the sopranos Meta Seinemeyer, who sadly died very young, Tiana Lemnitz, Frida Leider, Lotte Lehmann and Rosa Ponselle, as well as the great American contralto, whom he cited for her phrasing, Geraldine Farrar, aunt of the composer Samuel Barber. He also added a single phrase of Nellie

Melba, the word 'Bada' in Mimi's Farewell from Puccini's *La bohème*. He also urged Elisabeth to study the phrasing of Fritz Kreisler in his recordings of his own violin trifles, when she tackled operetta.

When after quite a delay I did meet Schwarzkopf at the Hampstead house, I naturally asked what singers had influenced her development. She immediately replied on cue, 'My husband modelled my voice on six singers . . .' I later learned that that was far from the whole truth, for Schwarzkopf was far too individual an artist to be bound by mere reflections of others.

It was when Legge, to everyone's surprise, announced the disbanding of the Philharmonia that I was able to witness the crisis from a privileged position. I was sad that Walter took the stance he did, but there was nothing I could do to budge him. As I later learned, he had just had an unfavourable report from his doctor about his heart, and in addition he was very well aware that the LSO, prompted by such leading players as Neville Marriner (in those days the principal second violin, having only just founded the Academy of St Martin in the Fields) and Barry Tuckwell, were turning the LSO into a serious rival to the Philharmonia. So much so, that Legge was worried that the pre-eminent status that he had built up for the Philharmonia would before long be undermined.

It was during the crisis that Legge asked me to go and see Harold Wilson, Leader of the Opposition at the time but poised to become prime minister later in the same year, 1964, to make him aware of the situation. I did just that, and Wilson issued a statement suggesting that a Labour government would seek to help orchestras such as the Philharmonia. That alarmed the LSO, who were immediately anxious not to be put at a disadvantage, so one morning I was rung up by Neville Marriner, who wanted me to meet the orchestra's new general manager, Ernest Fleischmann, and suggested dinner that evening. I pointed out that I was already scheduled to have dinner with Legge, but in the end I had to eat two dinners, the first cooked by Mollie Marriner at their Kensington flat, the second at the Savoy.

Several years later, when Walter had negotiated an agreement with EMI to divest himself of the royalties that until then he had received for Philharmonia recordings, he generously invited me to lunch in his suite at the Savoy. He was pleased to have contracted the agreement, even though it turned out to be far from advantageous for him. He expansively boasted, 'Of course I was the Pope of recording!' A little later he went on to lament the fact that, since he had left EMI, no one had wanted to employ him for recordings. I then cruelly had to point out that 'No one employs the Pope.'

In the years that followed it was always a joy to meet up with Legge during the Salzburg Festival, as he always seemed to choose a similar period to mine for his stay. He would demand that I should ring him every morning, and see whether he was free to meet up that day. As often as not, he would say he was expecting 'Herbert to call', meaning Karajan. In the event Karajan never did, as he kicked aside those who had furthered his early career, Walter more than anyone. Thus I would spend delightful times with Walter, usually over a meal, when as ever he was full of reminiscences. Again I so regret that I was unable to record them.

EDWARD HEATH

It was during my time in the Parliamentary Lobby for the *Guardian*, when I was also the paper's record critic, that I got to know Ted Heath, the Right Honourable Edward Heath, at that time Chief Whip for the Macmillan government and later the minister responsible for negotiating Britain's entry into the European Community. We found we had many points in common, both having been born to lower-middle-class parents, on opposite banks of the Thames estuary, each with music and politics as our principal interests – and both called Ted.

I remember writing to congratulate Ted when he was elected as Leader of the Conservative Party. Back came a duplicated form thanking me for my support, to which Ted had added, under an asterisk, 'support as a record collector', knowing that a dedicated *Guardian* man was unlikely to be a Conservative voter.

The development of the boy Ted's love of music came when his parents for his ninth birthday bought him a Thornton Bobby piano on hire purchase for £42. The family would hold sing-songs round it when Heath's father would sing ballads such as 'Roses of Picardy' and even a Verdi aria in translation. The boy's earliest musical training came as a choirboy in the local parish church, and as he grew older he took to attending Henry Wood Promenade Concerts in London.

When he reached Balliol College, Oxford, where he subsequently won the organ scholarship, he spent a high proportion of his tiny allowance on hiring a piano and occasionally buying 78 rpm recordings to be played on his wind-up portable gramophone. Among them were the HMV recording of Elgar's First Symphony conducted by the composer and one of Bruckner's Fourth, both involving half a dozen or so short-playing discs. It was at this formative period that he first started to conduct a carol concert each Christmas in his home town of Broadstairs in Kent, an event that continued into his years as prime minister and beyond, eventually transferring to the improbably named Crook Log, just outside his Bexley constituency.

He seriously thought of pursuing music as a profession, but was dissuaded after consulting his musical mentor in Oxford, Hugh Allen – for principally financial rather than musical reasons. That set him thinking all the more seriously of politics, for he had become president of the Oxford Union and Chairman of the Oxford University Conservative Association. Yet there was no lull in his devotion to music – rather the opposite. He heard Toscanini conducting Beethoven's *Missa solemnis* on the eve of war and Bruno Walter conducting Mahler in New York, when he was on an English-Speaking Union debating tour. It is characteristic of him that he meticulously kept the programmes of all the concerts he attended, preserving them as he would Cabinet documents.

During army service in wartime he managed to keep up his music, even conducting a dance band in one unit, with 'Tiger Rag' as the climax of each concert. In the army he was still able to attend the occasional concert. In uniform, he attended the first performance of Vaughan Williams's Fifth Symphony, conducted by the composer in a half-empty Albert Hall. His notable achievement as a colonel in Hanover, after Germany was occupied, was to ensure the opening of an opera house in the city, at the old Palace of Herrenhausen on the outskirts. I remember myself seeing Wagner's *Tristan und Isolde* for the first time in that improvised opera house. Opera had become increasingly important to Heath, and over the years the Salzburg Festival and Glyndebourne became regular features of his always busy itinerary.

When Ted became prime minister, I would get invitations to the informal concerts he organised, whether at the prime minister's country home at Chequers or in 10 Downing Street. I remember going to a concert by the Amadeus Quartet in Downing Street, to which I was invited by one of his press secretaries, Barbara Hosking. He was surprised to see me, but obviously pleased. I was talking to my contemporary at Cambridge, Patrick Jenkin, a Treasury minister at the time, who plainly did not recognise me even though I had been much more active than him in the Cambridge Union. I fear my small-mindedness came out when the prime minister came past and, ignoring his Treasury minister, invited me to go up to his flat above to hear the hi-fi. I swept away in triumph.

On another occasion Ted rang me up one Sunday evening, as he occasionally would do, wanting a late-night chat about music. It was the Sunday immediately following the birthday of a friend who had been in the navy, but who had sadly become alcoholic. When the operator on the phone said she had a call for me I immediately thought it must be my ex-naval friend, who always reversed the charges. Instead, it was quite a different sailor, who challenged me, asking, 'I don't suppose you came to my concert yesterday.'

In fact, prompted by his invitation, I had attended the Youth and Music concert he conducted very capably on the Saturday morning. I had then written a review of it for the *Guardian*, and was rather pleased with my opening line about approving his unpatronising manner with young listeners, being a 'bachelor Uncle Ted myself'. I added that I had likened him to Stokowski (I can't think how), and Ted's response was to bridle at being compared with someone as old as that.

On another occasion when Ted was still prime minister, I went to a concert given by the Berlin Philharmonic under Karajan. Their programme was very short, consisting only of Beethoven's Fourth and Fifth Symphonies. I complained in my review of being given short measure without even an encore offered. As I liked to do, I left promptly at the end, but so had another member of the audience, Ted Heath, and his private secretary, Robert Armstrong. My guest was my dear friend David Hart, who was taking me to the Royal Albert Hall and back on his motorbike. As was usual for him he was wearing total leather, not as common in those days as it became later. I was on the back of his bike when we had to stop at the traffic light just opposite the Royal Albert Hall. David suddenly whispered to me (this was before crash helmets were compulsory), 'It's him!' There next to us was the prime minister's car with Ted and Robert Armstrong on the back seat. I was acutely embarrassed, and turned my head the other way. We then roared away, but we were stopped again by the next traffic light.

I happened to see Ted at a reception at the Festival Hall a week or so later, and by way of light conversation I said, 'Oh, by the way, I saw you after the Karajan concert.' He replied sharply, 'I know you did. You cut us dead!' He then proceeded to criticise the review I had written, in which I complained of short measure. With some justice he pointed out that the programme had offered superlative perfor-mances of two of the greatest masterpieces in the repertory under a supreme conductor: 'And yet you also wanted a waltz by Streowss.' I shall never forget his curious pronunciation of the 'ow' sound.

It was when Ted had not been in Downing Street very long that André Previn, as principal conductor of the LSO, asked him to conduct an overture at a Festival Hall concert. He chose Elgar's *Cockaigne*, a difficult choice, with its different sections, replete with starts and stops. In the event the performance was a great success, and a recording of it quickly appeared on the EMI label. One of the only criticisms to be made was that, at the first appearance of the great love theme, he allowed the music to expand in a way more fitting for the reprise of that melody.

If until then Heath had been regarded as a cold, unbending figure, here was a positive demonstration of the emotional warmth behind that exterior, something I increasingly came to recognise. If the love theme was performed with even greater warmth than was merited, that simply demonstrated how moved this conductor was. Never had a prime minister displayed such artistic sympathy in the art of music. Here was a red-blooded performance of *Cockaigne* that still holds its own against any rival version in the catalogue.

It was after Ted had been both ousted from 10 Downing Street and replaced as Leader of the Conservative Party by Margaret Thatcher that I got to know him even better. I loathed Thatcher as much as he did, having encountered her when, as a newly elected MP, she was lucky in the ballot for Private Members' Bills, and sought to introduce a measure of which the National Union of Journalists disapproved. As Secretary of the Parliamentary Branch of the NUJ, I was persuaded by Joe Haines to attend a meeting to be addressed by the new MP.

I felt my hair standing on end; I had never come across anyone who was so completely convinced of her own rightness, and the wrongness of everyone else. I was horrified. In my years in the Press Gallery I came to like MPs from every political spectrum, left and right, but Margaret Thatcher was the one exception. Years later on one occasion when Ted came to have dinner with me at my house in Folgate Street, I suggested to him that, if he had known as soon as I did what Margaret Thatcher was like, he would never have promoted her off the backbenches. 'She would have become a megalomaniac monster rather like Dame Irene Ward,' I concluded, citing a notorious but far from influential eccentric who had remained confined to the backbenches. Ted leaned back in his chair, and said sadly, 'I rather liked Dame Irene Ward.' In fact my timing was wrong, as Mrs Thatcher was already on the ministerial ladder when Ted became prime minister, and in the early days she proved one of the most capable of his ministers.

Another memory I have is from television, when at a party given by the Queen on board the decommissioned *Britannia*, Ted was lecturing the then US Secretary of State, saying that he should have gone to see Saddam Hussein, adding, 'I did!' At that the Queen chipped in, saying with a smile, 'But you were expendable!' She immediately repeated the remark. I suggested afterwards that the Queen must have been very fond of him, if she felt she could tease him like that.

I also remember seeing Ted at the Snape Maltings Concert Hall in the interval of an Aldeburgh Festival concert. He said how delighted he was by my review of a version of *Cockaigne* by Eugene Ormandy. At first I failed to understand, and then it occurred to me that as one of two selected comparisons for *Cockaigne* I had listed the LSO–Heath recording. The prime minister was plainly more gratified by that musical compliment than by any political comment.

After Ted left Downing Street, he quickly enjoyed great success with his lavishly illustrated book on sailing. I met him at a party and I suggested that he should follow it up with a book on music. He was at once interested, asking me to arrange a meeting. I went along to his house in Wilton Street near Victoria, rented to him on extremely favourable terms by the Westminster Estate, and there I outlined my ideas for a book on music that concentrated on his personal enjoyment of music, surprisingly something rare in books on music. I outlined a sequence of chapters as a suggestion, and I was gratified to discover that his first draft, which he asked me to read, followed exactly the pattern I had suggested. In *Music: A Joy for Life*, as in the music-making itself, Ted revealed a warmth and openness that few had suspected. It is one of the cherishable few books that tells purely and directly of musical enjoyment.

During that same period, the late 1970s and early 1980s, Ted realised his dream of conducting the Berlin Philharmonic, plus several prestigious American symphony orchestras including those of Chicago and Cleveland. There is an extraordinary recording from the States of his rendition of Aaron Copland's *Lincoln Portrait*, later to be recorded in the studio by his nemesis Margaret Thatcher. I know which version I prefer. Ted also helped Lionel and Joy Bryer to establish the European Community Youth Orchestra, conducting that fine band on its summer tours of 1978, 1979 and 1980. No one who attended a packed Salisbury Cathedral for one of the five concerts Ted gave to celebrate his eightieth birthday in 1996 is likely to forget it. It was an electric occasion, featuring one of Ted's favourite pianists, Ivo Pogorelich, playing Chopin, and culminating in an almost impossibly slow, ecstatic performance of Bruckner's *Te Deum*.

Shortly after that great event, the head of his private office at the time, Michael McManus, convinced him to revise and update the book. I was glad again to be able to help, as Michael drafted some new chapters in Heath style. In the process I went down to Ted's house in Salisbury a number of times, to give him ideas, including one when the wives of his personal bodyguards were visiting along with their husbands and, rather to my surprise, they showed their devotion to a master who could be very demanding. Sadly, the production standards for the book were not at all impressive, with a number of howlers in the text and, more embarrassingly, in some of the picture captions, all of which could and should have been easily avoided with just a little more care and attention. It was still a project worth tackling, however, not least because it turned out to be an invaluable test run for the writing and editing of Ted's award-winning political memoirs, *The Course of My Life,* again undertaken by a team with Michael at its head, just a year or so later.

I would also make an annual visit to Salisbury to act as adviser on music for the Praemium Imperiale, a project sponsored by the Fujisankei Corporation of Japan to provide an artistic equivalent to the Nobel Prizes. I was one of Ted's two advisers on music, the other being his former private secretary and later head of the Civil Service, Lord (Robert) Armstrong. It was disconcerting when one year we had nominated Michael Tippett as musical choice to find the jury in Japan changing that to Andrew Lloyd Webber, something of which we strongly disapproved.

ERNEST FLEISCHMANN

Ernest Fleischmann was a man of many talents, and knew it. He was born in Frankfurt, Germany into a Jewish family who emigrated to South Africa when Ernest was just a boy. He came to London to take over the job of general manager of the London Symphony Orchestra in 1959, after Neville Marriner, the great horn-player Barry Tuckwell and other leading members of the LSO decided that Walter Legge's Philharmonia had kept pride of place among London orchestras for too long, while the LSO had been seriously lagging, at one time at the bottom of the league. Marriner was behind the move to weed out string-players who were no longer first rate, and to build a band of strings of the first order. The LSO also persuaded fine wind-players to join up, such as the clarinettist Gervase de Peyer and, later, Jack Brymer. When they visited Africa to take part in the Bulawayo Festival, they also spent time in South Africa, where they met Ernest Fleischmann, then intent on taking up a career as a conductor.

He had turned down the idea of leading the Cape Town Symphony Orchestra, when the LSO directors invited him to be the orchestra's go-ahead new general manager. In that role he certainly found his true métier. Though his management of the orchestra was often controversial and regularly high handed, it was undoubtedly inspired.

It was the brisk progress the LSO had already made under Fleischmann that made Legge worry that his Philharmonia was falling to second place, which seems to have persuaded him to try to disband the orchestra in 1964, in a sort of self-imposed *Götterdämmerung*. In the event the Philharmonia refused to be disbanded, and they became the self-governing New Philharmonia, a title that persisted until after Legge's death. Meanwhile the LSO was surging ahead, prompted by Fleischmann's original and sometimes controversial ideas of making concerts more attractive. It made headlines when he hired Pierre Monteux, then eighty-six, as music director on a twenty-five-year renewable contract.

Sadly Monteux died all too soon, after impetuously climbing many storeys up to his hotel room following a power cut. Fleischmann then imaginatively chose István Kertész as his successor. He had great success, but sadly was drowned during one of the orchestra's trips to Florida for the Festival, a visit inspired and organised by Fleischmann. The next conductor chosen was André Previn – after Fleischmann had left the LSO, having almost inevitably been sacked by the Board for overstepping the mark. He then joined the CBS Record Company in London as the European Head of Masterworks. André Previn subsequently enjoyed a longer period as principal conductor of the orchestra than anyone up to that time.

Fleischmann meanwhile was not really happy in the record industry, where he remained from 1967 until 1969. In that year he wrote a vigorous article for *American High Fidelity*, underlining the problems of American orchestras, who regularly depended on rich patrons for funds, necessarily deferring to their foibles and personal tastes. He outlined just the situation that the Los Angeles Philharmonic was facing, obsessed with the idea of ridding the city of its reputation as simply the film capital, and prompted by Dorothy Chandler, wife of the editor of the *Los Angeles Times*, the orchestra was determined to bring culture to the city.

As well as raising enough money from her friends to build the Dorothy Chandler Pavilion in the new Music Center, Mrs Chandler was behind the appointment of the young Zubin Mehta as the orchestra's new principal conductor. Fleischmann's appointment then followed, after his *High Fidelity* article was regarded as little short of a job application. In Los Angeles Fleischmann had just the job he needed and luckily found no opposition from Mehta when he took over far more of the duties of selection that a general manager usually has. He became a sort of dictator, and a very successful one too. When Mehta left on being invited to become the music director of the New York Philharmonic, Fleischmann chose Carlo Maria Giulini, a conductor who hated the cut and thrust of running an orchestra. That left an even greater array of decisions to Fleischmann.

In popularising the orchestra, he organised such events as *Star Wars* concerts along with a light show. As the American critic Alan Rich has written, 'He functioned as impresario, talent-scout, super-organiser, arts politician par excellence. He was the inventor of a whole new brand of cultural citizen, the concert manager as star.' Needless to say he did not please everyone with his arrogance and, among others, Martin Bernheimer, then chief music critic of the *Los Angeles Times*, made a savage attack on his dictatorial ways.

He almost met his match in André Previn, who after his early Hollywood career seemed a natural choice as principal conductor, but Fleischmann won the battle, going on to promote rising stars such as Simon Rattle and Esa-Pekka Salonen to take a prominent part in the orchestra's programme. Indeed it was Salonen who was appointed, by Fleischmann on his own initiative (and when Previn was still nominally music director), to conduct an important international tour. That made his appointment as the next music director almost inevitable.

One of Fleischmann's last projects in Los Angeles before retiring was to promote the idea of a new hall specifically for the orchestra, since the Chandler Pavilion had serious acoustic drawbacks as a multi-purpose hall. He found the necessary sponsor in the widow of Walt Disney, and so the new Disney Concert Hall with a daring modern design by Frank Gehry can be regarded as Fleischmann's final achievement in the city, as everyone concedes, a great success, in every way a fitting close to his often spectacular career. He died in 2010.

SIR CLIVE GILLINSON

When, unexpectedly, the London Symphony Orchestra was looking for a new general manager, they lighted as a temporary choice on one of the backbench cellists in the orchestra, Clive Gillinson, who ran a small antiques business on the side. Clive proved to have a natural gift for running a business, so instead of him being simply a stopgap, he was quickly chosen for a permanent post, almost certainly the most successful general manager that the orchestra has ever had.

Clive not only had plenty of good ideas for developing the orchestra, but managed to carry them through with the co-operation of the committee of self-governing players, not always an easy task. It meant that the orchestra's engagements not only for concerts and tours but for recording sessions were kept at a healthy level, and it was largely through Clive that the LSO developed a special relationship with the City of London, and so became the resident orchestra of the then newly opened Barbican Hall. In the early days of the Barbican not every project was a success, and for a time the orchestra ran up a deficit, but thanks to Clive's know-how and shrewd handling of finances, the problems were all sorted out.

Clive was also a brilliant diplomat in handling sometimes temperamental artists, and his relationship with the cellist Mstislav Rostropovich was especially close and musically fruitful. The LSO Live label, which he founded, is a model of its kind, at the time of writing approaching its hundredth release, a remarkable achievement for all concerned. It is a sign of Clive's success that, when he was tempted to step down as general manager of the LSO, he went to New York as the newly knighted general manager of Carnegie Hall, having been head-hunted, another well-deserved success for one of the nicest, as well as one of the most capable, musician administrators in the world of classical music.

RODERICK GRADIDGE

My relationship with the architect Roderick Gradidge was initially very variable, with wonderful periods of pure companionship punctuated by fearsome rows, when one or other of us proved unreasonable. Happily, the relationship quickly settled down when Roddy proved an excellent companion for a reviewer to take to concerts. He knew little or nothing technically about music, but he was the perfect responder, unfailingly detecting the electricity behind a performance. So, if I was jaded on any occasion at a time when I was regularly reviewing five concerts a week, Roddy would put me right over any performance, particularly in orchestral music.

I would share in Roddy's successes as an architect, which were very variable, despite the brilliance and ingenuity of his architectural ideas, as he managed to alienate far too many clients with his demands. It was Roddy who suggested that I should try to get one of the derelict houses in Spitalfields, when I ran out of space in my Highgate flat. Even better, he produced superb plans to renovate a house that was initially derelict with a hole in the roof. His ideas for renovating the rear of the building included fitting authentic Georgian windows instead of the metal-framed modern windows that were originally there.

He also devised a downstairs kitchen and toilet over the office block on the ground floor, which allowed me to have a completely panelled dining room, where I might have had to settle for a partially panelled kitchen–dining room, an unsatisfactory solution. Having the kitchen extension on the back also allowed me to have a terrace leading from my study, another great advantage.

The only problem was expense; though initially the builder we hired estimated a cost of some £60,000, that proved a complete underestimate, and in the end I spent many times more than that, a sum made easier to cope with when it was spread over a long period. It also helped greatly that Roddy agreed to supervise the work, charging a flat fee, which meant that I could ring him up about even the slightest query over the authentic restoration of any section of the building.

I remember Roddy's delight when he was elected to be a member of the Art Workers' Guild, something he regarded as a great compliment. It was only when I retired from the staff of the *Guardian* at sixty-five, that I myself became an active member too. I was able to help a friend over his mortgage payments, when otherwise he could not have been able to accept the offer made by the Guild's Trustees to become the paid Secretary of the Guild, so minimal was the remuneration. Possibly because of that I was made an honorary member of the Guild (writing not being considered a craft in Guild terms), and I decided to take an active part in the Guild's work, quickly being elected to the Committee. It so happened that I was able to help defuse a long-running feud between the Guild's Trustees and the Committee, represented by Roddy, who pointed out that by the constitution the Trustees could in theory sell the Guild's property, 6 Queen Square, over the heads of the members, and no one could prevent them from doing so.

It required a simple amendment, which should not have been difficult to pass, but Roddy was so aggressive in his arguing against the Trustees, who were popular figures, that it became an emotional issue, Trustees versus Gradidge, and invariably Roddy lost in the voting. It required a degree of diplomacy to sort the problem out. With the active co-operation of the Master at the time, I played my part.

Each year the Past Masters of the Guild, of whom Roddy was one, would meet to nominate a Master for a year ahead. Twice over Roddy reported to me that my name had come up, and he had off his own bat suggested that I could not possibly do such a job. When for the third year I knew the Past Masters' Dinner was coming up, I said to Roddy that I wanted the chance to refuse any offer myself.

Of course I accepted the idea eagerly, as I had very positive ideas of the programme I wanted to present, half devoted traditionally to Arts and Crafts subjects and half to music. I also wanted to do interviews with the speakers, rather than getting them to do formal lectures, which I thought would be livelier as I count myself a skilled interviewer. It also made it easier for a lecturer to accept the offer of a talk.

My year began with my interview with Janet Baker, and continued with Joan Sutherland, the violinist Tasmin Little, the cellist Julian Lloyd Webber and the conductor Richard Bonynge, husband of Joan. For each of my musical interviews I prepared a sequence of musical illustrations, which again helped to aerate the results, and I like to think that in living memory the Guild has rarely had so starry a year.

I also enjoyed the formality of the office of Master, wearing a scarlet robe of office and a chain, and conducting meetings as considerately as possible, not letting individual guildsmen hog an occasion too much. Sadly, though Roddy had warmly approved my proposals for the year, he died suddenly a year before I took office, simply not waking up one morning, having suffered a massive heart attack. I like to think he would have enjoyed my year as Master as much as I did, when much of it was devised as a tribute to him.

JOHN STEANE

John Steane and I met and instantly became friends when we were both sergeants in the Royal Army Educational Corps doing our

National Service at Oswestry. It was a meeting of minds such as I had never known before, an experience to be cherished. John vividly described the period in the memoirs that his splendid friend and neighbour in Coventry, John Karran, put together for him, something that greatly cheered him in the days before his death.

On balance I did profit from those years of National Service, and am infinitely thankful that I didn't go up to Cambridge raw from school. I also met a life-long friend in Sgt (as he was then) Edward Greenfield. The future music critic of the *Guardian* was as much a fish-out-of-water as myself, and together we faced the Sergeants' Mess. The legitimate residents were fairly successful in concealing their scorn for these bespectacled aliens forced upon them. We (there must have been a dozen of us) were talkative enough among ourselves, but awkward and stand-offish with them, and it must have been something of an affront to them that our puny arms should carry the three stripes for which they had probably been through battles, bombardments and beach-heads untold. In fact some of them were told, and at mealtimes between chattering about T. S. Eliot and W. H. Auden we listened to their exploits and their sexploits like the inexperienced schoolboys we were.

From Ted I learned about modern music, Stravinsky, Bartók, Walton. In return I didn't think I had much to offer, but ten or so years later he wrote a book with the dedication 'For John Steane who in exchange for Bartók gave me Puccini'. We met again at Cambridge, and summer days at his home in Leigh-on-Sea were vintage occasions, with records (solid works in albums) and orchestral scores, a great broadening of my musical horizons. At the university he lived amid Union politics and important persons, while I led a laidback existence, centred on my own college. When I arrived there, Jesus was famous as a rowing college; but when I went down we may no longer have been head of the river, but had become more noted for our attention to medieval music and drama. I can claim a small part in the degenerative process, for I produced two of the plays and acted in others. My speciality was old men.

Already John's hair was thinning, and he began regularly to adopt the stance of an old man, not in his needle-sharp mind but in his movements. We were within four months the same age, but I have kept my hair. Those four months at Oswestry in the autumn of 1947 were blissful for both of us; so much so that, a few years later, I wrote a sequence of poems for John, setting down my memories. John as a present for my eightieth birthday collected them and other poems in a book prepared by the wonderful John Karran. The one I have chosen celebrates the time when at our Christmas party at Park Hall Club, where we were in charge, we both got drunk together for the first time.

Housey-housey spurn the Sergeants' hop,
But organise our own with watered beer,
Frothing from kegs, our jollity non-stop,
When wind a clockwork toy that runs from drear
Compulsion. Whip them up a sing-song. Raffle
A packet of fags. But drink, yes, drink! Who's here
To look with sober eyes? Our army will snaffle
All blood it can from us, so say goodbye
To boyhood's chill. But what when you baffle langouste
My sodden attempts to get you home? I try
In vain to push your arm down greatcoat sleeve:
Huddled, I bear you mess-wards. Sudden cry:
'Look at the stars, they're moving!' Drunk, you perceive
What galaxy will spangle make-believe!

Those four months were made the more intense given that John was expecting daily to be posted away from Oswestry. Ironically, in the event it was I who got posted – up to Chester HQ Western Command. I wrote at once to John, and he immediately wrote back saying he had never known words written down to bring a person to mind so vividly. That simple note told me instantly how in future I had to write, imitating my own voice. So it was that John, on top of everything else, set me on the path to becoming a writer, journalist and critic, yet another of my debts to him.

TONY PALMER

A great iconoclast among British film directors today, Tony Palmer is one of the liveliest and most productive of his generation with well over a hundred films to his credit. Most of them are on musical subjects, notably biographical studies of composers who interest him. His magnum opus is a film about Wagner, starting in the year of revolution, 1848, which lasts nine hours in its full form, divided into three parts. For that he got no less a star than Anthony Burton as Wagner and Vanessa Redgrave as his wife, Cosima, looking surprisingly like that lady.

He also includes the only scene on film to feature all three top actor knights – Laurence Olivier, John Gielgud and Ralph Richardson – in a trio, quite a coup. He even got William and Susana Walton to take the cameo roles of the King and Queen of Saxony. When Wagner as an unlikely courtier was conducting one of his early overtures, William as the king woke from his sleep to comment, 'What's that fearful din!' – a very apt remark from Walton who loathed Wagner's music as much as he loved Rossini's.

Tony has also made a tripartite study of Stravinsky, and one on Shostakovich similarly long, but one of the most moving of Tony's films is a study of William Walton, *At the Haunted End of the Day*, shot only a year or so before Walton died. He did a comparable study of Britten shortly after the composer's premature death, *A Time There Was . . .* His study of Vaughan Williams on the occasion of the fiftieth anniversary of the composer's death had a scoop in revealing for the first time that Ursula, the composer's second wife, had an abortion in the 1930s, when she was still just the composer's amanuensis. Tony's study of Carl Orff similarly reveals many facts previously unknown, for he is meticulous in his research. Hyperactive, he is devoted to researching in detail the inner recesses of composer's lives.

I first got to know Tony when he was still in the BBC, early in his career. He was one of the brilliant team of directors assembled by Huw Wheldon in the Features Department of BBC Television, and took the opportunity at a vintage period of doing all sorts of adventurous programmes, with individual directors allowed a degree of freedom unthinkable later. Even that did not satisfy Tony, and he left to become a freelance director, immediately prospering thanks to his imagination and energy.

In those days he was quite a lothario, and it came as a surprise when years later he settled down with Michela, originally his secretary and later his wife. Hailing from Italy, she is a superb cook, and the marriage has brought happiness to them both. They began married life in Tony's super penthouse flat in a warehouse on a bend of the Thames at Wapping, with superb views down the river one way to the Dome, down the other to Tower Bridge. It was a most unsuitable flat for children, however, so when two offspring arrived they moved to a large suburban house in Ealing, which Tony immediately expanded to give him studio and editing space within the house.

It is always exciting to meet Tony, as he invariably has new projects in hand, so many it is hard to keep pace with them. He is also a superb driver, and I shall never forget one day when I drove back from Glyndebourne with him, and he drove far above the speed limit all the way. It was certainly exciting, even if I was glad when we arrived safely in London. One just hopes that he will continue and flourish in the years to come.

BRIAN REDHEAD

Brian Redhead arrived in Cambridge a year after me, in 1950, having spent quite a time on a local paper in his native Tyneside. He made it clear to all of us that he knew the lot about newspapers and journalism, never bothering to hide his arrogance, yet such was his charm that he came across – as he did later on radio – as a most attractive personality. In due course he followed me on to the *Guardian* and, right from the start, he made it plain that his ambition was to be the paper's editor. In effect he became features editor, and very successful he was too, transforming the features pages, but happily not interfering with my weekly record column.

On one of my visits up to Manchester I remember him showing me his wedding photos. One of them had him and his bride in front of a large Gothic door. Brian explained that it was not the cathedral, at which I naughtily suggested that it must have been the biggest church he could find. Slightly shamefacedly he admitted it was. That was well before he turned to the BBC and became an affectionately regarded presenter on Radio 4's *Today* programme.

In that, he had certainly found his métier, and when he was cruelly overtaken by cancer and prematurely died, he was given the most spectacular memorial service in St Paul's Cathedral, which was packed in tribute to a much-loved figure whose mortal illness and his finding of comfort in his faith were followed very publicly on the *Today* programme.

JAMES NAUGHTIE

I first got to know Jim Naughtie when, for a relatively brief period, he was the *Guardian*'s chief political correspondent. We shared our joint devotion to music and politics, and it has always been a joy to entertain him and his novelist wife, Ellie. Like me he was regularly invited down to Ted Heath's house in Salisbury for the Praemium Imperiale sessions. On one occasion I remember we narrowly missed our train back to Waterloo, and had to wait two full hours till the next. At least we were able to amuse ourselves drinking the station bar dry. Jim's contributions to the *Today* programme on Radio 4 are always illuminating, a splendid counterpart to the masterfully abrasive John Humphrys. If only the whole team was on that level.

BELINDA NORMAN-BUTLER

There are few with such a distinguished background as Belinda Norman-Butler. Her grandfathers on both sides were celebrated. On her mother's side her grandfather, Charles Booth, was the founder of the Booth Shipping Line, using his wealth to research the reasons for poverty. He was also a campaigner for old-age pensions. He bought one of the copies of Holman Hunt's celebrated painting *The Light of the World*, and sent it on his boats round South America on a highly successful evangelical mission. He owned Grace Dieu Manor in Thringstone near Loughborough in Leicestershire, and Belinda would recall how, when she was a little girl, she used to spend Christmas in this Victorian Gothic building, consigned to the North Wing, which was completely unheated. Children of the upper classes had to be tough in those days.

On her father's side in the Ritchie family her great-grandfather was the Victorian novelist William Makepeace Thackeray. Although he died half a century before Belinda was born in 1908, she was very close to her grandmother, Thackeray's daughter, Anne Isabella Thackeray Ritchie, always known in the family as Anny. She was a great character in her own right, treated recently to a delightful biography, *Anny*, by Henrietta Garnett. Her husband, Richmond Ritchie, had a career as a civil servant in the India Office and, as a chief adviser to the Secretary of State in the early 1900s, played a crucial part in commissioning Edwin Lutyens to design New Delhi.

Sadly, he died young in 1912, having become a Companion of the Order of St Michael and St George, CMG, in 1898. He was knighted in 1907. Through him the family is related to such leading Victorian figures as Macaulay, Darwin, Trevelyan, and the family of Leslie Stephen, who was the first editor of *The Dictionary of National Biography*, and was the father of Vanessa Bell and Virginia Woolf, the novelist, who married Leonard Woolf. On her mother's side, through her Booth grandmother, Belinda is also related to Beatrice Webb, one of the many Potter sisters, who with her husband, Sidney, was one of the leading members of the Fabian Society. Belinda then through marriage added the Butler family of Cambridge to her relatives. The group Anny belonged to also included such notable Victorian figures as Charles Dickens, Alfred, Lord Tennyson and Henry James.

Belinda, who lived to be a hundred, loved reminiscing about all these relations, giving a marvellous insight into the 1920s in particular. In this she was the opposite of boastful, simply delighting in her revelations, which were always candid and often surprising. Yet she used her connections most effectively to achieve what became her great project in life, founding the music scholarships of the English-Speaking Union, and chairing the project for over forty years, until in her nineties she went into semi-retirement, still keeping her finger on the pulse.

Her great project began when she organised a performance of Handel's *Messiah* in Westminster Abbey in 1953. It was so soon after the Queen's Coronation that the blue and gold chairs for the ceremony were still in place. It helped too that the extra platforms installed were still there, so that as at the Coronation itself those present could look and hear better. Reginald Jacques conducted the Bach Choir – of which Belinda was a member – with the Jacques Orchestra led by Emanuel Hurwitz, who remained on the adjudication panel of the Scholarship until, in December 2006, he died in his eighties.

It was Belinda's determination not to be fobbed off that led to that *Messiah* performance, given in aid of the Westminster Abbey Appeal Fund. Even earlier, during the Second World War, with her husband away in the forces, she first did voluntary work for the English-Speaking Union in the Cambridge Centre. When after the war she and her husband moved to London, she joined the ESU Education Committee and was then appointed to be one of the ESU Board of Governors.

As she remembered, 'I had a rough time.' Though she greatly approved of the chairman, Lord Baillieu, too many of the others, she felt, were businessmen and academics with no time for music. She proposed that Ralph Vaughan Williams and Benjamin Britten should become ESU vice-presidents, but was roundly attacked by an economist who proclaimed, 'We don't want any of Mrs Norman-Butler's long-haired musicians.' She promptly blew up and pointed out that, 'Vaughan Williams is an OM, if you know what that means!'

Undaunted, she organised a series of exchange scholarships between young people here and in the United States, four every year from each country. It was a time when exchange controls prevented almost anyone from travelling to America except on business to win dollars for Britain. It meant that the scholars on exchanges were entertained by ESU members in the United States, while the American scholars came here, similarly hosted by ESU members. Belinda had prepared the way through her contacts, first with Frank Dobie, Professor of American History at Cambridge, whom she had known during the war, and then by her first American hosts in 1948. James Lawrence became Chairman of the Boston Branch of ESU, and remained a lifelong friend and helper.

She already had other contacts in the United States thanks to her family, for Thackeray made two visits to the United States, which affected him profoundly. She also reported that her grandmother, Thackeray's daughter, sold the manuscript of *The Rose and the Ring* to the Pierpont Morgan Library, to help educate her sons. In other ways too as the friend of Henry James and at the centre of a literary and artistic circle, her grandmother cemented the American connection. This meant that Belinda's family connected with the world of politics as well as with the world of the arts and education. Regularly, that helped to expand the scope of her projects.

It was in 1969 that she devised the ESU Music Scholarships. She organised a concert in the Banqueting Hall in Whitehall for the visiting Boston Chamber Players, from which she raised enough money to start the scholarship scheme. Even then, advised by Robert Mayer, she waited until a really outstanding young artist emerged, before launching the first scholarship at Tanglewood, the summer school associated with the Boston Symphony Orchestra, the most prestigious of the American summer schools. In 1976 the violinist Nigel Kennedy was chosen, then in his teens and still at the Yehudi Menuhin School at Stoke d'Abernon. The following year Simon Rattle was chosen, only to be turned down by Seiji Ozawa, music director of the Boston Symphony Orchestra. Rattle of course has had his own back since, teasing Ozawa.

Since then, thanks almost entirely to Belinda's energy in exploiting contacts, her scheme has been expanded to include the other major summer schools – Aspen, Banff (in Canada), Yale and Ravinia. The list of scholars sent each year demonstrates what success the adjudication panel has had in spotting the stars of the future, among them Steven Isserlis, Robert Cohen, Tasmin Little, Lorraine McAslan, Grant Llewellyn, Michael Collins and many others. Loyally, the scholars have given their services in later years in the many cathedral and other concerts Belinda organised in aid of the Scholarship Fund, often using the excellent orchestras of the Menuhin School and the Purcell School. The ESU, as she said, is above all a place for ideas.

My own first contact with Belinda came when we were both on an adjudicating panel for the scholarships promoted by Robert Mayer. On the panel with us were Lord Harewood and Eva Turner, as well as Sir Robert himself. I remember vividly that Belinda and I, who sat next to each other, were amazed at what we both thought the perversity of the others in our distinguished team. The two of us agreed wholeheartedly on each candidate. The test we both naturally applied was the opposite of requiring mere mechanical perfection. Technical ability is obviously necessary, but for us both the essential ingredient is for the performance to convey warmth of feeling as well, charisma on whatever level. It was soon after that that Belinda contacted me direct to come and join the ESU panel, which she chaired.

As years went by, I became the principal questioner. As a journalist and a professional interviewer, I have always sought above all to find out about each candidate and his or her ambitions, when many of our always distinguished panel were more concerned to deliver their own wisdom to the candidates rather than seeking to find out about them. It was through Belinda that we were regularly joined by Ruth, Lady Fermoy, favourite lady-in-waiting to the Queen Mother and grandmother of Diana, Princess of Wales. Lady Fermoy was trained as a professional pianist before she married, and always proved a quietly persuasive adjudicator.

So in effect latterly I chaired the adjudication, while Belinda remained the official chairman, and I felt honoured to take on that role, until disability prevented me from continuing. After morning and afternoon sessions of adjudication I was regularly so exhausted I had to rest through the evening afterwards. Meanwhile Belinda would often go on to an evening concert. Her energy was extraordinary.

I also have a vivid memory of the ceremony at Buckingham Palace, when I received a relatively modest honour. It was typical that, when Belinda arrived with my two other guests, they were shown into the most privileged seats in the Investiture Room, a tribute to Belinda's effortlessly commanding dignity. I feel honoured to have known Belinda as a great and unique friend.

QUITA CHAVEZ

For well over half a century now, Quita Chavez has been a pillar of the record industry. In her youthful nineties she remains as active as ever, monitoring what the record companies are doing, and vetting the pages of *Gramophone*, the leading magazine for which she worked for twenty-five years or more. She also keeps her finger on the pulse of the operatic world, notably at Covent Garden, where there are few productions she misses, however much she dislikes the 'concept' productions latterly so popular with opera directors, if not with the general run of opera-goers.

Quita, who despite her exotic name retains a strong London accent, was interested in records and operas back in the 1930s, when she attended legendary performances at Covent Garden including one of Puccini's *Turandot* with Eva Turner and Giovanni Martinelli, conducted by Beecham. From there it was a natural move when she became a shop assistant in Imhof's, in New Oxford Street, and soon after was an assistant with her lifelong friend, Peggie Cochrane, at EMG, London's most exclusive record shop, which refused to stock any record that was not approved by its panel of critics.

War Service in the ATS with Peggie interrupted her career in the record world, before she ended up as the promoter of discs for the Decca label, soon after the introduction of the LP. She was brilliant in her handling of the critics, detecting those she counted time-wasters, out to get free records, but treating serious critics with an ideal generosity and consideration. From there she went to the Philips company soon after the label was launched, and on to the then newly established CBS label, before returning to Philips for a period. She was also brilliant at rallying her sales staff, regularly urging them 'to get their football boots on'.

It was only after this that she was persuaded to change her role completely and join the staff of *Gramophone*, and there was no one sharper at weeding out mistakes in the proofs each month, complaining of lax standards all round. It was in that role that she remained until she finally retired when nearing her eighties, as sharp as ever.

She was fortunate in having been given a generous legacy by a relation, which meant she could indulge not only her love of going to Covent Garden but of patronising smart West End restaurants, above all The Ivy, haunt of celebrities of stage and music from the years before the war. Booking a table at The Ivy was a problem for most would-be diners, but Quita was always given a welcome. Expense was no object.

Her loyalties have always been strong, but so has her list of those she disapproves of. She was devoted to Colin Davis as music director of the Royal Opera House, and to his successor, Bernard Haitink, both of whom would frequently find a place for her in their personal box, but she disapproved of their latest successor, Antonio Pappano, even though he is much more of a dedicated opera conductor than either Davis or Haitink, great conductors who happened to conduct opera. One hopes that Quita will go on for many years yet, and present signs could not be more hopeful.

ROBERT AND LINDY RUNCIE

The first time I met Robert Runcie, Archbishop of Canterbury, he was doing the washing-up. It was in the private flat that he and his characterful wife, Rosalind, had in Lambeth Palace, a place that Rosalind – or Lindy as she is always known to her friends – helped to renovate and decorate in a building that had been sadly neglected under previous archbishops. As an enthusiastic gardener, Lindy also took on the restoration of the gardens at Lambeth Palace.

It was typical that Lindy had got Robert doing some housework, and it says much for Robert that he had chosen as his wife a partner you would never have imagined marrying a priest, let alone an archbishop. Robert had met her when he was Dean of Trinity Hall, the Cambridge college that I myself attended. Very surprisingly, that unpretentious post has led over the years to the appointment of some of the most distinguished clerics in the Church of England.

These include not just an archbishop, and a whole raft of bishops, but an OM (Owen Chadwick, later Master of Selwyn College and a distinguished theologian) and at least two Regius Professors of Divinity. Those I met when I was invited to address the college Music Society were those of Oxford and Glasgow. Robert met Lindy when she acted as a part-time secretary to him while he was Dean of Trinity Hall, and that developed in due course into their mutual love, for it was indeed a very happy marriage.

It was only some years after I got to know Lindy that I discovered that she was the daughter of my favourite Law tutor at Trinity Hall, Cecil Lewis, who as an agnostic would have been deeply surprised, if not amused, to have an archbishop as son-in-law, had he lived that long.

Robert's background was modest. Coming from a lower-middle-class family in Liverpool, he went to the local grammar school as preparation for going to Oxford. When the war intervened, Robert, rather surprisingly, went into the Guards, which was usually reserved for public-school candidates, and in due course became a tank commander. It was in France in 1945, when his tank was hit by German shellfire, that he won the Military Cross for very bravely rescuing one of his crew from the blazing tank.

No one who knew Robert as a Guards officer would have dreamed at the time that he would become a priest. Yet that is what happened. It is a transition that has remained largely unexplained, and it was a development that sadly was omitted when, just before Robert's death, his son, the television producer James Runcie, undertook some intimate interviews with his father, which were otherwise most revealing.

The only obvious flaw that Robert had to my mind was his voice, for his bleating ecclesiastical manner was quite alien to his true character, which was consistently strong and forthright, a match for Lindy.

In my experience his sermons were a model of their kind, compact with a clear message and always including a streak of humour.

I always remember after a particularly fine sermon he had preached at St Mary's Bourne Street in London, I congratulated him, and sincerely suggested that the scandal of the time, which erupted when Humphrey Carpenter published his biography of Robert, would quickly rebound in his favour. So it proved.

In the biography Carpenter quoted him as having occasional doubts, which for many, if not most, Christians made him the more sympathetic and less doctrinaire. More seriously, Robert was quoted on his opinion of Princess Diana and other public figures. What had happened was that Robert chose Humphrey Carpenter as his biographer, when he had written a series of highly readable biographies and was in any case the son of a friend of Robert's, a former Bishop of Oxford.

Robert knew that Carpenter always liked to have an intimate interview with his subject before writing, as a help in sorting out biographical details. That is why the interview he gave was unusually forthcoming. He did not realise for a moment that Carpenter, who was an excellent journalist, would immediately register that, with his comments on the Princess, the interview was a dynamic piece of information. So instead of using it as background, he made it the main subject of the biography, much to the horror of Robert and many others.

Robert's progress in the Church had been swift after leaving Cambridge, for he became Principal of Cuddesdon Theological College before being appointed Bishop of St Albans. It says much for his happiness at St Albans that after he retired as Archbishop, he and Lindy went to live there. It also says much for their marriage that Robert at one point was offered the post of Archbishop of York, which he refused when Lindy, who had inspected the Palace at York, said that she could not possibly live there.

Robert as Archbishop was a temporising force, not least in reconciling the liberal wing and the High Anglican wing of the already troubled Anglican communion. His own sympathies were fundamentally with the Anglo-Catholic tradition, yet he held the balance so much more successfully than his successors have so far done, for all their worthy attempts to heal breaches.

I need not repeat the story of his years at Lambeth Palace and in Canterbury itself – which Lindy actively disliked, always preferring Lambeth. Enough to say that here was a great man whom it was a privilege to know, and one who has left a legacy for me. Equally Lindy has become one of my closest and dearest friends, a regular visitor to my house, her visits always a cue for gales of laughter.

Lindy herself is a professional musician, a trained pianist. In Robert's period as Archbishop she gave dozens of charity concerts in aid of many good causes, and when he retired she continued to do so. After that, during her widowhood, she concentrated on giving piano lessons, for she became a strong and positive teacher, who drew impressive results from her pupils, including her grandchildren. Characteristically, she gave opinions straight from the shoulder, and would not hide from any weaknesses she saw. Perhaps she ought to have been a music critic.

MERVYN HORDER

Mervyn Horder was eccentric in a way long established in the world of upper-class Englishmen, and was the more lovable for it. He was the son of the first Lord Horder, ennobled when he was the surgeon in the early 1930s to George V. Mervyn by contrast was the most unlikely member of the House of Lords and, to give him credit, he never took his seat in the upper house, at a time when he was fully entitled to do so.

Mervyn was a man who did not have any regard for formal etiquette. He would arrive at even the grandest event on his bicycle, wearing a frayed tweed sports jacket and grey flannels, usually still wearing his bicycle clips. His dress was unconventional, yet he would always be allowed in to such an event, and would be warmly greeted by his many friends.

He lived in a strange cottage in the grounds of what had been a grand mansion in St John's Wood in London, with bedroom and bathroom upstairs and a single living and dining room downstairs. As you entered, you would be lucky not to knock over the bicycle he propped up just inside. His supply of food and drink was always generous, and he would usually offer delicious beef stews, which yet had rather watery gravy. He did not believe in using any thickening agent as he felt it was somehow immoral, no doubt an attitude instilled by an early nanny.

He appreciated my hospitality in return, but would note almost invariably that the windows needed cleaning. He would then devote himself as a priority to cleaning the windows on the ground floor, and at subsequent visits would remember to bring cleaning equipment, just as Lindy, widow of the Archbishop, would bring materials to polish my dining-room table.

Mervyn was an amateur composer, a musician who had had an early musical training, so that his songs were warmly lyrical, and sensitively enhanced the poetry he chose to set. Happily, a small record company was persuaded to issue a CD of a good selection, something that plainly delighted him. Towards the end of his life he could no longer ride his bicycle, and the last times I saw him he was in an NHS nursing home, plainly frustrated that he was bedridden, but still as cheerful and full of good conversation as ever. He was the sort of friend whom one goes on missing for ever.

DAME NORMA AND SIR JOHN MAJOR

It was when I received for review a new biography of Joan Sutherland that I first registered the name of Norma Major. I myself had written a short book on Sutherland, and I was full of admiration for a biographer who over ten years had done so much more original research than I had, and had written up her material so well. On the book jacket it said simply that Norma was 'married to a Minister of State in the British Government'. That was when Margaret Thatcher was prime minister.

I had barely heard of John Major at the time, and so when I first met Norma – in fact it was at a Downing Street reception – I immediately said that for me, 'It was you who made your husband famous', which pleased and amused her. It was soon after the book appeared that John Major's rapid promotions in various departments including the Foreign Office and the Treasury took place, culminating in his election as leader of the Conservative Party and prime minister in succession to Margaret Thatcher.

Getting to know Norma was a delight, for in total contradiction of the colourless figure that some hostile commentators pictured, she is among the most stylish and enchanting women I know; one who even when dressed simply glows naturally with good will. She makes a splendid match for John Major who is almost unique among top politicians in empathising with even his worst enemies. It was this man who had chosen Norma as his wife, when they were both working for the Conservative Party in South London.

I noticed this quality of empathy first when John was interviewed before his election as Leader in 1990. As I had been at Cambridge with Douglas Hurd, I naturally favoured him, but John's eyes would twinkle when he was faced with a catch question, which he unfailingly answered deftly and honestly. In an interview long after he left office he even claimed that he had tried to empathise with one of the worst terrorist leaders in Northern Ireland.

Norma, when John was PM, went on to write another book, on the history of Chequers, the country estate given for the use of the prime minister, where John and Norma enjoyed spending weekends. Norma's book on Chequers was published in the form of a coffee-table volume with plenty of pictures, but in the depth and detail of the writing it was far more than that, another splendid achievement for her. She was also keen to write a biography of the American soprano Jessye Norman, but she had to abandon the idea when far too many difficulties were put in her way.

With John out of office and concentrating on his business interests, Norma has devoted herself to charitable works, continuing what she had started when John was in office. For that most deservedly she was awarded a DBE, establishing her claims independently of those of her husband.

DAVID MELLOR

My first contact with David Mellor came one year at the Salzburg Festival. My friend Roddy Gradidge had shown me an article in the *Spectator*, praising one of Elgar's rarer works, *The Spirit of England*, and I was most impressed that a government minister could write so knowledgeably and perceptively about music, with detailed analysis of the kind of which I greatly approve. The author was David Mellor. When we met in Salzburg we immediately had much to talk about, and I was amused to be able to introduce David to Ted Heath, who was also at the Festival. Though they were both Tory MPs, they had not made contact before that.

In the years that followed, my contacts with David were frequent, for he was a generous host. On one occasion I was having dinner with him at the House of Commons, and he arrived at the table, having shared a joke with the head waitress of the Strangers' restaurant en route. He laughed when he told me that she had asked whether I was his 'Old Dad'. Ever since then David has always greeted me as his 'Old Dad', though I am considerably younger than his genuine father, whom I have since met.

It was the period when David was constantly being targeted by the tabloids for his infidelities. Some of the stories were pure fabrication, as for example that he had worn a Chelsea strip (the shirt players wear on the field) when having sex, though the affair was genuine enough. David did his best to keep his job as Minister of Culture, a post specially devised for him by his friend and fellow Chelsea supporter, John Major. It suited him perfectly, and he managed in his period in that role to set up the National Lottery among other things. That did not prevent him from being very active in his role as MP, and I was deeply grateful to him when a very dear friend, one of his constituents, was in danger of being made homeless after the break-up of her marriage, and David managed to get her a council flat.

In the end events conspired against him as his affairs got more and more publicity, and he was forced to resign, but in the event it was a blessing in disguise, for he was then available much earlier than the ministers who were put out of office in 1997, when John Major's government fell in face of the Labour landslide. The next I knew was that David had left his charming wife, Judith, and set up with Penny, Lady Cobham, who had been married to the elder brother of my friend Richard Lyttelton, president of the classical division of EMI. Richard knew nothing of the development in advance, news that burst in the papers like a bomb.

Penny, much tougher than David's estranged wife, was a more suitable partner, and I was delighted to meet her when David invited me to a party at his superb Regency house in St Katharine's Dock, in the shadow of Tower Bridge. It was the first of many visits, for David and Penny are generous hosts, and three times I went for lunch with them and also to a large party on Christmas Day, as theirs was a house I could reach on foot at the time. On the last occasion I went for Christmas lunch, we sat in the small bower in the garden, on which David had had a glass front installed, and the place heated. Sitting drinking champagne in comfort in the shadow of Tower Bridge was a luxury such as one can enjoy only rarely.

Penny is as active in public life as David, who after losing his seat at Putney in 1997 found a niche in business, and has made a fortune from his shrewd operating, reflected in the many beautiful objects he has collected in his house. As well his business affairs, which involve frequent visits to the Far East, the ever-hyperactive David manages to make regular appearances as a broadcaster on Classic FM, very effectively so, in promoting music that his listeners might not know, something of which I heartily approve. Though since my disability came on me, I see David and Penny rather less, I greatly value their friendship.

LIZ FRANCIS

Liz Francis – or Elizabeth Francis-Jones to give her full name – was the last and dearest of all the many wonderful BBC producers I had monitoring my broadcasts, whether on Radio 3 or the World Service, which was where Liz operated. She was tough but always constructive, and very soon we became close friends. It was always a joy in the days before I was disabled to take Liz as my lady companion to the important events I was invited to – lunches, dinners, concerts and opera, most of all at Glyndebourne. It was a special joy going there, when instead of having to return to London, whether by train or car, after the opera, I was able to stay with Liz and her partner Pru in their house in Lewes near Glyndebourne. We would picnic on the lawns at Glyndebourne in all weathers, enjoying ourselves enormously, and latterly we have reminisced endlessly about our many glorious outings together.

RODNEY BICKERSTAFFE

I first met Rodney Bickerstaffe at a vegetarian lunch hosted on the edge of the Chilterns by my then *Guardian* colleague Ed Pearce. As founding General Secretary of the big trade union Unison, he had become notorious for organising a strike that had totally disrupted the collection of rubbish. Yet here was a wonderfully civilised man who first of all accused me of encouraging him to buy far too many CDs thanks to my recommendations in our *Penguin Guide*: 'You're the man who's cost me all that money!' I also learned that he was an eager and scholarly book collector.

On that first occasion he ferried me home in his car with his delightful wife, Pat, and we then had drinks back at my house. I then learned of another remarkable side to Rodney's character, his love of champagne, making him a dyed-in-the-wool 'champagne socialist'. We became immediate friends, and each year he never fails to ring me on my birthday, and then comes round with a bottle of champagne. Since his official retirement from Unison, he has become very active in promoting the cause of pensioners and their welfare, not least the money they receive.

He told me that at Chequers Tony Blair as prime minister had urged him to accept a life peerage, but he totally refused. I myself lectured him, urging him to accept if a similar offer ever came his way, pointing out that Emanuel Shinwell, a militant trades unionist of an earlier generation, had become a much-loved pillar of the House of Lords, but Rodney, alas, was not to be budged, even though it would have given him a wonderful platform for his work on behalf of pensioners. Happily, our disagreement has never got in the way of our friendship, for with his wonderfully resonant Yorkshire voice he is a joy to be with, not least for his many anecdotes.

Interlude 3: Evacuation and Belper

I arrived at Westcliff High School for Boys ('WHS') in September 1939, having won a place from my council school, at what was the most unpromising time. The war had just started and, as first years, those of my generation were delayed until the air-raid shelters had been completed, potentially dangerous places buried just below the ground. There we would go when we had to practise when there was an air raid and, indeed, whenever the air-raid siren sounded.

I had a large bar of Aero chocolate in my gas-mask container. I never consumed it, as the visits to the shelter were invariably short. Lessons were otherwise barely disrupted, except that several teachers were borrowed from the Girls' High School next door, as a number of WHS masters had already gone into the forces. Miss Chatterton, against all the normal WHS conventions, insisted that everyone in the class, 1A, should stand when she entered the room and say in chorus, 'Good morning, Miss Chatterton!' This caused much amusement for any prefect who stood in for her from time to time, taking over the task of ensuring we kept reasonably quiet.

The big disruption came in the spring of the following year, 1940, after the end of the so-called 'phoney war', when at three days' notice we had to be evacuated from the Borough of Southend-on-Sea. It was not so much that bombing was expected in our area, but there was a fear that there might be an immediate German invasion after the fall of France and the evacuation from Dunkirk. On Sunday, 2 June 1940, we had to get up very early indeed, and somehow reach the railway station at Southend to board trains to our various destinations.

We had no idea where we were going, and the journey was unbelievably slow in our special train. Happily, I was with a lot of sixth-formers and they decided to keep siblings together, so I went with my brother, who was captain of the school at the time. Until this time we had been incurably hostile to each other, for he had for years resented the arrival of a brother six and a half years after his own emergence into the world. From that moment, however, we became the closest of allies, an alliance that remained firm until my brother's premature death from cancer in the 1990s. I cannot praise my brother highly enough for the extraordinary care and attention he gave me for the rest of his life.

Sunday, 2 June 1940, was an incredibly long and wearing day, as we did not arrive in our chosen venue, Belper, just north of Derby, until the afternoon, and then had to wait to go to various schools in the area there to be chosen by our potential foster parents. I was much the smallest in our group and, as I found out later, a number of Belper citizens, who were circling round our group in a school playground as if we were exhibits in a cattle market, wanted to take me as an evacuee. That was until they were told that they would also have to take an eighteen-year-old.

In the end we were both taken to various potential foster parents, finally finding our new abode at 5 Far Laund, the home of Luen and Phyllis Banks, who counted themselves a little superior to most Belperites, because Luen was a draughtsman in the offices of the LMS Railway in Derby, which was then devoted to war work, designing tanks. Sadly, my brother had to leave school to go into the forces at the end of the school year, and returning to Belper after only two weeks' summer holiday, I was more homesick than I have ever been before or since. That I weathered my misery was partly due to the fact that friends from Leigh-on-Sea had also followed the school and were staying at Bridge Farm in Belper, next to the mill of the British Sewing Company.

There I would go every Saturday afternoon, invited not just by our family friend, Mrs Glover, but also by their neighbours in Leigh, Miss Queenie Tattersall and her ailing mother. From then on Miss Tattersall, a devout Baptist, was an unfailing mentor, and I would live the whole week looking forward to Saturday afternoons, when she would take us on walks or would get us making posies from beech-nut husks in the gaslight, which was all that Bridge Farm could offer. Miss Tattersall would finally take me at the end of the evening up the hill towards my foster home. I would return totally happy for a brief, blissful moment.

The other reason why I stuck it out in Belper was that, by some fluke of having classes that had to be rearranged, I was able to move from a stream destined to take five years before the School Certificate to one taking only four, leaving most of my original classmates behind. Realising that, I was determined to soldier on. I was not going to miss the chance of doing a four-year course to the School Certificate when I returned to Westcliff High School.

It was a very fortunate decision, for at WHS I was only one of the three or four in each year whom the music master, John W. Bates, would select to do music as a main subject. Bates was a mentor of the old-fashioned school. This was in total contrast to my earliest mentor, my singing teacher, Freda Parry, who had taught me impressionistically that music was above all about enjoyment: that message has become the watchword of my whole life.

Bates, by contrast with Freda Parry, was a marvellous teacher of harmony, counterpoint and musical theory generally, dinning into us all the grammatical rules about parallel fifths and octaves or how to deal with perfect fourths. Having such individual tuition meant that, by the time we had finished our first year with Bates, still in the Third Form, we had completed not only the School Certificate syllabus but the Higher Certificate one too. It was that intensive training from then through the rest of my time at WHS that convinced me that it would be a waste to read Music at university. I was confident that I had already progressed far enough never to feel ill equipped on the subject. As I have always said in my years as a music critic, I can analyse twelve-note music as well as anyone academy trained.

Though I had many friends at Westcliff High School, there have been only two who remained close friends over the years, both of them dedicatedly musical. Eric Sams, two years ahead of me, was by far the most brilliant pupil at WHS, having won an open scholarship at his first attempt at Corpus Christi, Cambridge, after gaining distinctions in all four subjects he took in the Higher Certificate. I remember seeing him on a bus not long before he left Cambridge, when he told me he was going into the Civil Service. I complained at once that that would be a terrible waste. In fact Eric treated his main job in the Ministry of Labour as a part-time occupation – he was so quick in responding to any problem that he got through official work in double-quick time – leaving him free to become one of the world's leading experts on the art of *Lieder*.

Over the years he wrote a definitive book on the songs of Hugo Wolf, following it with similar studies of the songs of Schumann and those of Strauss. He was also invaluable in helping the Schubert specialists to compile a definitive listing of the composer's many hundreds of songs. Such was his fame, corresponding as he did with the most distinguished musicologists in the world, that his boss, the then Minister of Labour, Edward Boyle, was astonished to find that the musicologist he so admired was a civil servant in his own department.

Back at WHS Eric would display to us his astonishing facility in sight-reading Beethoven sonatas; he was not far short of the phenomenal gifts in that direction of André Previn and Antonio Pappano, whom I got to know much later. Hearing Beethoven sonatas played that way even before I had heard many of them on disc was a great joy and a privilege I cherished. My only response was that I was probably even better equipped than he was in talking about the history of music and of composers.

That was something that would endlessly occupy me when talking to my other great friend from WHS, Garth Plowman. He was in the year following mine, and was officially on the science side. That fortunately did not prevent us from becoming close friends, and we both greatly enjoyed hearing the compositions that each of us was writing at the time. We even developed the strange gift of improvising piano duets, each responding to the other, usually attributing our efforts to a fictional composer, presumably from darkest Eastern Europe, whom we dubbed 'Huriczaczek'.

Garth was extremely tall and thin and suffered from asthma, with the consequence that he was not able to go in the forces, as the rest of us had to at the time. Instead he went straight from school to Magdalen College, Oxford, on a major scholarship, and switched from reading Modern Greats (Politics, Philosophy and Economics) to reading Psychology. It was a joy to me, many years later, when I got my first job on the then *Manchester Guardian*, that Garth at the time was a lecturer in the Psychology Department of Manchester University, which meant that for quite a time I was able to have lunch with Garth and his colleagues in the university before I went in to the *Guardian* soon after 3 p.m.

Garth finally became Professor of Social Administration at the London School of Economics, but unfortunately had to retire early. It has been good to keep him as a close friend over the years, even after, during his second marriage, he emigrated to Cyprus for half the year, where his asthma was not nearly so troublesome.

Chapter Four

Composers

This chapter really speaks for itself. Some of the people in the following pages truly are household names – and not just the Beatles. From lost titans to those whose best days may yet be ahead of them, the names here resemble a 'wish list' of those great composers who are still (in some cases only just) within the span of living memory.

IGOR STRAVINSKY

Shaking the hand that wrote *The Rite of Spring* was one of the great thrills of my early years as a critic. Stravinsky was visiting London for the last time in September 1965 and, at the last minute, a press conference was called in his suite at the Savoy for a Saturday afternoon, the time when most serious critics were taking the day off or writing their reviews for the Sunday papers.

It was a motley group of journalists who assembled in his room at the Savoy, most of them duty reporters who knew little or nothing about Stravinsky or his music. One of the questions, I remember, was on what he had had to eat in Frankfurt airport. I decided to take the opportunity to ask a serious question. I pointed out that Maestro Stravinsky had recorded *The Rite of Spring* three times, the first in 1929 when the Paris players could not even play the notes correctly; the second time in New York in 1940, very fast and clipped; and lastly in 1960, also in America, one of the finest ever recordings. Interpretatively, I pointed out in my question, the performances were quite different from one another. Did Stravinsky intend the differences and, if so, what did he intend to convey?

Plainly the old man did not realise that there were any differences between the three recordings, and he fudged his answer, rather as I expected. Then at the end of the press conference he stood up, and extended his hand to me in the second row of chairs. It was a wonderful moment for me, which happily was caught on film, though sadly my question was not included in the finished film.

What especially delighted me was that when the next book of *Conversations* was published, written up by his devoted amanuensis, Robert Craft, it included a section commenting on different versions of *The Rite of Spring*, though at that stage not his own. The typically sharp remark I remember was on the version from Karajan and the Berlin Philharmonic which understandably he found too polished and civilised, a tame animal rather than a wild one: 'I do not mean that they are out of their depth,' he said, 'but that they are in my shallows.'

Another remark of Stravinsky that I specially treasure is also about *The Rite of Spring*. When for CBS he made a spoken commentary on the composition of *The Rite*, he explained that 'I heard and wrote down what I heard. I was the vessel through which *Le sacre* passed,' one of the most profound comments I know on the creative process of a composer. On the other hand his wit could be devastating. In his memoirs he wondered why, when he happened to meet Glazunov in Paris when both were exiled, he was at first disconcerted by Glazunov's chilly reception. Maybe, said Stravinsky, he had heard his remark that Glazunov was 'no more than a Carl Philipp Emanuel Rimsky-Korsakov'.

On the day after the press conference I was privileged to attend Stravinsky's rehearsal for the *Firebird* Suite, which he was due to conduct that evening at the Royal Festival Hall, the final item in an all-Stravinsky concert otherwise conducted by Robert Craft. At the rehearsal Stravinsky spotted at one point that some of the wind instruments were playing something slightly different from what was printed in the orchestral parts. He questioned them, and they explained that the amendment had been inserted in pencil. At that

Stravinsky flapped his arms like an angry bird, exclaiming, 'I do not write in pencil!'

Happily, Stravinsky's performance is caught on film with the camera facing the old man, but getting that full-face shot was touch and go, as the camera was out of action until that moment when it came to life, much to the relief of the television director. At the very end of the performance, the audience in its standing ovation continued to applaud and would not let the composer go, sensing perhaps that this would be the last time we would see him in London. In the end, to signal his very last bow, he came on wearing his overcoat.

SIR WILLIAM WALTON

It was in May 1943, when I was still only fourteen, that I had one of the great 'Road to Damascus' moments in my musical life. It was during the war, when I was still evacuated from my home town in Essex to Belper in Derbyshire. I had been alerted to the name William Walton by a snatch of *Popular Song* from *Façade* on a radio programme about future broadcasts, and I then read in the half-page of serious music criticism by Ralph Hill, that the much reduced wartime *Radio Times* was offering, of the imminent broadcast of the first performance in Britain of Walton's Violin Concerto, written in 1939 for Jascha Heifetz, who retained exclusive rights to performing it for several years.

During the war he was unable to visit Britain to play it himself, so this British premiere was played by Henry Holst, a noted orchestral leader rather than a star soloist, with the orchestra he led at the time, the Liverpool Philharmonic. I was fortunate that on the day of the performance I had the house to myself, and so by great good luck was able to listen to the performance undisturbed at a time when, before the age of transistors, any household would have at most a single radio.

During the performance, my ears were on stalks. I had never heard such magical music before, at a time when I had not even heard a complete Beethoven symphony. From that moment I devoured every note of Walton's music I could hear, and as soon as I could the following December I bought the recording that Heifetz had made with Eugene Goossens and the Cincinnati Symphony Orchestra, a thrilling performance. I was still puzzled a bit by music that with its dissonances was, by the standards of the time, strikingly modern. I played the discs twice a day, loving the music more and more. I have never been afraid of any music, however difficult, ever since.

As I quickly realised, William Walton was placed in my mind in my canon of priorities somewhere between Jesus Christ and God Almighty. That was something I reported to Walton himself, much to his amusement, when to my delight I got to know him and his sparkling wife, Susana, on the LSO's tour of Russia in 1971. As I said, if I had known as a teenager that I was going to get to know Walton as a friend, I think I would have had a seizure on the spot, such was my boyhood devotion.

Walton's career, as I learned, was an extraordinary one. He was the son of struggling music teachers in Oldham in Lancashire, and his only distinction as a young boy was the beauty of his treble voice. Mrs Walton saw in the paper – I like to think it was the *Manchester Guardian* – that choral scholarships were being offered at Christ Church Cathedral, Oxford. Mrs Walton applied, and young William was accepted for audition.

Yet, on the morning of that Oxford appointment, they discovered to Mrs Walton's horror that the previous night Mr Walton had drunk away the money for the train fare. In desperation, as Walton told me, when I interviewed him to celebrate his seventieth birthday, that was an explanation that had never previously been published. He remembered how embarrassing it was for Mrs Walton to borrow the money from the greengrocer on the corner.

It meant that mother and son missed the train they had planned to take, and consequently missed their connection at Crewe. They arrived at Oxford just as the auditions were finishing. Initially the examiners refused to hear young William, but Mrs Walton with Lancashire determination argued that William ought to be heard, when they had come so far. They did hear the boy, and he was at once accepted for a place in the Christ Church choir.

As he reported, he quickly lost his Lancashire accent, under the chaffing of the other boys in the choir and, in due course, because of the beauty of his voice and his musical skills, he became the chief chorister. When later his voice broke, the Dean of the College pulled every string he could, and the sixteen-year-old became the youngest Oxford undergraduate since the time of Henry VIII, being accepted to do a degree in music.

The trouble was that William proved totally unable to get through exams, conceivably because he was what we now call dyslexic. Yet Walton's luck came to his help. He made friends with Sacheverell Sitwell, the youngest of the three Sitwell siblings, Osbert, Edith and Sacheverell, who had already established themselves as prominent figures in the world of the arts.

Osbert was looking for a composer to sponsor, and so it came about that young William was given a flat at the top of Osbert's house in Chelsea. At sixteen he wrote a Piano Quartet which was accepted for a Carnegie Award, but his first really successful piece was the music he wrote to accompany Edith Sitwell's poems, *Façade*, with music recited to fit the rhythm of the poems. The first performance was a *succès de scandale*, breaking up before the performance was finished, but soon enough with more and more pieces written for the series over the following years, the *Façade* Entertainment became very popular. An orchestral arrangement of some of the pieces was then issued separately, and was used for a ballet.

Walton, meanwhile, quickly became one of the leading young composers of his generation, alongside the even younger Constant

Lambert. The trouble was that young William, for all his musical success, had no income and, as he admitted to me, he became 'something of a gigolo', one who found himself attracted to women much older than himself. Fortunately, he was left an allowance of £100 a year, a fair sum in those days, which helped his finances. One exception to the rule of older lovers was the German Baroness Imma von Doernberg, who received the dedication of the First Symphony, even though by then the affair was over. Exceptionally, the First Symphony received its premiere without a finale, as Walton, who was always slow in his composing, had a serious blockage.

In the end Walton did complete a finale, but by that time he had another lover, Alice, Lady Wimborne, whose husband had no objection to his wife having her young admirer. As Walton explained to Walter Legge, the great EMI record producer, he changed girlfriends between movements, and that accounts for the noticeable difference between the tortured music of the first three movements and the relatively warm and confident music of the finale, anticipating the style of Walton's highly successful film music and the Coronation march of 1937, *Crown Imperial*. If Imma von Doernberg inspired the first three movements, Alice Wimborne inspired the finale.

A year or so before that Walton had been commissioned to write a choral work for the Leeds Festival of 1930, at which Thomas Beecham was due to conduct Berlioz's *Requiem* with its attendant brass bands. Beecham suggested to Walton that he might as well include brass bands himself, as he was never 'likely to hear his piece again'. Despite that prediction *Belshazzar's Feast*, the subject chosen by Walton in collaboration with Osbert Sitwell, has become one of the most popular choral works in the repertory. Here was barbaric music quite different from anything in the English choral tradition, and initially it was turned down for the Three Choirs Festival as not being suitable for performance in church. Walton once suggested to me that had he written *Belshazzar* a few years later, he might well have called it a choral symphony instead of an oratorio, so flexible had our ideas of a symphony become.

It was at the end of the Second World War that Alice succumbed to cancer, and her painful death had a powerful effect on Walton. To help him overcome his loss it was suggested that he should be one of the British delegates to a conference in Buenos Aires convened by PEN, an organisation celebrating the work of creative artists in different fields. At one of the first parties he was asked by an Argentinian journalist what he thought of Argentinian women. Promptly Walton pointed to a striking young girl on the other side of the room and boasted that he was going to marry her.

He had not even spoken to her at the time, but later in the party he introduced himself to her, Susana Gil, daughter of a banker. He quickly came to the point of asking her to marry him. Susana's response was to think to herself, 'another drunken Englishman', but Walton repeated the offer on the phone the following day, and continued for more than a week. His persistence paid off, and in the end Susana said yes. It was the beginning of one of the happiest marriages any composer has enjoyed.

They came back to post-war England after their marriage in Buenos Aires, cold and grey in the period of austerity. Susana and William both agreed that England at that time was not the place where they wanted to live, and quickly settled for Italy, which under the influence of the Sitwells, Walton had come to love. They found their ideal retreat on the island of Ischia in the Bay of Naples, a place where Walton could avoid the sort of commitments to committees and the like, that he loathed.

At first the conditions were anything but luxurious, and Susana remembers sitting on what had been the back seat of a car doing her crochet while William was hard at work writing his first opera, *Troilus and Cressida* – like most of his works the product of a love affair, this time a happy one. Walton chose a traditional grand-opera setting and a traditional story, intending to counter the operas of Benjamin

Britten, which consistently relied on offbeat stories. It was Walton's great disappointment that, despite excellent reviews initially, the piece was not counted a success.

Walton even included a role for Britten's partner, Peter Pears, as Pandarus, and the casting was excellent, though the role of Cressida, designed for the great soprano Elisabeth Schwarzkopf, was never sung by her on stage, only in excerpts from the opera on disc. There was outright disaster when the opera was given its premiere outside Britain at La Scala, Milan, and the soprano singing Cressida found that the dagger with which she should have stabbed herself was missing. She rushed round the stage looking for it like a dog after a bone, until the audience collapsed in laughter. That was the end of *Troilus* in Italy.

In the years that followed, Walton wrote a fine sequence of beautifully crafted works, but something of the fire that had marked all his pre-war works – the Violin and Viola Concertos and *Belshazzar's Feast* – was missing. His later works, *Troilus* excepted, tend to have less memorable if often subtler melodies, and there is not quite the high-voltage electricity that so marked out Walton's pre-war music.

One aspect of Walton's character that I increasingly came to cherish, the more I got know him, was his wit. I remember once over tea at the Ritz he said drily, 'Oh, I don't think that Bernstein's *Mass* is as bad as everyone says it is.' He paused. 'It's almost as good as the *War Requiem*.' In that way he shot at two targets, Britten and Bernstein, without seeming to attack either. On another occasion I remember him saying that he had just had a phone call from Michael Tippett, who said he was writing another opera. 'Keep it simple, old man,' was Walton's advice, in the full knowledge that Tippett never kept anything simple, so complex were his thought processes.

It was always a joy to witness the love between William and Susana, a love that survived any number of minor trials, so devoted was Susana. After William died in his early eighties, she dedicated herself to developing the house and garden which together they had created on the island of Ischia. So much so, that *La Mortella*, the name they gave this wonderful sanctuary, became one of the principal tourist attractions of the island.

LORD BRITTEN

My devotion to Walton and his music was so extreme that it took me some years before I could listen to the music of Benjamin Britten in any way dispassionately, so intense was my resentment over the arrival of a composer who in my mind was the usurper, ousting Walton from his prime position as the leading young British composer. Where Walton was painfully slow in composing, Britten's facility was phenomenal, so that he quickly built up a formidable list of works to establish his role as leading composer, backed up by his gift as an interpreter of his own music, and his lifelong collaboration with his partner, the tenor Peter Pears, who inspired so many of his works.

The work of Britten's that for me provided a breakthrough was the *Serenade for Tenor, Horn and Strings*, which a friend in the army insisted I should hear. I could not resist, and from then on I built up a devotion to Britten's music second only to my devotion to Walton's. That devotion was intensified when I became a regular visitor to the Aldeburgh Festival, which Britten and Pears had established in the Suffolk seaside town where they lived. In that way every year for two or three weeks in the summer, the capital of musical Britain moved from London to Aldeburgh, and I relished that more and more.

Knowing Britten's aversion to music critics, I was not surprised that I never got an invitation to the party at the Red House, the home of Britten and Pears, at the end of each Festival. In the year of the great fire that consumed Snape Maltings, however, I felt things were different, as I had loyally stayed in Aldeburgh for the full length of the improvised Festival. To my delight I was indeed finally invited, yet I still did not have an encounter with Britten himself. Then in the end we both turned, and we found ourselves face to face with each other. I began by complimenting him on his driving, as I had driven immediately behind him one day when he was going to a concert.

That eased the atmosphere and so, more daringly, I asked him why he hated critics so much. He explained that, soon after the pre-miere of his Coronation opera, *Gloriana*, much misunderstood at first, he had been rung up by a friend, who excitedly informed him that there was a wonderful review of the new opera in the *Daily Telegraph*. Britten, who detested that publication as being alien to his own political views, reluctantly paid the tuppence for the paper. There was indeed a very long review, but it was a blistering diatribe against the piece, which the sensitive Britten found extremely painful. It was symptomatic of what I detected then and elsewhere on the rare occasions when I had a brief word or two with him. He suffered from having a dozen skins too few to withstand criticism.

On one such occasion, in 1971, it was I and not Britten who needed a thick hide, when a selected group from the LSO, along with Walton and Britten, was invited to a reception held by Madame Furtseva, the notorious, hard-drinking Soviet Culture Minister. I was delighted to be invited too, though when Madame Furtseva heard that I came from the *Guardian*, she described it as 'the worst paper of all'. This was at a time when Victor Zorza, the leading Kremlinologist, was writing the most revealing pieces in the paper. I felt, if anything, even more proud of working there.

I spoke to Britten at that reception and happened to mention that André Previn, principal conductor of the LSO, was about to conduct Beethoven's Ninth for the first time. 'Not a very good piece,' was Britten's dismissive remark. I was shocked at the idea, but sug-gested gently that perhaps Beethoven was not a composer for whom Britten would have had much sympathy. He denied that and said that, some years before, when he was in his teens, Beethoven had been one of his principal heroes. Walton's comment, when I told him this story was a brusque 'He's a bloody liar!' Yet years later in a photo of Britten's study when he was a boy, there in the middle of the desk was a portrait of Beethoven, validating his claim.

My first visit to Aldeburgh and its Festival came in 1961, when the great Russian cellist Mstislav Rostropovich was visiting Aldeburgh for the first time, to give the premiere of the Cello Sonata Britten had composed for him. At the last minute, to everyone's surprise, the Soviet authorities allowed Rostropovich's wife, the soprano Galina Vishnevskaya, to come to Aldeburgh as well, unannounced, resulting in some thrilling last-minute changes to the programme. Such spontaneity marked out the Aldeburgh Festival in that golden era and made it an essential event in my yearly calendar as the *Guardian*'s music critic, but that is another story.

SIR MICHAEL TIPPETT

Next to Walton and Britten, both of them precocious, Michael Tippett was a relatively late developer. Though he studied at the Royal College of Music in the 1920s, he did not produce any work that he felt he could acknowledge until 1935, with his First String Quartet. It was even later that he delivered what has become one of his most popular works, the Concerto for Double String Orchestra, with a heavenly melody in the slow movement and outer movements with gently jazzy syncopations.

He was teaching and conducting at Morley College, initially with an orchestra of unemployed musicians, and later becoming head of music there. In his oratorio *A Child of Our Time*, inspired by the shooting of a Nazi official in Paris by an anti-Nazi activist, he wrote his first really large-scale work in which he used settings of American spirituals in just the way that Bach had used chorales, to memorable and moving effect. Tippett was always slow and deliberate in his composing and, when he planned his first opera, *The Midsummer Marriage*, he first wrote to T. S. Eliot asking him to provide a libretto.

Eliot not surprisingly told him to write the libretto himself. That he did, simultaneously with composing the score, page by page, an extraordinary procedure, which nonetheless suited his inspiration.

It was a work that was initially misunderstood, so complex was the story and so arcane were the references. Yet before the run of performances at Covent Garden was over, many of us felt that this was one of the most beautiful of all post-war operas.

His next opera was quite different. *King Priam* marked a complete change of style in what in effect was his second period. Where *The Midsummer Marriage* was warmly lyrical, *Priam* was angular and crisp, and it took some time before the change of style was accepted, and one realised that here was an opera in its way just as powerful as *Midsummer Marriage*.

Tippett's choices of subject, like those of Britten, have always been offbeat, for his next opera, *The Knot Garden*, takes a psychiatrist as a central character and has moving roles for two gay characters, Dov and his black partner, Mel; quite a development for opera, when, by contrast, Britten's impliedly gay characters were never explicit in their orientation. In fact Tippett had already paved the way in his portrayal of Achilles and Patroclus in *King Priam*.

The Knot Garden marked another new development in the spareness of the writing, and so it was in the operas that followed, *The Ice Break* with its rather self-conscious use of popular forms such as the blues, and the 'space-age' opera, *New Year*. Other works of the period included *The Vision of St Augustine*, disconcertingly thorny in its textures, but ultimately most rewarding. These led to the massive oratorio *The Mask of Time*, in which strange characters appear, including a dinosaur.

Meanwhile, Tippett wrote a sequence of symphonies, with No. 3 in two long movements, starting with a blues-inspired vocal movement, which seemed at first not to have much relationship with what followed. No. 4, written for Solti and the Chicago Symphony Orchestra, encapsulated the process of life, starting and ending with breathing effects, and including sections on the mature periods of life.

Tippett from the start was always obsessed with the subconscious, having been psychoanalysed at an early age, and when he was interviewed for BBC Radio in a series called *In the Psychiatrist's Chair*, he quickly turned the tables and in no time at all was psychoanalysing his interviewer, asking all the questions. His philosophical concepts were always highly involved, and often difficult for the layman to follow, but one always had trust in his final judgement.

Tippett's very last work, *The Rose Lake*, written as he approached his nineties, was also one of the most beautiful. It was inspired by a visit to a lake in West Africa, which at a certain time of day turned pink, a strange phenomenon, which moved Tippett greatly, drawing from him some of his most atmospheric music. Cleverly, he used some African-inspired instruments, miniature drums called roto-toms, with memorable effect. Some of Tippett's later music is disconcertingly wild in its expression, and from having been a slow worker he became quicker and quicker, not always to the benefit of the work involved. Just how he will ultimately be judged is still in doubt; and, though he had great success late in life in the United States, a country he loved, some of his works may soon be forgotten, not least in America.

MALCOLM ARNOLD

The first time I met Malcolm Arnold came when he was conducting the film music Walton had written for the film about the Battle of Britain. I was introduced at the first pause, and his initial remark was to say how he hated music critics. To his surprise my response was to say, 'And so do I!', reflecting my lack of sympathy with critics who regard their role as a negative one, making them intent on picking holes in performances rather than seeking to bring out the positive qualities of a performance.

From then on Arnold and I got on famously, but it was right at the end of his life that I got to know him best of all. Sadly, Malcolm's later years were marked by excessive drinking and bouts of psychiatric illness, which sometimes grew very severe, resulting in at least two suicide attempts. For a time in the early 1980s he left hospital and moved into a pub in his home town of Northampton, having separated from his second wife and fallen out with his children. Aware that his health was growing precarious – not for the first time – he decided to settle in a comfortable bungalow in Attleborough, a village near Norwich. He wanted a housekeeper, and a colourful character, Anthony Day, who also lived in the village, became not only his housekeeper, but also his devoted carer for over two decades.

The odd thing was that Malcolm had always possessed a streak of homophobia, yet Anthony had 'come out' and was unashamedly gay. That seemed to cement the relationship still further. On his own birthday in 1986, Anthony challenged Malcolm, suggesting that he should write a piece for him. He cannot have expected the astonishing result of this suggestion: Malcolm, now in his mid-sixties, immediately set to work on his Ninth Symphony; and three weeks later it was finished.

The problem then was to get it performed. A number of conductors were approached, and each rejected the idea of performing the piece, as the textures were alarmingly thin. It was Charles Groves who agreed to perform it in an impromptu concert, which was recorded. Anthony gave me the tape to play for myself, and I remember listening to it on the train from Norwich to Liverpool Street, and getting increasingly excited. It struck me that here was a piece that benefited from its spareness, so that the long slow movement, the most substantial section, was like Mahler slimmed down.

I was lucky enough to receive the first recording for review in *Gramophone*, and was a little apprehensive that my enthusiasm for this Ninth Symphony might be ridiculed by less sympathetic critics. I need not have worried, as soon enough what I had appreciated in this spare score came to be praised generally, a wonderful example of a piece of music written out of affection for the composer's carer.

SIR HARRISON BIRTWISTLE

The first time I met Harrison Birtwistle was at the Aldeburgh Festival, when I was reviewing the first performance of his first opera, *Punch and Judy*. I attended not only the premiere but the dress rehearsal too the night before, and emerged from both with a violent head-ache, so abrasive was the style, with woodwind predominating in the chamber accompaniment. Not only that, I found Stephen Pruslin's libretto most unsympathetic, with its childish dependence on nurs-ery rhymes. I wrote a blistering review attacking the piece, but as I have often told Harry since, it was the only time when I knew I had completely misjudged a piece of music, before I had even heard it again, so vivid was its impact, and I came to relish it. I even objected when later in the year the piece was given in London, and a central interval was inserted.

From then on I followed Birtwistle's operas eagerly. I couldn't always follow what he was trying to say, as some of his textures were rather thorny, but I never had a moment's doubt that this was great music in the making. When I went to see his epic opera *The Mask of Orpheus*, on its penultimate performance, I found the experience so compelling, and to a degree baffling, that I had to go to the final performance as well.

It was a delight too to get to know Birtwistle personally, for his dry Lancastrian sense of humour is irresistible. I remember when I went to the comic opera he wrote for Glyndebourne, *The Second Mrs Kong*, I was rushing back to my seat at the end of the interval, and happened to see Harry similarly finding his way back. I said to him enthusiastically, 'Harry, this is marvellous!' and his dry response was to say, 'It isn't over yet.' Then again when he was being interviewed by his fellow composer Nigel Osborne, during a Birtwistle Weekend at the Queen Elizabeth Hall, Osborne told him that they were getting schoolchildren to improvise on a certain Birtwistle theme. 'What do you think of that?' asked Osborne. 'I don't know,' came back the reply. 'I haven't heard it yet.'

SIR PETER MAXWELL DAVIES

It is a curious fact that the very first premiere that Peter Maxwell Davies had as a boy composer was a little piano piece played by Ena Sharples of *Coronation Street*, the actress Violet Carson. Before she became a national celebrity in *Coronation Street*, she was the resident pianist of BBC Northern *Children's Hour*, and when the young Max had a piece accepted for performance, naturally she was the performer. Later he played his piano pieces on the radio himself, a precocious composer who had started writing at the age of six.

That Violet Carson was chosen for a leading role in this pioneering soap opera was thanks to another young contributor to the Northern *Children's Hour*, Tony Warren, who devised the whole scenario of *Coronation Street*. Asked to suggest someone to take the role of Ena Sharples, he thought back to his days on *Children's Hour* and suggested Violet Carson, who was not in her own personality a battle-axe, but looked exactly like one.

Tony Warren and Max became good friends, and they would go out together and visit 'tin tabernacles', evangelistic chapels, and would make rude comments during the service. On one occasion they remember being run up the street by irate members of the congregation, strange experience for two figures later to achieve prominence.

For his formal musical training Max went to Manchester University, but met up with his contemporaries, Alexander Goehr, Harrison Birtwistle and John Ogdon from the Manchester Royal College of Music to form the Manchester New Music Group, establishing themselves as leading the British avant-garde. After graduating Max took a job as a teacher at Cirencester Grammar School, writing works specially for the pupils to perform, a key factor in his development.

Later he worked in London, and formed first the Pierrot Players, dedicated to performing new music, but replaced a year or two later by the Fires of London. I always remember going to a Fires of London concert at Queen Elizabeth Hall, when my companion and I were greeted in the foyer by Max who enthusiastically told us his new work was really a very good piece.

He did not exaggerate, for it was *Eight Songs for a Mad King*, setting the ravings of George III in an extraordinary vocal line, which involved not just singing but shrieking. Not everyone was convinced, and I remember it was interrupted in the middle by cries of 'rubbish' from the back of the hall. Even when the protester was put out, he managed to open the door and to our intense amusement shouted, 'It *is* rubbish!'

Max's amazing facility has led him to write a great sequence of symphonies, not all of them as effective as they might be, for his facility gets him writing at great length, as in his First Symphony. Yet, when he has deliberately limited himself, it is different, as in the Seventh Symphony, in which the one-movement structure echoes that of Sibelius's Seventh, and the results are most impressive.

When I last saw him for an extended interview I asked him whether he might be in danger of writing too much. I wrapped up the question as tactfully as I could, but he bridled at the idea, and explained that his mind is constantly buzzing with musical ideas. He would have one on his way to the bus stop, he said, and would later note it down. The problem, then, is knowing good from not so good, and there have been works such as the Violin Concerto he wrote for Isaac Stern, which run the risk of falling into mere note-spinning.

That work was first performed by Stern at the Orkney Festival that for many years Max organised on the remote island where he made his home, cut off from his usual contacts. For some years he did not even have a phone, and would wait by the public phone box some distance from his house, when he was expecting a call. His lifestyle was primitive, but the landscape of Orkney did inspire a number of his works, some among the finest.

It is typical of Max that he accepted a commission to write a series of concertos for the Scottish Chamber Orchestra and later from the Naxos record company to write a series of ten string quartets, two a year, a schedule he readily maintained, with the quartets promptly issued on the Naxos label each year, an attractively varied sequence.

I also remember asking Max, well known for his left-wing views, why he had accepted a knighthood, and very openly he told me that it had been suggested to him that having a title would help to raise money among rich but musically unskilled potential sponsors. It is a sound argument.

CARL DAVIS

If there is a busier composer in Britain than Carl Davis, it would be hard to find him. I remember him arriving for an interview, precisely on time, when that very morning he had completed a Clarinet Concerto for the Greenwich Festival. His precision on timing chimes with the requirement in writing for films, and particularly for the blockbuster scores he has devised for accompanying great films from the silent era, starting with Abel Gance's *Napoleon*, three hours long and an early experiment in wide-screen presentation with three projections side by side. For that he used various works of Beethoven as well as other music from the Napoleonic period.

Yet Davis is not just devoted to music; he is also a great talker, and is hyperactive in everything he does, including the conducting that has inevitably followed on his writing for films. He realised that no one else could present the scores as well as he could. He then came to enjoy conducting, and has branched out as a conductor generally, not just in light music.

When I first met him, he was devising a score to accompany a classic film of Douglas Fairbanks Senior, *The Thief of Baghdad*, for which he used various fragments of Rimsky-Korsakov music, not just *Sheherazade*. When he first started conducting for films, he was concerned to instruct the orchestra in every single bar. He then on one occasion knocked his spectacles off just as he had started a precisely timed take. He had to break off conducting, and then found in the finished result that the players had continued perfectly, even when he was not conducting. It taught him not to worry too much about every single detail, once the rehearsal was finished.

His path to success in Britain has been a curious one. Despite the Welsh surname, his background is Jewish. He was born in Brooklyn, and as an only child was taken to concerts from the age of four, either in the sculpture court of the Brooklyn Museum or in the parks. He became an avid listener to the radio, and even before he became a standee at the old Metropolitan Opera House, he was regularly listening to the Saturday afternoon opera broadcast. High spots for him were *Khovanshchina* in 1949, Flagstad's last appearance in 1951 and the New York City Opera's production of Prokofiev's *Love for Three Oranges*. Records he loved included Beecham's set of Mozart's *Magic Flute*, Heifetz in the Sibelius Violin Concerto and Edith Sitwell's early recording with Constant Lambert of Walton's *Façade*.

In his teens a lot of creative energy went into his painting, and his composing was fitful, but that changed when he went to study at the New England Conservatory. He then discovered that he had a phenomenal ability to sight-read at the piano, and he was snapped up as accompanist and *répétiteur* for choral concerts, including those conducted by Toscanini's former choirmaster, Robert Shaw, appearing all over the United States.

He might well have made that his whole career, but his

contribution to a highly successful revue presented by the college led him to realise that composing was his forte. He came to Europe, not immediately to Britain; in Berlin by chance he met his collaborator on his college revue, who suggested he should come to Britain. Once there he never looked back, writing music for television plays from the start, and preparing music for such television series as *The World at War* and *Destination America.*

That led him to look outside light music and his old repertory, which in turn fired up in him an ambition to conduct more generally. He will never become primarily a conductor, for he enjoys composing too much and is consistently successful at it, but so active a musician will never be idle.

SAMUEL BARBER

My meeting with the American composer Samuel Barber could not have been more delightful. I was on my way to the Van Cliburn Piano Competition in Fort Worth, and I had had the worst flight I have ever had from Britain to the United States. It had begun well enough, but we were just settling down, and were flying over Ireland, when the captain announced that one of the engines was not firing properly, and we had to return to Heathrow. This we did, and were divided in two. I opted to go with those on Pan Am, as that was the airline I was booked on, yet when we got to New York all our luggage was stuck in the TWA terminal half a mile away.

We finally retrieved our luggage, and were offered overnight hotel accommodation. I finally got to bed at 4 a.m. US time, 9 a.m. by my body-clock time. I then caught a plane to Dallas-Fort Worth from La Guardia Airport, and reached my destination, not even knowing whether anyone from the Van Cliburn Competition would know that I was arriving and on what flight. To my delight there was someone there to greet me, and they came out with quite the most wonderfully welcoming question I have ever had posed to me: would I mind sharing the Cadillac with Samuel Barber?

In the car Barber recalled the first time he had arrived at Fort Worth, when he was a raw conscript in the Army Air Force. As he had studied at the Curtis Institute in Philadelphia, which did not believe in exams, he had no paper qualifications, and so was treated to the worst possible jobs, sweeping up katydids from the latrines, and generally cleaning around the camp.

Fortunately, there was an officer who had been a Hollywood star, who knew exactly who Samuel Barber was, and so memorably the raw recruit in his dirty fatigues was summoned before the colonel, and was promptly asked if he would sit down, something that flabbergasted the sergeant who accompanied him. The colonel said the Air Force was anxious to get every man into an appropriate role – round pegs in round holes – and suggested that Barber might write a symphony celebrating the Air Force.

Barber pointed out that he could not write such a work in the camp, and so suggested he should do it at his home in New England, which is how he was able to do his military service without leaving home. The only trouble was that the officer to whom he was told to report progress was an enthusiast for serial music, and rather resisted Barber's very tonal composition.

None the less the three movements were completed, and the colonel then wrote to Serge Koussevitzky in somewhat patronising terms suggesting that they thought him the best person to conduct the first performance. This indeed is what happened, and Barber, by this time a corporal, took his bow in Symphony Hall, Boston. Afterwards he was approached by a formidably tall figure of a woman, Mrs General Patton, who brusquely asked him, 'Tell me, corporal, have you had any musical training?'

At that time I had just organised a new recording of Barber's two symphonies, taken up by a conductor friend, David Measham, who as a reward for helping a pop composer had been given a series of free sessions to use as he wanted. In the car I discussed the recording with Barber – or Sam as one was quickly encouraged to call him – and I chided him on having withdrawn the outer movements of his Second Symphony, leaving only the middle slow movement, *Night Flight*. He explained that he no longer liked the outer movements, but I disagreed; I already possessed an early recording of the full three-movement symphony.

The reason for Sam's involvement in the Van Cliburn Competition was that he had been commissioned to write a short piano piece for all the candidates to play. Sam was to be the judge, and in the end he chose as the winner of his special prize Christian Blackshaw, a distinguished British pianist who went on to have a good if hardly starry career. Over the week when the competition was being held, I got to know Sam much better. We would regularly be invited to unbelievably rich oil millionaires' houses, and would each hate their vulgarity. During the week I took the opportunity to do an interview with Sam, while we drank up my duty-free gin, of which I knew his carer, Valentino, did not approve. Yet in my recording of what he said, he was happily at his most uninhibited.

He told me of going each summer to Italy with his friend and housemate Gian Carlo Menotti, as well as with another composer, Nino Rota. While there they would visit Toscanini in his summer retreat. On the first occasion Toscanini asked Barber to send him a short piece that he might perform with the NBC Symphony. Barber, flattered, responded by arranging the slow movement of his First String Quartet for full string orchestra, and that was what Barber sent to him, the *Adagio for Strings*, which has become one of the most popular of all twentieth-century pieces.

When they returned to Italy the following summer, Barber had not heard anything from Toscanini, and so thought it best not to accompany Menotti and Nino Rota to see him. The veteran conductor asked where Barber was, realising that he was inhibited by not having heard about the *Adagio*. Whereupon the great conductor told Menotti and

Rota to inform their friend that Toscanini was about to include the *Adagio* in his next series of concerts. They returned with the glad news.

Barber had bad luck over some of the big works he wrote. A commission from one of the big railway companies was unveiled on the very day that the company went into liquidation, and his major opera, *Antony and Cleopatra*, written for the opening of the new Metropolitan Opera, was poorly received, largely because it was inadequately rehearsed. It has since emerged as a beautifully written opera with some great moments for the heroine, a role designed for Leontyne Price who was also the interpreter of many of Barber's songs, most of them very much rooted in the British literary tradition.

OLIVER KNUSSEN

Oliver Knussen first attracted attention when, at the age of sixteen, he conducted the LSO in his First Symphony. It was an astonishingly confident piece, very well scored, and André Previn as the orchestra's principal conductor suggested that Knussen should conduct one of the two movements at Carnegie Hall at one of the orchestra's concerts there. At Kennedy airport reporters were waiting to interview the boy composer, but they completely missed him; the sixteen-year-old was already six foot and chunkily built, looking far older than his age.

Knussen had the advantage of being the son of Stuart Knussen, the LSO's principal double-bass-player and for many years the chairman of the self-governing body. Yet the boy was not unduly favoured, for his symphony was far more than a conventional student exercise. He had begun composing at the age of six, and was so advanced so early that his father sent him to a composition teacher, John Lambert. That led him in turn to study at the Purcell School, devoted to training promising young musicians.

Since then Knussen has produced a sequence of very well-crafted works, much tauter in style, when he has adapted serial techniques for his own ends, and writes very deliberately and slowly. He thinks very carefully before he writes a single note, and it is only rarely that he is seized with an urgent inspiration, though it was so when he lighted on the children's books of Maurice Sendak with their strange grotesque beasts.

He had been commissioned to write an opera for Glyndebourne, and he chose as his subject *Where the Wild Things Are* and, unlike most of his works, that one-act opera flowed relatively easily. The result is a charming piece, which he promptly followed up with another Sendak adaptation, *Higglety-Pigglety Pop*, making a useful double-bill in productions.

I have known Ollie from the time he wrote that First Symphony. He is one of the warmest and most genial of companions, who has latterly turned to conducting concerts of new music, not just his own works, very successfully, particularly with the London Sinfonietta. When his works come only rarely, one might even argue that he is now more of a conductor than a composer, but always an inspirer.

Ollie has always had many enthusiasms, not all of them predictable. For example, he was devoted to the conducting of Leopold Stokowski long before we witnessed that great conductor's rehabilitation thanks to the appearance of so many of his classic recordings on CD. Ollie remains a devoted aficionado.

JAMES MACMILLAN

My first interview with the Scottish composer James MacMillan, early in his career, was unique in that we made no mention of music in our first half-hour together. I was fascinated by the fact that James was a devout Roman Catholic, and at the same time politically an extreme left-winger. I wondered at that apparent contradiction, and he claimed that he came from an area of the county of Ayr where the shipbuilding workers, many from Ireland, were similarly devout Catholics and dedicated left-wingers, many of them Communist.

When we did talk about music and his works, it was exciting to find a composer so eager to develop his talents. His first break-through came when his early work *The Confession of Isobel Gowdie* was heard at the Proms in 1990, scoring an instant success. This was a vivid commemoration of a medieval nun who was walled up and died a martyr's death.

Another remarkable occasion was two years later, when *Veni, Veni, Emmanuel* was given its first performance by the dedicatee, the deaf percussionist, a fellow Scot, Evelyn Glennie. This is in effect a percussion concerto with the soloist surrounded by a vast array of instruments, tuned and untuned. The dramatic scheme was to continue the main concerto until near the end, when the percussion soloist made her way up to the back of the stage to a high platform with enormous chimes hanging down. Meanwhile the orchestra tinkled small bells. Then, with the arrival of the main melody of the traditional hymn, '*Veni, Veni, Emmanuel*', the soloist plays the great chimes with thrilling effect.

It is an astonishing moment that makes an unforgettable impression, though so far MacMillan's operas have not been so dramatic as that orchestral work. Yet MacMillan is so prolific there is no knowing where his inspirations will take him. It is a wonderful success story, and MacMillan adds to his activities various academic appointments in different universities. I have yet to discover whether his worldly success has helped to modify his left-wing stance in any way. He is such a determined character that I imagine not.

THE BEATLES

I have rarely dabbled outside the classical repertory in my record reviewing, but I made a big exception when I first registered the quality of the Beatles, notably when their album *Revolver* appeared. In that more than elsewhere the gifts of Paul McCartney as a supreme tunesmith came out superbly in such numbers as 'For No One' and 'Here, There and Everywhere'. I have long felt that McCartney was the musical genius behind the group, just as John Lennon was the inspirer with words and ideas. Sadly, I missed out on interviewing the group in their heyday. I was asked by BBC Radio 4 to go to their hotel to do a radio interview, but at the last minute the plan was cancelled, as there was a trivial dispute in the group, so I never did meet McCartney, much as I wanted to.

I did, however, interview George Martin, the EMI recording manager in charge of the Parlophone label, who over the years, particularly with Paul McCartney, devised some highly original musical effects, such as the idea of using just a string quartet to accompany the glorious McCartney melody 'Yesterday', and having Alan Civil playing a horn *obbligato* on 'For No One'. After I interviewed Martin I wrote a piece for the *Guardian* beginning, 'They call him the fifth Beatle.' I was delighted when, a few weeks later, the satirical magazine *Private Eye* had a piece by 'Edward Greensleeves', beginning, 'They call him the fifth Turdie', *Private Eye* language for the Beatles.

Martin told me that when he heard the tape of the Beatles they sent to him, he was by no means certain that he wanted to record them, but felt it was worth hearing them further. Notoriously, they had been turned down by Decca, and the group came down to London highly suspicious, if not hostile, towards any recording manager. Happily they discovered that Martin had been responsible for the Parlophone recordings of the Goons, which they loved, and that helped to break the ice. The rest is history, and before long Martin resigned from EMI to form his own company, to his enormous benefit.

When in the *Guardian* we had to choose some figure with whom we would like to change places, I chose McCartney, suggesting that the next thing he might try was to write an opera. The *Guardian* for once was highly appreciative of what I wrote, and memorably had a row of photos, McCartney at one end and me at the other, with a digital transformation gradually changing one face to the other. I like to think that McCartney might have seen what the *Guardian*'s chief music critic had written.

My suggestion that he should go on to write an opera, so brilliant and original were McCartney's melodies, never fully came about, but at least he did produce several substantial choral works with the aid of such musicians as Carl Davis. It is a thing of wonder that the Beatles as a pop group had one member, John Lennon, giving his name to Liverpool airport, and another, McCartney, being knighted for his services to charity – something never likely to be matched again.

The other group that at the time of the Beatles' heyday made an impact and also impressed me were the Beach Boys. I did meet them at a party given by their record company, CBS, and I complimented them on the fact that plainly some of their numbers suggested that they had had a classical training. They were delighted, and told me that when they had their first big hit, they went out and celebrated by buying a disc of a Beethoven symphony. Memorably one of them said, not meaning to be pompous, 'Beethoven was our inspiration,' a remark I cherished.

Interlude 4: The Army

y two and a quarter years in the army, doing my National Service, brought me a number of unexpected benefits, not least that in that time, between 1947 and 1949, I met at least a dozen of my closest friends for life; friends who have brought me joy ever since, though sadly a number of them have now died. The other great benefit was that, when I arrived at Cambridge University, I was far more mature than I had been when I left school and far better equipped to appreciate the enormous benefits that university life can bring you, most of all for anyone at Oxbridge.

My personal D-Day was 6 February 1947, when, with mountainous apprehension, I walked with a troop of other conscripts up the hill from Brentwood station to the grim buildings of Warley Barracks, built in Napoleon's time for wars against the French. They were made the grimmer in that month, as Britain was at the start of the worst winter weather for a hundred years, an ice age so complete that the ice did not melt on some of the hills until midsummer.

It meant that there was neither heat nor running water in our barrack room. The nearest toilet facilities were across the yard where there was a row of very basic latrines that the whole camp had to use. For heat we had to light a fire in the primitive grate, and over the flames I remember trying to melt the thick grease that was enveloping the rifle with which I had been issued. It had not been used since the First World War and, when I did rid it of the grease, I found that the barrel was so terribly scored that no officer would believe I had been desperately trying to clean it. Fern-like growths would appear down its length as soon as I had (illicitly) used a gauze to clean it. It was the happiest day of army life when, on starting to train for the Royal Army Educational Corps (RAEC), I handed my rifle in.

That was six months away from the misery of my primary training at Warley Barracks. I was the most cack-handed rookie in our platoon, relying on friendly colleagues to help bail me out from many practical tasks. With no running water, even washing my face was a problem, and it did not help that, mollycoddled as I had been, I at once caught some formidable bugs and had to be taken at one point into the sickbay.

I was also hopeless at doing the sort of tasks that were given to us when we were required to peel potatoes or to wash down floors. I had no idea how to squeeze a floorcloth to wipe up the dirt on a floor until someone showed me, but I was a willing worker when, on a day I greatly enjoyed, a handful of us were deputed to help a sergeant move into new living quarters. He repaid our help when at the end of my six weeks' primary training we had stocktaking and I had had several items of kit stolen or at least lost. This sergeant promptly restored them without charging me.

In those first six weeks, being among the first National Service recruits, we were inspected twice over by Field-Marshal Montgomery, who gave his usual pep talks, and twice or three times by General Horrocks, who was Commander-in-Chief of Eastern Command, a man who somehow had the gift of making everyone like him. Later, as I witnessed at first hand when I was in the Parliamentary Press Gallery, he was appointed Black Rod and carried out his duties better than anyone else I have ever seen in that role, whether in person or on television.

One benefit of having ice and snow on the parade ground was that we could not be intensively drilled, but we still had to tackle the assault course. I could scream well enough when we were required to plunge our bayonets into sacks representing human bodies, but I was hopeless trying to walk along a narrow beam eight feet off the ground, and to swing from the end back to the ground.

Our so-called aptitude tests were so simple that I finished them absurdly early, discovering later that, although the clerical test was devised to find clerks, it was hopeless for that purpose and was kept on the list to discover 'officer material', as only the persistent and determined rookie could finish it. Asked to suggest which branch of the army I wanted to go into, I nominated first the Intelligence Corps and then the Educational Corps.

For the Intelligence Corps I was given a language test at Hobart House in London near Victoria, which evidently I failed, for I discovered that I was chosen to go into the Educational Corps, which had just been honoured with the prefix 'Royal'. It was only at the end of my six weeks' primary training that to my horror I discovered that, far from going straight to train for the Educational Corps, I had to do full infantry training designed to toughen and smarten up a notoriously slack regiment.

So I duly arrived at Oswestry station, bound for Park Hall Camp at Tinkers Green and attachment to the North Staffordshire Regiment. Our only consolation was to discover they had put all the potential Educational Corps recruits into the same barrack room. This had the effect of making the North Staffs recruits resent us all the more, thereby dividing the platoon sharply. So it was that a man going by the name of Shutler was ironically called 'Shootler' by us, imitating the North Staffs men, and 'Shatler' by the North Staffs, they in turn seeking to imitate what they heard as our posh accents.

It was a tough course, culminating in two weeks of battle camp at Kington in Herefordshire. By a happy chance Whitsun leave and a long weekend break came in the middle. That followed immediately on our night of bivouacking on a Welsh mountain, followed by a twenty-mile route march, made the more taxing as we were still in our heavy winter serge, and not in shirt-sleeve order: we sweated profusely, shouldering our heavy packs.

I was still determined not to drop out of the march and, although during the latter stages I couldn't keep up with my platoon, I did somehow stumble to the end, knowing that I had a blister on my heel. It turned out to be over five inches long, and the corporal insisted on getting the North Staffs chaps round to look at it, complimenting me on having finished the course even with such a blister, something he thought few of the others would have done. That was one of the few compliments I ever had during that time. The other was when an officer of the day called Dalziel-Payne made me the leader of our guard-duty group of four, much to my astonishment, as the smartest of them.

The benefit of having our Whitsun leave in the middle of battle camp was that, when I arrived home, my parents insisted that I should go to the doctor, to have my blister attended to. He at once prescribed penicillin, which had only just become available. It cured the blister almost instantly, and only later did I discover that the doctor's over-prescribing would leave me allergic to penicillin for some years.

When finally we finished our infantry training, the start of my Educational Corps training was still delayed, as the School of Army Education was in the process of moving from Alton Towers on the Derbyshire–Staffordshire border to Buchanan Castle, twenty miles north-west of Glasgow. My group was in the rearguard party, which meant that we had to do a lot of cleaning and clearing up, which in its way was fun. Finally arriving at Buchanan Castle, to our horror we found we were under the tutelage on the parade ground of sergeants and warrant officers from the Guards regiments, another scheme for toughening up the Educational Corps.

Before we finished Educational Corps training I had incidentally come to know John Steane, who became my closest friend, and I shared a bunk with another lifelong friend, Geoffrey Best, with whom I did a study of the Glasgow Docks for our final task on the course, which evidently was much approved of by the RAEC authorities at Buchanan Castle. When as a final hurdle we had our viva in front of a panel of officers, I was asked whether I had ever thought of staying in the army. That of course was the last thing I had in mind, but instead of rejecting the idea in a way that might have offended the panel of officers, I pretended surprise and, in apparent delight, said I had never thought of the idea, but then, 'I was due to take up my school at Cambridge.' It was the best answer I could have given.

The other event of my RAEC course at Buchanan Castle was that I was roped in as pianist at the end-of-term concert in a company entitled 'The Buccaroos'. I accompanied a rather formidable officer, Major King, who fancied his voice but had no idea of keeping time, which he at once confessed to me. In fact he was touchingly appreciative of the way I followed him – simple enough. The only hitch was not our fault. When he sang a ballad with the couplet, 'Up in the attic away from the din, someone is playing an old violin', Major Gladwell, positioned behind a curtain, was due to play the first phrases of Beethoven's Minuet in G. The inevitable happened: whether or not because the major had been imbibing, he missed the cue and didn't come in at the right place. He then belatedly tried to do his bit, which was worse than anything.

My other role was to play what I called my *Prague* Concerto, a ham-fisted use of popular tunes of the day echoing various piano concertos including Tchaikovsky's, Rachmaninov's and Grieg's, not forgetting Addinsell's *Warsaw* Concerto. The man who was acting as compère, one Vivien Daniels, didn't like that title and insisted on calling it my 'Concerto Galantine', a title no one understood.

The great advantage of training to become an instructor in the RAEC was that, on passing out, one immediately became a fully fledged sergeant, with appropriate pay. I was first of all posted back to Park Hall Camp, where I had trained only six months earlier. It was quite a delight to come across corporals who had previously been difficult, now one had an extra tape on one's arm. The only one I remember was in fact the corporal who had complimented me on my guts in completing the twenty-mile route march, and he was the last person I wanted to treat shabbily.

He was the only one to come into the library I ran at Park Hall Club, the recreation venue in the centre of the camp. Our routine was simple: an easy morning and, after lunch, a fairly relaxed time until the club officially opened for the evening, when we often had a busy time. That routine allowed us to devise a very happy schedule of having a three-day break every other weekend, leaving on the Friday and not returning until the early afternoon on the Monday.

That worked well until we were unexpectedly visited by the senior officer who regularly put us in fear and trembling, Colonel Scriven, a tough old soldier who had been an army schoolmaster in the days before the Educational Corps was founded. He would tell us of primitive conditions in the Sudan before the war, and he always emphasised that we didn't know what hard work was – which was, in all candour, true enough. On one particular Monday 'Scriv' had decided to inspect Park Hall Club, finding half the complement of NCOs absent. I arrived back on schedule to find one of the privates who had managed to act as hanger-on, saying that we had all 'had our chips'. Luckily Scriv was mainly annoyed with the warrant officer in charge of us, and I escaped with no more than a word of disapproval.

What was a complete joy was that John Steane was my regular companion – so much so that in the sergeants' mess we were known as 'Nig and Nog', indubitably two of the least soldierly soldiers in the army. That hardly troubled us and, after having our evening meal, usually with a main course involving either 'bullet' peas or 'sludge' peas, we would go in ritual fashion down to the level crossing at Whittington, to watch one of the expresses from Paddington go past on its way to Gobowen, the exchange station for Oswestry.

We had very little contact with our fellow sergeants in the Royal Artillery mess, partly because we had little in common with old sweats who had fought through the war. That did not satisfy the sergeant major who hauled us before him, and complained that we were falling short in our duties to the mess, and that we were 'obstroporous'. It hardly assuaged his anger that, as we pointed out, our busy time of day was in the evening when other sergeants were generally free, but we promised to do what we could to be good members of the mess.

John was deeply afraid that he was about to be posted away from Oswestry and Park Hall Club. A colleague who had been in the Intelligence Corps, Harry Davenport, had discovered on John's typewriter a letter he had incautiously written, which made a passing reference to the Coventry Communist Party, something severely frowned on then, at the start of the Cold War. In the event it was not John who was posted away, but me. I arrived off Christmas leave to find I had been posted to Chester to the headquarters of Western Command with the job of looking after the Textbook Library of the area.

Painful as that was, it gave me the chance to make friends with another group of colleagues, for at Oswestry it was not just John who became a friend but also Jon Curle, later an announcer in the BBC. At Chester I was billeted along with other sergeants at Blacon Camp at the beginning of the Wirral, some three or four miles outside the city. We would be ferried in every morning by truck to Western Command HQ, returning for lunch and again in the evening.

It was an agreeable routine, and among the friends I made over my months in Chester were Ian Anderson – who did a brilliant Cubist portrait of me – Michael Pilkington, later at Cambridge with me, and Derek Whitehead, also due to go to Cambridge, who was the education officer with the Signals Unit at Blacon Camp and was housed in a very comfortable little flat not in the sergeants' mess but in the Education Centre. He would organise what he called 'salons' when we would read extracts and poems we had enjoyed, a tradition that we carried on when we both got to Cambridge, usually in Derek's rooms at St John's. The novels of Jane Austen were always among our favourite readings, all the more effective when read out loud.

Sadly, just when I thought I was safely stationed in Chester for the rest of my two years' National Service, a posting came through, the kind of nasty surprise in which the army so often excelled. This time I was due to report at the RAEC HQ in Buchanan Castle, where I had previously trained. Luckily my cousin was already there doing his Corps training in the RAEC, and it was good to meet up with him, and to celebrate my birthday, having an enormous high tea in the restaurant in Glasgow celebrated for its Arts and Crafts designs by Charles Rennie Mackintosh.

Yet in our week of preparation we had to undergo an especially severe inspection with kit to be precisely squared off, preferably with wood (goodness knows from where) as we met together in a group of ten or a dozen, all bound for the British Army of the Rhine (BAOR) in Germany. Immediately, I made friends with Peter Marchant, who was my regular companion not just over the period of our travelling to Germany, but also throughout the months that followed. I confess that I was just a fraction disconcerted when we were filling our forms together and I saw that, under 'Religion', Peter had put 'Jewish'.

I had never had a close Jewish friend before and, it is sad to relate, tended to follow the automatic suspicion of Jews that was still a part of conventional culture in Britain, a leftover from before the war. In the event it was a revelation. By the time we were due to be given our various postings in Germany, Peter and I were inseparable. He suggested that we should say to the posting officer – a warrant officer who was rather formidable – that we wanted to be posted together. He could only refuse, as Peter pointed out, but fortunately, he responded to our plea and together we were posted to the headquarters of the BAOR in Bad Oeynhausen, Westphalia, between Bielefeld on one side and Minden and Hanover on the other.

It was fun having a friend with whom to share (and laugh at) our experiences, often involving unpronounceable German. We acquired absurd-sounding little catchphrases from notice boards, such as *Strumpfhaus Mundhenke* or *Moebel Knupp*, and we laughed to see in a window a very old-fashioned hat with a feather at a jaunty angle labelled '*Eleganter Damenhut*'. Peter and I shared a room in what looked like a seedy brothel. An old man would appear every morning with a bowl of water, and luckily Peter thought of getting a little water heater for our ablutions.

There was no bathroom in our seedy billet, so we had to go some ten minutes' walk into the centre of the *Kurpark* opposite the house, and there had an enjoyable hot bath in the health-giving brine of the Spa waters. It was in the *Kurpark* too where there was a club for sergeants and warrant officers, which we called the Wo's and Jo's Club, where we had what for us were exotic meals and drinks at heavily subsidised prices.

We had heavily subsidised leave centres too, and I greatly enjoyed going to one in the Harz Mountains. One day from there I walked to the border with East Germany, going up a path under the Brocken which was plainly going right up to the border itself. I was disconcerted when, standing on the border, I came across a policeman looking very officious. I trembled in case he was East German and would arrest me for straying over the border. Happily, he was a West German policeman, with whom I had a happy conversation in my very halting German.

What came out of my nine months in BAOR (extended by three months because of the Berlin airlift) was that, far from regarding Germans as having horns and devils' hoofs, as we had been told during the war, I liked them consistently, just as I came to love Germany. It has always seemed strange that the foreign countries in which I feel most at home are both German-speaking, not just Germany but Austria too where, for over thirty years, I made an annual pilgrimage to my favourite music festival in Salzburg.

I shall never forget the day in Bad Oeynhausen when I had to go to a discussion group outside the military enclave of Army HQ. It was on the British Constitution, and I spent days boning up on the subject, making copious notes. To my horror, on arriving at the venue I found I had left my notes behind. In fact, it was the best thing that could have happened, for I had to rely on memory, so the resulting talk was much freer and more spontaneous than it would have been.

At the end one of the questions to me was a ticklish one, particularly in 1947 so soon after Germany's defeat. What, I was asked, was the British attitude to the Fascist Party of Great Britain? I had to pause for a moment, and then I said that we allowed Oswald Mosley to say what he liked, but no one took any notice. My audience was visibly appreciative of this clear demonstration of British democracy in practice.

My other contact with a group of Germans came in the Anglo-German discussion group which I chaired in the YWCA in Bad Oeynhausen. Some dozen or more elderly Germans, mainly women, came every week, and alongside a YWCA helper I did my best to entertain them. At the end we offered them all a cup of tea and a biscuit. Sadly, they always looked and sounded terribly gloomy, and my YWCA colleague went to their leader, wondering whether we should close the discussion group down. That horrified them, for the leader – a formidable dowager – explained that their visit inside the Army HQ was their big event of the week, and they specially appreciated the tea and biscuits.

When I was due to be demobbed in March 1949, I wanted to celebrate my departure with a different sort of event. I was writing quite a lot of music at the time, so I composed two piano preludes especially for the group. I carefully copied them out and gave the manuscript ceremoniously to the leader of the German group. Dare I say that such a sentimental, very Germanic gesture drew tears of appreciation from the old dears?

One of our daily duties was to give lessons morning and late afternoon in the Education Centre. It was not easy giving a lecture at 8 a.m., particularly after a heavy night out, and many of those who attended had no interest whatever in education, and regarded it all as a great bore. I felt my task, above all else, was to prevent those attending from being bored. In that I found it was much easier with the privates and corporals rather than the sergeants and warrant officers, who all felt that they had better things to do.

One problem was that one rarely had the same pupils twice, though, in one instance, those who came from the Royal Engineers depot, thanks to their commanding officer's keenness on education, had the same soldiers coming every week. The sappers and lance corporals were a rowdy lot, but I loved teaching them, as they were all so lively. I would interest them by putting all the desks in a different position, as though the classroom was a debating chamber, and then we would have a good discussion. The only trouble was that it took a great deal of concentration on my part to prevent their rowdiness from getting out of hand. On one occasion my successor found them trying to push one of their weaker colleagues out of a window on the first floor.

At one stage we had to give tests in maths and English to all in HQ Company, which we did. Generally, things divided predictably between sergeants and warrant officers on the one hand and privates on the other. When the tests were marked, there was one striking exception. A private in the Black Watch, small, smart, with a monkey-like face, was outstanding, and beat most of the sergeants. He was put in the upper group, which dismayed him. He pleaded with me to stay with his mates among the privates, to which I quickly acceded, but I gave him a lecture that I hope he took on board. I pointed out to him that he could readily outshine all those around him if he tried. I have often wondered whether, after his demob, he ever made a success of his life after the army, maybe, I hope, becoming a millionaire as a Glasgow entrepreneur.

One unique experience came when I was sitting with a friend, Peter Jackson, drinking coffee one morning, and I was experimenting with my webbing belt to see if it could be put on backwards. It was then that someone rushed in, pointing out that we were missing pay parade. So we ran up to HQ Company office and were just in time to hear our names called out. I, of course, had completely forgotten about my reversed belt, so when I went up to collect my pay, saluting smartly, the eyes of the officer at the desk nearly popped out to see a belt back to front. 'It was only a joke,' I said rather lamely, happily saluting and departing before I could be charged and put in 'jug'. I was very lucky to escape, but I feel a little proud of presumably being the only soldier ever to appear on pay parade with his belt reversed.

One joy of being stationed in Bad Oeynhausen was that we could easily take the bus to Bielefeld ten miles away and go to the opera there. Then, venturing rather further afield, I went with Gordon Deeble to Hanover to see my first *Tristan*, or rather most of it, as we had to struggle out during Act III to catch a bus into central Hanover and the last train back to Bad Oeynhausen. The opera at that time was housed in a *Kurhaus* outside the devastated centre of the city, and I discovered much later that the idea of starting an opera there had been the brainchild of one colonel, Ted Heath, the future prime minister and later my friend, encouraged by his CO at the time to indulge in a fantasy.

The other adventure came when, with Peter Marchant, I went illicitly up to Hamburg on the CCG train, wearing civvies. As mere sergeants we were not supposed to use it. We stayed at the Atlantic Hotel on the banks of the Alster. By some miracle the hotel had survived the war almost completely intact, and our room in dark crimson had plainly not been touched since before the start of the war in 1939. Peter amusingly looked up the telephone directory for Hamburg in our room, dated 1939. There he found a whole page of Cohens listed, plainly Jewish. It seems that Hamburg as a Hanseatic port was much more cosmopolitan than most of Nazi Germany, and in many ways defied the dictates of the *Führer*.

That had not prevented Hamburg from being nearly destroyed, thanks to British bombing, in a more terrifying way than I had seen even in devastated Hanover. I remember a concert we attended with the Boyd Neel Orchestra playing Britten's *Variations and Fugue on a Theme of Frank Bridge*, which had been written by Britten for Neel and his orchestra, to be played at an early Salzburg Festival in the 1930s.

A great joy of being in Bad Oeynhausen was that, even more than in my previous postings, I made so many close friends, as it proved for life, not just Peter Marchant and Peter Jackson but also Colin Haycraft (who became the most adventurous of publishers as managing director of what in effect was a one-man business, Duckworth), Richard or Gordon Deeble and Peter Mansfield, like me due to go up to Cambridge, equally destined to devote himself to the Labour Club and the Cambridge Union, though as a Wykehamist wisely treating it all less seriously than I did.

A delay to my release from the army was caused by the Berlin airlift, which necessitated a degree of mobilisation. It did not worry me at all, for I knew there was no chance of going up to Cambridge until the Michaelmas term the following October. It gave me seven months of the laziest, least-stressed period of my whole life. The snag was that, as I was living on the dole, cash was short.

I spent my time reading in the most relaxed way, and during the summer spending many hours on the beach at Chalkwell, doing my best to learn to swim. I could keep up in the water easily enough and on my back could move reasonably well, but attempts at an Australian crawl were hopeless. Even so, it was all a great delight. In May 1949 I received a letter from Charles Crawley, senior tutor at Trinity Hall, with whom I had corresponded when I was taking my Scholarship Exams. He said that 'a man called Janner' had been to see him, said he knew me and was willing to share rooms, as 'all men will have to double up in the coming year'.

Chapter Five

Instrumentalists

So many of the dominant personalities in music have been the great soloists, many of whom (Oistrakh, Rostropovich, Previn) have also ventured into the realm of conducting. Again and again it is they who inspire fervour in audiences and creativity in composers. Some of these men and women endured the worst excesses of the cruel regimes that afflicted much of Europe during the last century.

SIR YEHUDI MENUHIN

What, I boldly asked Yehudi Menuhin, did he feel were his faults? Such a question was apt, I felt, rude as it might seem, when Menuhin's reputation for saintliness was so universally accepted. Plainly, the question took him aback, but he promptly answered that he was impatient with those he loved. That, when you think about it, is hardly a fault, when impatience with those you love reflects that love: you do not need to hold back on any feelings.

His second fault, he felt, was impatience with jacks-in-office, officials who like to throw their weight about in exercising their duty. At that point, Yehudi's vividly characterful wife, Diana, entered the room and explained, 'He means customs officials.' Indeed, Menuhin's delightful and witty autobiography, *Unfinished Journey*, gives some fascinating examples, as when he went to visit Moscow for the first time during the Cold War.

He had to change planes in Berlin, going from the West to Tempelhof airport in the East. Menuhin reports that there to deal with his case and give him his visa was the sort of woman 'whom only the Soviet Union could produce with all the qualities of a man including a moustache'. She asked him whether he had any prizes, and whether he knew David Oistrakh. In the end she was satisfied, and he was allowed to continue on his way to Moscow. The other example came when also in Berlin he was taken off the train for not having the right visa, and had to spend a night or two in a cell. His reaction was to say that, although he knew there were many fine people in East Germany, he would not play there again.

Menuhin, one must remember, was arguably the most amazing child prodigy in music since Mozart, and had been brought up in the most sheltered way by his devoted parents. When Menuhin's mother wanted to do some match-making between a nurse she had met in hospital and their lodger, she invited the lodger to have dinner with the family and the nurse. Young Yehudi spoke boldly to the lodger, saying, 'You know why you have been invited? You are meant to marry that lady.' This promptly put an end to any attempt at match-making. Another occasion was when their rabbi, the employer of Menuhin's father, came to a meal. Young Yehudi noted that the meat was pinker than usual, letting it out that they usually ate ham.

Menuhin's close ties with Britain date back to 1932, when with the composer conducting the LSO, the sixteen-year-old *Wunderkind* was the soloist in Elgar's Violin Concerto. Yehudi often told the story that Elgar did not want to discuss the interpretation in detail, but that is not strictly true. What Ivor Newton, the pianist accompanying the boy, remembered is that, at the first two or three rehearsal sessions, Elgar was meticulous in discussing what he wanted, with Yehudi immediately understanding and responding.

Only with the final rehearsal, on a beautiful day, when Elgar felt he had covered the whole work, did he suggest that the session should be abandoned, so that he could go to the races. Menuhin's ties with Britain were later cemented when he married Diana as his second wife, his first marriage having foundered, largely because, until then, he had led such a sheltered existence, guarded closely by his parents.

What comes out from his early recordings, including those he made with his pianist sister, Hephzibah, was not only his artistry but his dazzling virtuosity. Only later did his technique develop flaws, even when the artistry remained magical.

One of my happiest memories of a recording session with Menuhin came when, in partnership with Wilhelm Kempff, always one of my favourite Beethoven pianists, he recorded the complete set of Beethoven violin sonatas. The venue was the intimate Conway Hall in central London, excellent for chamber music, and it was fascinating to witness their style of preparation.

Instead of rehearsing they simply played straight away and, as great musicians, they instantly responded to the individuality of the playing of each other, the distinctive phrasing and tonal or dynamic gradations. The result is a cycle that is flawed on detail, but is vibrantly alive from beginning to end. One really feels one is in the living presence of great artists enjoying themselves. I also heard Menuhin and Kempff playing the three Brahms violin sonatas at the Gstaad Festival, but sadly they never got round to recording them.

Over the years it was a delight to meet Yehudi, not least in Gstaad, where the Menuhins lived in the chalet Chankly Bore, and where he founded a music festival, inviting many of the most distinguished musicians of the day, including the pianists Wilhelm Kempff and Sviatoslav Richter. At the chalet, Diana Menuhin was unmistakably in charge, and I became very fond of her, when she had such a wonderful fund of stories to tell.

Until she met Yehudi, Diana always claimed, she was dogged by a black fairy, who undermined everything she did. As a ballet dancer, she was the last dancer to be engaged by Diaghilev, but he promptly died, and the company disintegrated. She was so tall and thin that her French colleagues nicknamed her 'L'Asperge', the asparagus.

At Gstaad I found she enjoyed my company, when I would prompt her to go on telling stories. That is how I was invited every day up to Chankly Bore, a rare honour, which gave me much enjoyment.

When interviewing Yehudi it was imperative that Diana was not present, as she immediately took over the whole conversation, and I could no longer ask the questions I wanted. I would get as much material from the maestro as I could, before he suggested that Diana should join us. She was his helper in everything and, although some thought her attentions to her husband were excessive, to me her attitude confirmed this as one of the most devoted marriages I have known. There was a period when Yehudi decided not to travel by air, for at that time so many musicians had been killed in air crashes. For Diana that was a penance, until planes became much more reliable and air flights were restored to their lives.

It was towards the end of his career that Menuhin took up conducting seriously. His playing had become disconcertingly erratic, and the extraordinary thing was that he himself could not tell whether he was playing well or badly.

Previn told me the story of a performance Menuhin gave at the Iceland Festival, when Yehudi was playing the Beethoven Violin Concerto on a bad day with erratic intonation. Diana whispered to Previn, 'Ah, dear Yehudi, communing with God alone.' So it was, though always Menuhin retained his unique gift of bringing magic to the music with individual tone or phrasing, something that never left him, however variable the intonation was. Happily, in the recording studio the technical problems that beset Yehudi after his golden boyhood were at least minimised.

The last time I saw Yehudi was only a week or so before his sudden death in Berlin from a stroke he suffered on a weekend when he had been conducting a concert performance of Mozart's *Die Zauberflöte*. At our final encounter he had conducted a scratch band in a performance of Leopold Mozart's *Toy Symphony* (including Tasmin Little as leader, Philip Jones on toy trumpet and

David Willcocks as continuo – I gladly draw a veil over my own playing of the toy drum) to celebrate the ninetieth birthday of a mutual friend. He was hyperactive to the last, full of enthusiasm for his latest project, to record all the Beethoven symphonies afresh. It was less than five years since he had recorded a similar Beethoven cycle with one of his favourite orchestras, with which he had a special relationship, the Warsaw Sinfonia, and here he was tackling the whole massive cycle all over again. Sadly, he died before he could carry out that project, but it was typical of him that he was still looking forward.

Here was a Jewish musician, son of immigrants from Russia, brought up in the United States, who amazingly broke all rules, and became in the end not only a British citizen but a life peer in the House of Lords and an OM. He also demonstrated rare courage and integrity by defending Furtwängler in the post-war era, when it was far easier to damn him. What an inspirational partnership they forged as well, which, happily, was recorded on several occasions. Yehudi had a rare gift to reach out beyond music too, occupying a genuinely international position, championing environmental and other worthy causes, before such outspokenness became the fashion. I remember Diana Menuhin specially marvelling at all this, when, as a further incongruity, Yehudi was giving a charity performance in an Anglican church, Salisbury Cathedral. Whoever could have predicted such an amazing and unique career?

MSTISLAV ROSTROPOVICH

I first met Mstislav Rostropovich (or Slava as he was always known) in the Kensington hotel where his Soviet masters had insisted he stayed. I spotted him at the far end of the foyer, and I could see he immediately registered who I was. He came rushing over and gave me the first Slavonic hug I had ever received, a mark of Slava's friendship.

He was accompanied by Marion Thorpe, who was acting as his interpreter. He went to his room, but the door was locked against him. His wife, the soprano Galina Vishnevskaya, seemingly suspected him of having an affair with Marion Thorpe, and took some time to be pacified. She never did let him in while I was there, and we conducted our interview in the open foyer.

I had first heard Rostropovich in an intimate setting in the concert he gave at the Aldeburgh Festival in 1961, accompanied by Benjamin Britten. Britten had been so moved by a performance by Rostropovich of the Shostakovich First Cello Concerto at the Royal Festival Hall that he promised to write a cello sonata for him, the first work he had ever written for the cello.

The Cello Sonata proved an interesting work, in that Britten seemed to adopt some of the mannerisms of Shostakovich, while remaining very individual himself. The performance was a great success, but when we heard the news that, against all their usual practice, the Soviets were allowing Slava's wife Galina Vishnevskaya to come to Aldeburgh too, there was great excitement around the box office, as people fought their way to get tickets for the impromptu concert in Jubilee Hall. That proved a thrilling occasion, with Britten joining Rostropovich and Vishnevskaya in a sequence of varied items. Not only did Britten accompany Rostropovich; Slava as pianist accompanied his wife and the concert ended with items involving all three artists, a Bach aria, I seem to remember, with cello *obbligato*.

The other memorable concert from Slava's early appearances in Britain came in 1968 on the day when Soviet troops invaded Czechoslovakia, determined to put down the reforms instituted by the Czech president, Alexander Dubček. There was universal condemnation in Britain, but by an ironic twist the Prom performance at the Royal Albert Hall that very night involved the Soviet State Symphony Orchestra accompanying Rostropovich in, of all works, the greatest of all Czech masterpieces, Dvořák's Cello Concerto.

Protesters threatened to disrupt the performance, and there were a few half-hearted attempts to do so, but Slava's performance was so magnetic that he silenced the audience, not only in his deeply felt performance of the concerto, but in the encore he chose, the *Sarabande* from one of Bach's solo Cello Suites, with tears streaming down his face. His performance had such dedication, reflecting the suffering of the Czech people, that no one could miss the fact that Rostropovich was himself making his musical protest, a typically daring move against his Soviet masters.

The Cello Sonata was but the first of five cello works that Britten wrote for Rostropovich, the Cello Symphony and three solo cello suites being the others. Slava became a regular visitor to the Aldeburgh Festival, agreeing to play some of the works specially written for him by other British composers. At one of these offerings Slava jibbed and refused to play it. 'When I am in Russia, I have to play Soviet shit, but when I am in England, I will not play British shit.'

Slava commissioned more new works to play than any comparable artist, a tremendous achievement, and he performed each with that dedication and intensity that were the mark of all his playing, highly individual as it always was. His were never conventional readings but had the mark that only he could implant, a rare gift indicating the truly original artist. He was splendid in chamber music both before and after leaving the Soviet Union, making up an inspired partnership with such great artists as the violinist David Oistrakh and the pianist Sviatoslav Richter, creating the trio of artists that, with Karajan conducting, recorded Beethoven's Triple Concerto, a recording for which, as Slava ruefully complained, he never got paid a penny, the penalty of the Soviet system.

Slava was always alert to his role as a politically aware musician. When the Berlin Wall was coming down, he impulsively flew to Berlin, and took a cab to Checkpoint Charlie, the principal crossing point between East and West. He took his cello with him so as to play unaccompanied Bach, and it was only when he arrived at the Checkpoint that he realised he had no chair to sit on, a comic situation that he relished. In the end they found a chair from the Checkpoint, so that he could play, but the grand gesture had nearly been undermined by a simple oversight.

Similarly, when Boris Yeltsin was fighting back against the rebels who sought to overturn Gorbachev, Slava flew to St Petersburg, and stood on a tank, addressing the crowd, a crucial moment in the defeat of the attempted coup. Small wonder that in Soviet times Slava had fallen foul of the authorities.

It was typical of so multi-talented an artist that in due course he developed his gifts as a conductor, not least on disc. He was especially proud of his pioneering recording of Shostakovich's opera, banned for a generation and more, *Lady Macbeth of Mtsensk*. Shostakovich's revision, *Katerina Ismailova*, had achieved some currency, but the original, disapproved and banned by Stalin himself, is a tougher and even stronger score that pulls no punches.

Slava, I remember, counted his EMI recording of *Lady Macbeth* as his finest recording as a conductor. He received the test pressings on his way to the house he had bought in Aldeburgh, where Vishnevskaya loved to stay. He took the discs back, and in the middle of the night played them at full blast, so as to enjoy them to the full.

Not all of his discs as a conductor were as successful, and his readings of the Shostakovich and Prokofiev symphonies with French and American orchestras (he was for a time music director of the National Symphony Orchestra of Washington) were marked by exceptionally slow speeds, an expansiveness that he managed to sustain, but which made the results controversial. These were emphatically Rostropovich readings rather than performances to recommend without reservation.

His appointment to the Washington orchestra was a surprising one, but he sustained it well with his always characterful readings. The appointment of a Russian in the nation's capital was a strong gesture in what was still the Cold War period. Slava was such an individualist, one who hated to be regimented, and it was inevitable that he and Vishnevskaya chose to leave Russia for an extended period. While they were out of the country their citizenship was withdrawn, but Slava was very much a citizen of the world, and took delight in possessing homes in a number of different countries, the Aldeburgh pied-à-terre being only one.

In 1991 I was offered the honorary membership of the Guildhall School of Music, an honour I treasured. In the same ceremony honorary membership was also being bestowed on Rostropovich: the *Guardian* pictures editor, spotting the occasion, against all my previous experience decided to send a photographer along to take photos of Slava and me in our academic caps and gowns. The picture appeared in the *Guardian* the following day, a very jolly photo with both of us grinning broadly. I got my artist friend Jeffrey Spedding to make an oil portrait of it, which still delights me, a happy memento of a happy occasion.

EVELYN BARBIROLLI

Evelyn Barbirolli, who died in 2008 on the day after her ninety-seventh birthday, was not just the widow of the great conductor, John Barbirolli, keeping his memory alive for nearly forty years after his death, but also an outstanding artist in her own right, a leading oboist from the early 1930s onwards. Until her husband died, she still played under her maiden name of Evelyn Rothwell, and only after his death did she adopt the name Barbirolli in her performances.

She was trained at the Royal College of Music in London, the pupil of the leading oboist of the day, Leon Goossens, but Evelyn would talk about how bad a teacher he was, more concerned with his own career than with those of his pupils.

Goossens did at least develop her rich, fruity oboe tone, using plentiful vibrato, unlike previous generations of oboists who generally tried to avoid vibrato. Her outstanding qualities quickly earned her a place in leading orchestras, notably the Scottish Orchestra.

As the Scottish Orchestra had a break in summer, she accepted the invitation to join the ad-hoc orchestra, mainly drawn from members of the LSO, assembled to perform at the newly founded Festival Opera at Glyndebourne. Evelyn's distinctive oboe can be heard in the recordings of Mozart operas at Glyndebourne that were made in the Festival's earliest years with Fritz Busch conducting, most of them first ever recordings of the works, made at a time when complete operas on short-playing 78 discs were a relative rarity.

It was as a principal oboe that she was noticed first by a very different conductor to Barbirolli, George Szell, then the Scottish Orchestra's principal conductor, who out of the blue came to her and proposed marriage, much to her surprise. She promptly turned Szell down, to his irritation, but it was not long before her response to John Barbirolli was quite different. They immediately fell in love, and soon enough they were lovers. They were prevented from marrying immediately, as the conductor was unhappily married at the time and his Catholic family was shocked at the idea of divorce. Finally, some years later, they did get married, and Evelyn was John's greatest helper over the difficult period when he was the successor to Toscanini, no less, as principal conductor of the New York Philharmonic, during which the American critics, unlike the public, were determined to bring him down.

Evelyn always remembered their New York days as a happy time, stretching into the period when Britain but not the United States was at war with Nazi Germany. There then came the surprise invitation to John to become the music director of the Hallé Orchestra in Manchester, which he eagerly accepted, and they took up residence in Manchester while the war was still on.

During their Manchester period Evelyn regularly performed concertos, mostly with her husband conducting, and for her he made a number of baroque arrangements built from movements of works by such composers as Pergolesi and Corelli. Sadly, she did not make as many recordings as her admirers would have liked, but those she did make, mainly in the period before stereo arrived, are marked by magnetic artistry with each phrase turned to make itself memorable.

It was Evelyn who gave the first modern performance of Mozart's Oboe Concerto, the composer's own transcription of one of his own flute concertos, and she also recorded it. She inspired various composers to write for her and, as a member of various chamber groups, she was a popular performer, quite independently of her occasional appearances as principal oboe with the Hallé Orchestra.

Evelyn was always the solicitous wife, who encouraged her husband to indulge in the cooking he so enjoyed, particularly after conducting a concert. Their flat in Manchester became a welcome venue for many friends and colleagues, as their flat in London also did when they moved to the capital after Barbirolli's Hallé period. It was his achievement there that, at a difficult period for players at the end of the war, he built the Hallé into Britain's leading orchestra. Only in 1945 with the founding of Walter Legge's Philharmonia and Beecham's Royal Philharmonic did the capital regain its primacy in orchestral playing.

My own friendship developed over Evelyn's eighties and nineties, and we both especially enjoyed such occasions as when I brought two outstanding wind-players together for lunch, with the clarinettist Thea King in attendance, as well as Evelyn. Most delightful of all were the lunches we had when Evelyn would come to my house, brought in their car by Janet Baker and her husband, Keith. Her reminiscing on such occasions was always a delight, with the meal stretching on hours beyond lunchtime. It was sad that Evelyn died before she reached her centenary, but she was always most philosophical, and to the end looked back with joy on a richly fulfilled life.

LARRY ADLER

Michael Parkinson, himself no mean practitioner, has said that the harmonica-player, Larry Adler, was the world's most accomplished name-dropper. One of Larry's stories concerned his time in Hollywood in the early 1930s. He was rung up one morning by Charlie Chaplin, who wanted him to make up a foursome at tennis that morning. Naturally, Larry obeyed the summons, and arrived to find two others there besides Charlie Chaplin, the surrealist artist Salvador Dalí and a woman who was very down at heel, with dirty plimsolls (it was before the age of trainers), and long shorts. That turned out to be Greta Garbo, making up a unique quartet.

Born into a poor Jewish family in Baltimore in 1914, he established his virtuosity and inspiration on the harmonica at a very early age, and won some sort of fame on the music-halls of the time. That led in turn to his years in Hollywood and trips abroad, often to Britain, where he became a great favourite, and where he settled during the war in 1940, becoming something of an institution.

He inspired works for this long-underrated instrument from such composers as Ralph Vaughan Williams and Gordon Jacob, so individual was his artistry. I got to know Larry when he became a lodger in the flat of a dear friend. As he grew older, he took to writing about restaurants and food, and together they would enjoy meals at some of the most prestigious restaurants in southern England, even though they had frequent rows.

There was no doubt of Larry's star quality, which was well illustrated when he came to my seventieth birthday party. He had been ill, and sat quietly in a corner of the large and noisy room where I held the party. Yet somehow in his quiet voice he managed to quell the noise and announced that he wanted to play in tribute to me, *Variations on Greenfield*. It was of course *Greensleeves*, and the variations were almost all very quiet. The whole room listened, with everyone hardly daring to breathe, and I must say I found it a most

Above: André Previn walking with the author in front of the Royal Festival Hall at the Southbank Centre, London, in the 1970s.
Below: Joan Sutherland with the author in 1960, the first time they met.

Above: The author meeting Leonard Bernstein in 1989 at the Savoy Hotel, London. This and all subsequent paintings shown here are by Jeffrey Spedding.
Below: Elisabeth Schwarzkopf, Alfred Brendel, Walter Legge and George Szell at the recording of Mozart's concert aria 'Ch'io mi scordi di te?'

Above: The author entertains Yehudi Menuhin, Michael Tippett and other friends at his home in Spitalfields, London, in 1993.

Above: (top) William Walton, whom the author considered his hero from a young age – the two would later go on to form a close friendship; (bottom) Igor Stravinsky, whom the author met on what would be Stravinsky's last visit to London.

Above: (top) The author with Mstislav Rostropovich, at the Guildhall School of Music & Drama, 1991; (below) Michael Tippett's portrait is visible in the party scene shown in the preceeding pages, having been completed just weeks before.

Painter Jeffrey Spedding's particular interest in classical and contemporary music subjects mirrored Edward Greenfield's enthusiasm for the visual arts, and he became a great admirer of the artist. The paintings collected here evoke the atmosphere of Greenfield's home in Spitalfields, where they adorn the walls.
Opposite: (top) Jean Sibelius and (bottom) Edward Elgar.
Above: (clockwise from top left) Gustav Mahler, Johannes Brahms, Giacomo Puccini and Ludwig van Beethoven.

Above: Jeffrey Spedding's portrait of the author for the Art Workers' Guild, 2002.

moving tribute and a great demonstration of Larry's magic for which I was deeply grateful.

LYDIA MORDKOVITCH

Lydia Mordkovitch is one of the most underrated violinists today, yet she has made a whole series of superb recordings, which bear witness not only to her masterly technique and gloriously varied tone colours, but also to her extraordinary dedication to playing long-neglected works, notably by lesser-known British composers. Some works have even been unplayed until she tackled them, other violinists having passed them over for being too difficult technically.

In recordings she has shown that such works can not only be played, but can convey a thrust and warmth unsuspected before she played them. Her list of recordings is astonishingly wide, and it is a pity that she has only rarely been asked to record the great central masterpieces. Maybe one day her talent will be fully appreciated.

Her background is remarkable. She was trained largely in Moscow, where her great mentor was David Oistrakh, whose example she has always revered more than any other. At an early stage in her career she found herself in Moldova, and it was typical of her that she played very successfully works by Moldovan composers, reflecting her ability to learn new music very quickly, thanks to intensive practising methods.

It was after she emigrated to Israel that she was discovered by Brian Couzens, then working for RCA, who prompted her first international recording, a version of the Brahms Violin Concerto, which only intermittently showed her gift as a recording artist of conveying the sense of a live performance. Soon after Couzens founded his own record company, Chandos, and since then Mordkovitch has made most of her recordings for that excellent label, an impressive legacy still continuing, when violinists contracted to major international labels have found their recording opportunities cut down or curtailed.

Like so many Russian artists Lydia has a deep streak of melancholy in her nature, and it has often been difficult to convince her of the fine qualities of her playing. Yet she knows in her heart what she has achieved, and when she rehearses – something she does with characteristic intensity – she forgets any reservations. Latterly, she has been a very successful teacher at the Royal Academy of Music in London, and the devotion of her students is warmly illustrated on the occasions when she has been encouraged to perform at the end of student concerts, as a climactic item. Lydia Mordkovitch might still be under-appreciated, but she will always be recognised by those with genuine perception.

VLADIMIR HOROWITZ

My meeting with the supreme piano virtuoso Vladimir Horowitz took place at his house on the east side of Central Park in Manhattan. It was the time when he was marking the sixtieth anniversary of his first recital in the United States, and his then record company, RCA, asked me over to cover the celebration. I said I needed a private interview as well as the public one they planned, if I was going to write a worthwhile piece, and his regular recording producer promised to organise it.

Day after day Horowitz would put the idea off, and in the end I saw him when I was literally on the way to the airport for my return flight, having brought my luggage along with me. Even then, Horowitz temporised, and for the best part of an hour I sat with his wife, Wanda Toscanini Horowitz, daughter of the great conductor, while we heard him striding up and down in his room upstairs.

Wanda was a very good companion to talk to, with plenty of anecdotes of her own, but I was relieved when Horowitz himself appeared. He seemed intent on making provocative remarks, as for example his suggestion that Chopin was only a second-rate composer.

I tackled him on the question of his coming to Europe again. He explained he would come only by Concorde in order to avoid a lengthy journey. He then pointed out that Concorde flew only in the morning, and he himself did not get out of bed until the afternoon, such was his self-obsession.

None the less it was an amiable conversation we had, and he seemed relieved that as an interviewer I was not more aggressive. The previous day or so when he held his public interview, the questions were almost all fielded by Wanda, a much more forthright character. One questioner wanted to know the explanation for the unique Horowitz tone colours, bright and exceptionally clear. He suggested that he might have had the keys of his piano varnished, at which Wanda exploded, 'That is the worst suggestion of all,' and she totally ridiculed the idea that he could resort to so cheap a trick. The tone colour was Horowitz's own, depending totally on his touch on the keys.

After that period Horowitz did of course relent and gave a series of recitals not just in England but notably in Moscow, where he was greeted rapturously. The live recordings appeared, and they were indeed amazing for a man already in his eighties, with an agility that beggars belief. I think particularly of his playing of Moszkowski's '*Étincelles*' ('Sparks'), which he used regularly as an encore.

Horowitz had originally been trained in Russia, before he left for the United States, exiled like so many artists by the Russian Revolution. That is why the Russian audiences late in his career were so thrilled at hearing this extraordinary home-grown phenomenon, a rival for their own Soviet artists.

Eccentrically, ever a law unto himself, Horowitz stopped playing in public for some years, and it was during that time that a young virtuoso called Ivan Davis went to see him, as he regularly did, to play and receive the great man's criticism. On this occasion Horowitz greeted Ivan, and suggested they should go down to Greenwich Village and have a meal. Horowitz was always concerned not to be recognised, and Ivan expected him to choose a table in a dark corner of the restaurant.

Far from it. He chose the most prominent table of all on the sidewalk. Ivan was apprehensive when he spotted two obvious young music-lovers walking up and down and eyeing them. He was even more apprehensive when they approached the table, and spoke. Ivan had only a few days earlier played a concerto with Bernstein and the New York Philharmonic, but little did he expect what happened. The two young men approached, and inquired tentatively, 'It is Ivan Davis, isn't it?' For a young beginner to be recognised ahead of him sent a message to the great pianist in temporary retirement, and very soon after that Horowitz announced his return to public performance.

On another occasion friends of mine on the editorial staff of *High Fidelity* magazine, for which I used to write reports from London, went up to see him at his home, as he had been awarded a special lifetime achievement prize, and they wanted to present it to him in person. He was delighted to see them, and they were thrilled (for this was still in his period of retirement), when he sat down to play. Wanda took a different view. 'There he goes,' she said. 'We have company, and all he wants to do is to play the piano!'

The last time I saw Horowitz was in Milan, when, most improbably, the record company DG had persuaded him to record Mozart's A major Piano Concerto, K. 488, as well as a Mozart sonata. Accompanying him at the Sala Abanela was the Orchestra of La Scala. The conductor Carlo Maria Giulini was disconcerted by Horowitz choosing to use a cadenza by Busoni, when there is a perfectly good one written down by Mozart himself. Typically, that controversial cadenza brought Horowitz's most inspired playing, a challenge to him when the rest was too easy for such a virtuoso. A film was made of the occasion, but I fear that that gives only a partial idea of the tension behind the event.

VLADIMIR ASHKENAZY

One Sunday morning I was rung up unexpectedly by the pianist Vladimir Ashkenazy, who by that time had left the Soviet Union with his Icelandic wife and was living in the West. He was mainly based in Iceland instead of London, as he knew that in London he would regularly be contacted by such friends as Daniel Barenboim to meet up and play music together. He wanted a quiet life instead.

His phone call was about a news story that had appeared in the *Guardian*. It said that Ashkenazy was free to go back to Russia whenever he wanted, and he complained that that was just not true. He wanted to have the mistake corrected. I tried to lull his fears, saying that no one would remember what had been written on so detailed a point. Instead, I gave him the phone number of Victor Zorza, the *Guardian*'s great Kremlinologist, who by meticulous study of the Soviet press regularly deduced developments in Soviet policy that were being kept secret. Ashkenazy and Victor immediately became close friends, and Ashkenazy in due course helped Victor with the project very close to his heart, a hospice where his terminally ill daughter was being looked after.

What neither Victor nor I appreciated, which as journalists we certainly should have done, was that this was a very hot news story. The *Guardian* sent a reporter out to Athens post-haste, where Ashkenazy was appearing, and indeed got an impressive exclusive story about Ashkenazy not being free to return to Russia.

In the section on Leonard Bernstein earlier in this book, I have already described the television film the BBC made when finally Ashkenazy did return to Moscow. The film offered a wonderfully detailed study, which brought out the direct warmth of Ashkenazy's personality, viewing him intimately as he arrived, and following him until he gave his first concert with the Royal Philharmonic Orchestra, of which he had become principal conductor, having by that time become as much a conductor as a pianist. As I have said, it was a

thrilling performance of Tchaikovsky's Fourth Symphony that he conducted, something that plainly moved his Soviet audience as much
as it did Ashkenazy himself.

Ashkenazy's conducting has always been exceptionally responsive,
and the recordings he has made tend to be even more spontaneous-
sounding than his recordings of piano music, in which the result can
at times sound too perfect, so flawless is his technique. His sets of the
Tchaikovsky and Sibelius symphonies are excellent, with the Sibelius
acquiring Russian overtones. Rarely has the often hackneyed-sounding
Finlandia sounded as exciting as it does in his hands, and the brilliant
Decca recording has always added to the impact.

As a pianist Ashkenazy was always the most sensitive partner to
colleagues when recording chamber music. I particularly remember a
set of the Beethoven violin sonatas he recorded with Itzhak Perlman,
whose strong personality dominated the preparatory conversation,
insisting that his violin should be placed nearer to the microphone
than the piano. Ashkenazy quietly allowed the balance to be altered,
but in the finished performance Ashkenazy's playing is at least as
magnetic as Perlman's, so responsive was he.

ITZHAK PERLMAN

Of all the young violinists who trained at the Juilliard School in New
York in the late 1960s, the most dazzling was Itzhak Perlman. Like his
slightly younger friend and fellow Israeli Pinchas Zukerman, he emigrated to the United States at an early age, thanks to the sponsorship of
the violinist Isaac Stern, who was so impressed with his playing in his
earliest years. Perlman's achievement was all the more remarkable, as
before he left Israel he had suffered an attack of polio, which left him
crippled. In any concert he would awkwardly manoeuvre himself to his
seat on two sticks, but once he was in place his playing was breathtaking.

There were those who found his playing almost too confident, lacking an element of vulnerability, and that was true of many of his recordings. He also insisted, like his great idol, Jascha Heifetz, on having his violin balanced well forward of rival instruments. I remember noting that when he was recording the Beethoven violin sonatas for Decca, and I was able to argue the point with him in detail, when I stopped off in New York to interview him at his apartment in Manhattan.

His answer was that in recordings he liked to have reproduced what he himself heard. I pointed out that his ear was only an inch or so away from the violin when he played, unlike ours, but that argument did not sway him at all, though I was able to get back at him, when we played a Heifetz recording, and he pointed out that the balance was even more extreme in the violinist's favour.

Perlman's earliest recordings were made for RCA, and very fine they already were, but then he gravitated to EMI, for whom he has made many of his recordings since, including new versions of what he had already done for RCA, notably the Tchaikovsky and Sibelius Violin Concertos, performances that were even more formidably powerful.

He also played along with developments in the record industry of the time, and made some very different recordings, for example of Jewish klezmer music and duets with jazz musicians he admired. It is hard to see how he can develop further, but his concerts are packed out in every part of the world where he is persuaded to perform, a happy situation.

PINCHAS ZUKERMAN

The reputation of Pinchas Zukerman has inevitably suffered with his career following so closely on that of his slightly older fellow Israeli, Itzhak Perlman. Like Perlman he was sponsored by Isaac Stern as a youngster and, also like Perlman, he quickly established his brilliance as a virtuoso violinist. His reputation might never have quite matched that of Perlman, but one of his great gifts is his extra versatility.

He readily switches from violin to viola, producing equally dazzling results on the bigger instrument, playing with flawless intonation and a rich tone. He was a contributor to the starry line-up of friends who assembled to play Schubert's *Trout* Quintet at Queen Elizabeth Hall in London, an event that was fascinatingly filmed by Christopher Nupen.

Daniel Barenboim played the piano with Perlman on violin and Jacqueline du Pré on cello, while Zukerman played the viola and, even more surprisingly, the conductor Zubin Mehta came specially from Hollywood, where he lived with his film-star wife, to play the double-bass, which he had studied at music college. Mehta and his wife were shown arriving in their chauffeur-driven car, a dazzling couple, where the others were all very much down to earth, as they prepared for their joint project. Mehta had to practise a little to get his technique back to what it had been, but the starry group worked wonderfully well together, and the result was a classic performance, the more effective when so well caught on film.

Zukerman has tended to be a degree more adventurous in his choice of repertory than Perlman, and more eager than his friend to play British works, such as the Elgar and Walton Violin Concertos. He has always played with flair, and sometimes his performances reflect his sense of humour. I always cherished the way that, as a fine mimic, he would address me in a crisp English accent, something that those with an American accent often find hard to adopt. Being sent up like that always struck me as a sort of compliment.

Zukerman has also been more ready than Perlman to conduct, and for some years he was music director of a chamber orchestra in the American Middle West, with some impressive results, even if he was never tempted to go over to conducting full time. Again, with the recession in the record industry, his star has latterly shone rather less brightly, but the recordings that he has given us are more than enough to ensure his high status among violinists.

KYUNG-WHA CHUNG

My first experience of hearing the violinist Kyung-Wha Chung came when I had her first recording for Decca to review. I had heard from friends in the LSO about the extraordinarily compelling young Korean violinist who had performed with them, and I was eager to find out about her myself. I was mesmerised by what I heard in this coupling of the Violin Concertos of Tchaikovsky and Sibelius.

I played the opening of the Sibelius to a number of my visitors, who all confirmed the extraordinary power of the playing, the magic of the phrasing, warm and individual, and the range of tone colours. It promptly established Kyung-Wha as an outstanding new personality, with André Previn and the LSO providing ideal accompaniment.

Within a year, in 1971, I got to know Kyung-Wha personally, when she was one of two soloists with Previn and the LSO on their tour of Japan, Korea and Hong Kong. Her vivacious personality was as winning as her playing, for she was always ready to share in a joke, as when she was rehearsing the Tchaikovsky in Japan, and the players naughtily started to play the opening of the Mendelssohn Concerto. Automatically, in a reflex action, Kyung-Wha started to play the Mendelssohn too, until she realised they were teasing her.

I also remember going shopping with her and Previn in the Ginza area of Tokyo. Kyung-Wha wanted presents for relatives and, in one department store, she pulled out all the handkerchiefs in sight, much to the consternation of the Japanese assistants. In another department she set all the clockwork toys going, with similar reactions from the assistants, conscious that the Koreans for their wildness have been called 'the Irish of Asia'.

On our way back to the hotel we stopped off at a pachinko parlour where they had a whole range of the bagatelle-board-like machines. Kyung-Wha started a whole series of them going, and was not satisfied until she had won on some of them. Again, her wildness was what came over endearingly.

I also remember several meals with Previn and Kyung-Wha when we persuaded her to tackle the Walton Violin Concerto, for Walton's seventieth birthday was due soon after. So it proved, and one of the birthday recordings was Kyung-Wha's wonderfully warm and expansive recording of the Violin Concerto, again with Previn and the LSO, quite different from the great original Heifetz recording, urgent and forceful, but just as compelling.

Kyung-Wha herself had the experience of meeting Heifetz, one of her heroes, when he agreed to hear her play. She arrived a few minutes early, and through a peephole in the door, he told her to come back on time. He was reasonably encouraging to her, but her real teacher at the Juilliard School in New York after her early training in Korea was Ivan Galamian, a figure to whom she owed much more. His only discouragement was that he was reluctant to spend much time on teaching women virtuosi, when they were so likely to get married, and waste all their training.

It was many years before Kyung-Wha did get married, and then she did indeed divert her attentions to her baby as well as her playing. When she travelled, she carried the baby, leaving her nurse to carry her precious violin. Over her later career she performed in chamber music with inspired results, often partnering her cellist elder sister Myung-Wha and her pianist brother Myung-Whun, later a very successful conductor. Impressive as her later career was, Kyung-Wha never quite recaptured the magical freshness with which her career had so brilliantly begun.

JACQUELINE DU PRÉ

My first encounter with the playing of the unique cellist Jacqueline du Pré came on television. I had read the ecstatic comments of various colleagues, and was frankly sceptical. It took only a few seconds of watching her television performance – she was only sixteen – for me to realise that here was a major new musical genius. I was then eager to hear her as much as I could.

Jackie was fortunate in having, after her mother, as her first important teacher, William Pleeth, known as Bill. She always referred to him as her 'cello daddy' and, thanks to being drawn into his family, she came to feel exceptional closeness to the Jewish life. Bill Pleeth realised that though Jackie's technique was unconventional, it was useless to get her going back to square one to adopt conventional techniques of playing; he devotedly developed her genius, knowing that it transcended everything. Contrast that with the teaching that Jackie's sister, Hilary, a flautist, received at the hands of Gareth Morris, principal flute of the Philharmonia. He insisted that she should unlearn her natural technique and for lesson after lesson kept her playing a single note, a killing process that completely undermined Hilary's confidence.

The first concert of Jackie's I remember attending was at a girls' school in Camden Town, when she partnered a favourite of mine among young Beethoven pianists, Stephen Bishop (as he then was), later Kovacevich, in cello sonatas, including one by Beethoven. I was enraptured, but was still critical of the balance between cello and piano. So much so, that I promptly received a letter from Stephen complaining that the balance had been wished on him, and he had not wanted his piano to dominate. Happily, that led to Stephen coming to have a meal with me, and to a warm friendship, only hampered by the fact that, for once, I felt that friendship might get in the way of my being impartial in what I wrote about him.

Jackie, meanwhile, was developing fast, and I quickly learned that her new partner was the pianist Daniel Barenboim. They had met at the house of Menuhin's son-in-law, Fou Ts'ong. As they put it later, instead of talking they played Brahms, immediately discovering a magic rapport. That exploded in 1967, when, during the Six-Day War in Israel, Barenboim insisted on going to Israel in support, with Jackie accompanying him.

Impulsively, they decided to get married, with Jackie being quickly converted to Judaism and John Barbirolli giving the bride away at the wedding ceremony, with Janet Baker as a witness. Barbirolli had been among the first to spot Jackie's talent, when, with the viola-player Lionel Tertis, he was on a jury to give scholarships. When Jackie appeared, not yet in her teens, he had promptly said, 'This is it!' And so it was.

Though du Pré and Barenboim had their musical partnership cemented, Jackie by this time had become closely associated with the Elgar Cello Concerto. I shall never forget the recording sessions at Kingsway Hall in 1964, when with Barbirolli and the LSO Jackie made her first recording of the Elgar. When at the lunch break I had to leave Kingsway Hall, I found Jackie in her anorak making for the door. I asked her where she was going, and she said she was going to the chemist's next door to get some aspirin, as she had a headache. Earlier in the day the record company had not even bothered to arrange a car for her, so she had had to go out and find a cab for herself.

Before that occasion I had heard Jackie recording the Delius Cello Concerto with Malcolm Sargent conducting, and had also reviewed for *Gramophone* her first recording, a collection of short pieces representing the cello in a series about the instruments of the orchestra, in which her reading of Saint-Saëns's *Le Cygne* stood out.

Even then I was not convinced her magic was being fully caught on disc, but when it came to the Elgar recording, there was no doubt whatever that here was a classic recording in the making. And so it has been, a disc that has never been out of the catalogue ever since, an irresistible bestseller, particularly when it was initially coupled with Janet Baker's equally magnetic reading of Elgar's *Sea Pictures*: 'A real Ted Greenfield coupling,' as Douglas Pudney, one of my contacts in EMI, commented.

Over the years it was a delight to witness the love of du Pré and Barenboim blossoming. He would tease her mercilessly. I remember her arriving for a television recording session for the Elgar with

Barenboim conducting. When she claimed to have been practising, his comment was, 'Practising *boeuf bourgignon*, more like.' He himself showed his virtuosity, when on the suggestion from the television crew that his music-stand got in the way of the cameras, he had overnight learned the score, and conducted from memory.

On another occasion, when at the Edinburgh Festival Barenboim and du Pré were recording the complete Beethoven cello sonatas live, he complained when she drew an expressive phrase out beyond what he thought was acceptable. 'You're not going to play it like that at the performance, are you?' he asked. She shrugged, and said nonchalantly, 'I might and might not.' Then in the performance, when she drew the phrase out even more, she said through her teeth, 'Hello!'

Jackie's career went from strength to strength, until she received the terrible news that she was suffering from multiple sclerosis, and that the prognosis was not good. She had noticed that on several occasions her fingers lost their feeling, and she found it extraordinarily difficult to play in tune, feeling the notes on the strings by intuition. It was months later that the doctors gave her the news of her grave illness.

It was in the period when Jackie could no longer play that I came even closer to her. She would ring me up and ask me to go to her flat for dinner that evening. In the early days it was invigorating to find that she remained so amazingly optimistic. She would ask innumerable questions about all kinds of subjects, as she always admitted that, thanks to her intensive musical training, her broader education had been wanting.

I always remember one day when she rang up, I think it was New Year's Day, and she asked me to come for a meal that evening. I saw in the *Radio Times* that one of Christopher Nupen's brilliant films about her was being transmitted, and I then assumed that there would be a party of us to watch the programme together. Not so. I was her only guest and I took over from Danny's mother, Aida Barenboim, who had been with her all over Christmas, a wonderfully generous gesture.

It was always a trial, when at the meal one had to hold her head still enough to feed her with food, for MS prevented her from keeping still for a moment. It was horrific to realise that here was a great artist so reduced, and one did one's best to comfort her.

That period of optimism sadly came to an end all too soon, when suddenly she became totally pessimistic, and nothing one could do would cheer her up, except that she still enjoyed listening to her own recordings, particularly the informal pirated ones of live performances.

Knowing that she was supposed to have an early bedtime she would, like a naughty child, get a performance played, which she knew would take her beyond her bedtime. She had a marvellous nurse and carer who literally helped her to live much longer than she might have done. The trouble was that the nurse was a strict evangelical Christian, and Jackie became obsessed with the idea that the nurse had said her illness had afflicted her because she had abandoned Christianity to become Jewish. However much one tried to ridicule that suggestion, she would determinedly not be convinced, which saddened us all greatly.

On one occasion, before her MS became really serious, she arrived unexpectedly at the house in France where her sister Hilary and her husband, Christopher Finzi, known as Kiffer, had their summer home. Like so many artists, Jackie was highly sexed, and Hilary understood completely, when Kiffer took Jackie to bed, and eased her serious depression, which had become suicidal.

It is a situation vividly illustrated in the film, *Hilary and Jackie*, which I saw for the first time when I was invited by Hilary to a preview. I sat next to her, and it could not have been more moving, watching a film about one's companion. Equally the film illustrated Jackie's pain when Barenboim – who was marvellous in providing all the care she needed – went off to live in Paris with his new girlfriend, with whom he had a baby. Jackie in one of her phonecalls heard the baby crying, which was very painful for her.

The other problem was the accommodation that she had to have when she needed so much nursing care. Originally they bought the maisonette that had been adapted by Margot Fonteyn to cope with the problems of her disabled husband, the Panamanian politician, Roberto Arias. It had a lift between ground floor and first floor, which made movement easy, but it was surrounded by trees with no sunlight able to get in and with heavy wood panelling. I always thought it a terribly depressing place. Eventually, Barenboim bought her a double flat near Notting Hill, which was much brighter and more convenient, but that did not please her at all, despite the obvious advantages, which I always emphasised to her.

As the MS progressed, so Jackie was increasingly unable to articulate her words, another factor that added to the stress of going to see her. In the end I felt it a reward if for a moment or so I had made her smile, but it remained a strain, and after a couple of hours with her one was physically drained. I simply don't know how her nurses and carers managed to sustain the situation day after day.

Finally it became almost impossible to go and see her any longer and I have to admit that, when she died, one counted it a happy release. Fortunately, we have all her recordings to remember her by, and that is what will always keep her legacy fresh.

JULIAN LLOYD WEBBER

It says much for the characterful cellist Julian Lloyd Webber that even in the face of the global success of his elder brother, Andrew, composer of musicals, he has carved out a distinctive place for himself in the world of music. When I met their mother Jean, widow of the organist and composer William Lloyd Webber, she said very boldly, 'The boys get their talent from their father, their ambition from me.'

I first got to know Julian when I gave a lecture to the Elgar Society on the composer's recordings and how they differed from the readings of others. He insisted on coming to my flat, and bringing his cello. He wanted to play me the solo in the Elgar Cello Concerto, a work he specially loved. He was halfway through the concerto when my cousin arrived, and Julian insisted on going back to the beginning, to play the first movement again.

It was some years later that he recorded the Elgar Cello Concerto with Yehudi Menuhin conducting, and he then demonstrated that he had learned from the example of Elgar's own recording with Beatrice Harrison as soloist, though that gives only a partial idea of how he wanted the work to be played. Since then Julian has tended to specialise in his recordings of British works, many of them half forgotten.

He has promoted concerts of music by William Lloyd Webber, a distinguished organist who simply composed in his spare time, and wrote in a way that was unashamedly old fashioned, with the influence of Rachmaninov important to him. His works were completely unknown and unperformed, until Julian found the scores among his father's belongings and promoted performances and recordings.

Julian also teaches selected pupils, but he prefers to perform and has established a significant career playing in Britain and in various parts of the world. If he is not the world's finest technician among cellists, he has great gifts as a communicator, and he gave a fascinating talk about himself, his playing and the work of his father, in my year as Master of the Art Workers' Guild. There seems to be no limit to Julian's energy, which will take him further still in whatever direction he chooses.

TASMIN LITTLE

Among British violinists a top favourite for me has long been Tasmin Little. The magic of her playing has consistently been irresistible, and to see her at the Last Night of the Proms keeping the rowdy audience rapt in attention, as she did once with Vaughan Williams's *The Lark Ascending*, with not a murmur disturbing the extended *pianissimo*s, is ample evidence of her qualities.

Similarly, I remember when I was attending the Bulawayo Music Festival in Zimbabwe before President Robert Mugabe's latter-day undermining of the country, she was amazing. When she had a noisy school in front of her, she quelled them by the sheer charm of her personality and her playing, not letting the children lose interest for a moment. Her charismatic qualities are very clear, even though she has never persuaded any of the major record companies to give her an important recording contract.

Some of her most important recordings were made for the Classics for Pleasure label and the Eminence label, subsidiaries of EMI sold at budget prices, and it is instructive to compare her version of the Brahms Violin Concerto with any of the most prestigious rival recordings. Little's comes out of the comparison with flying colours, for her relatively direct approach is still highly individual in its phrasing and rubato, with immaculate passagework and a magical range of tone colours.

Her technical prowess is also formidable, as she demonstrated when she performed the violin concerto by György Ligeti, with Sir Simon Rattle conducting. Only a tiny handful of violinists have mastered this piece, which is generally regarded as the most difficult ever written, even requiring the soloist to turn the music with his or her foot. When Rattle toured the piece internationally with the Berlin Philharmonic, he asked Tasmin to be the soloist, including performances at the Proms and in Carnegie Hall.

Her enchanting qualities readily translate to her recordings, and it is typical of her adventurous approach to her work that she has latterly offered her live recordings free online as downloads. Though she receives no payment for that service, she argues that she is rewarded by the extra exposure she gets.

She is similarly indefatigable over causes she believes in, such as the violin music and early works generally of Delius. She made an illuminating television film about the early life of Delius in Florida, and since then has concentrated on performing and recording all his violin works, not just the concertos but the sonatas too, including one long neglected that he wrote early in his career. That goes with Tasmin's delight in resurrecting all kinds of neglected works.

Her contribution to my year as Master of the Art Workers' Guild was remarkable, for as well as co-operating in an illustrated interview, she played on two important violins, not only the Stradivarius she had been lent, but also her own Guadagnini. She played solo Bach on each in turn, and it was fascinating to hear the contrast between the bright and brilliant Strad and the warmer, less forward Guadagnini.

With an artist who displays such energy there is no knowing what will develop next, and Tasmin remains one of the most vital of British artists before the public today.

NIGEL KENNEDY

My first interview with the violinist Nigel Kennedy was a delight. It was early in his career, but he was already married to a delightful nurse, who took good care of him. This was before he embraced pop culture in the violent way that marked him out later, though he was already adopting a cockney-style way of talking, and was devoted to jazz, as he had been from his earliest youth.

Nigel was the son of the principal cellist of the Royal Philharmonic Orchestra, a favourite artist of Thomas Beecham's. Sadly the marriage broke up, with the consequence that Nigel was initially brought up by his mother and his aunt. Yet by the age of five he had already been offered a place at the Yehudi Menuhin School, which has trained so many brilliant young hopefuls.

At the school he was a rebel from the start, largely because of his devotion to jazz, but when the jazz violinist Stéphane Grappelli visited the school at the invitation of Menuhin, Nigel was in his element, improvising alongside the great man with huge success when he was still only in his early teens.

It was when his own marriage broke up that he began to grow

more eccentric under the influence of a sequence of girlfriends who led him on. Even so, Nigel's artistry is so formidable that he was still playing, not just with amazing technical command but with the consistent imagination that has marked his playing throughout his career.

Kennedy's first recordings were made for the independent label Chandos, consisting of a jazz collection and an Elgar collection centring on the Violin Sonata with various short Elgar pieces added. Then, happily, Nigel secured a contract with EMI, first for the Eminence label and soon after for the premium-price EMI label. Since then he has made a long sequence of recordings which consistently convey his magnetism.

His oddities also brought him a great deal of media attention, and though he had always had an individual haircut, more and more he began to look eccentric and to dress in bizarre ways, preferring torn jeans and jacket to more conventional wear. Even so, I always enjoyed my conversations with Nigel, for even when his ideas grew ever more strange, he was always interesting, and plainly regarded me with some warmth. Not that his interpretations were uncontroversial, for he began to adopt very spacious speeds in such works as the Brahms Violin Concerto as well as the Tchaikovsky.

He also recorded the Walton Violin Concerto in a coupling with the Viola Concerto, taking such liberties with the speeds in the opening movement, that he ran the risk of sounding self-indulgent. What was impressive was his facility in playing on the larger instrument, and whatever the developments in his lifestyle, he never let his technique slide at all, evidently allowing himself plenty of time for practice.

Latterly, he has lived in Poland, and has developed the practice of conducting chamber orchestras there and on tours of the rest of Europe. It is still not clear where his career can go next, but he has effectively established himself as a pop star to a degree unmatched by any other artist in the classical music world, something that has become a mixed blessing. Yet his brilliance and warmth in such a work as the Elgar Violin Concerto remains a consistent delight, and always will be.

JACK BRYMER

My first encounter with the great clarinettist Jack Brymer reflects badly on me, I fear. It was my review of a performance of *The Barber of Seville* at Glyndebourne that caused the trouble. I was sitting in a seat in the old auditorium at Glyndebourne, which by some acoustic freak effect exaggerated the sound of the woodwind. I noted that the clarinettist of the RPO, then the Glyndebourne orchestra, was playing so loudly that the piece sounded like a concerto. I also noted what I described as a sloppy tone, as I deduced, loose-lipped in a jazz-like way.

That was emphatically not true, and the reason Brymer's tone was so fruity was his use of vibrato, observable in his many recordings, not least in the Mozart Clarinet Concerto with Thomas Beecham conducting the RPO, a classic recording. After my review Brymer sent a brilliantly written letter to the *Guardian*, in which he demolished what I had written, using a fair amount of irony about my knowledge of clarinet-playing.

Happily, a few years later I met Jack and we became firm friends. That friendship developed rapidly on the many overseas tours I went on with the LSO, the orchestra that Jack had joined, having left the RPO after Beecham's death, first of all going to the BBC Symphony Orchestra before being persuaded to join to the LSO. The LSO then had the two finest clarinettists in the country as co-leaders, for the first clarinet already in the orchestra was Gervase de Peyer.

The LSO players described Jack's playing as 'peaches and cream', while Gervase's was 'gooseberries and custard', a very unfair comment, though it highlighted the marked contrast in tone between the two. Jack was the more dominant of the two, and when Gervase decided to try his hand at conducting, that prompted a memorable incident.

It was during one of the LSO's residences at the Salzburg Festival, and Gervase was due to conduct the wind soloists of the LSO in Mozart's C minor Serenade, K. 388, for wind octet, a masterwork of the genre. On that occasion Jack and his wife, Joan, were late for the rehearsal, as they had had to wait for a bus from where they were staying out of the city. He arrived, and at once commented on the fact that the players were sitting in an odd formation. He demanded changes at once, so Gervase's authority was immediately undermined, and Jack it was who dominated the performance from then on rather than Gervase.

It was one of the conditions that Jack made on joining the LSO that he could take his wife, Joan, with him on any tour, a concession that he took advantage of to the full, so that Joan became a favourite with all the players. She was a great character, who had a copious wardrobe of clothes more appropriate for a trendy teenager than a matron of over sixty. She also sported pink hair, very distinctive. She would appear each day in a get-up ever more surprising, particularly when like Jack she had earlier been a teacher, with engineers' caps for headgear a speciality. In appearance she was quite the opposite of the aristocratic-looking Jack, but they were the most devoted couple, and he was devastated when she died before him.

Jack's career was unconventional in that, only after he had been teaching for some years did he gravitate towards playing in an orchestra, and it was Beecham's inspiration to discover him, bringing out his talent by making him one of the so-called 'royal family' of wind-players in the RPO, so starting an exceptionally distinguished career.

ALAN CIVIL

Horn sections regularly contain the biggest personalities in an orchestra. I never knew the greatest of British horn-players, Dennis Brain, much as I admired his playing, but I did get to know Alan Civil, his deputy in the Philharmonia Orchestra, who took over from Brain as first horn, after he was killed, driving overnight from the Edinburgh Festival, having gone to sleep at the wheel.

Civil was unkindly nicknamed Baroness Civil by Walter Legge, founder of the orchestra, but the impression of pomposity was only a façade. I remember sitting next to him at a concert in the Royal Festival Hall. It was not long after the Beatles' album *Revolver* had appeared, to my mind the finest they ever recorded. George Martin, the group's recording manager, had the brilliant idea of getting Civil to play a horn *obbligato* in the song 'For No One'. I asked Alan whether he had his *obbligato* written out, and he totally denied any such idea. He had simply 'busked it'. Since then cover versions of the number have all reproduced Civil's improvisation meticulously.

The group of horn-players I got to know well was the quartet in the LSO in the early 1970s, led by the brilliant player Jeff Bryant. During one of the Salzburg Festivals, they were having a dispute with the LSO management. To the surprise of the rest of the orchestra, they confided in me, and I had several meals with them at the *Peterskeller* in Salzburg. I did my best to act as a helpful go-between between them and the management, but with little success. The next I knew, Jeff and his principal colleague had defected to the RPO, and Jeff had many successful years as first RPO horn, at one point becoming chairman of the self-governing orchestra and making some stunning recordings.

GEORGE MALCOLM

George Malcolm won his reputation first as the choirmaster of Westminster Cathedral in London. He it was who more than anyone first transformed the old idea of British trebles, who traditionally sang with a slightly squeezed tone quite different from the open-throated sound preferred for boy trebles on the Continent.

Benjamin Britten was so impressed with the sound of the Westminster Cathedral boys that he was inspired to write his *Missa brevis in D* for Malcolm and this choir, a work they recorded with great success, establishing the vigour of their singing. Britten also included them in some of his later choral works.

I got to know Malcolm slightly at recording sessions in the 1960s and 1970s, notably as a harpsichord continuo-player in Menuhin's Bath Festival Orchestra's recordings, and later with the Menuhin Festival Orchestra. The Bach recordings they made have stood the test of time, remaining perfectly viable even in this age of 'period' performance.

It was only later that I really got to know Malcolm. I was returning from taking part on the jury of the Montreux International Record Award, travelling back by rail from Montreux to Geneva before getting my flight back to London. My colleagues, who all had first-class train tickets, urged me to join them, but I insisted on travelling separately in second class, for which typically I had opted.

When the train stopped at Lausanne on the way to Geneva, who should get into my carriage but George Malcolm, and we enjoyed a vigorous chat all the way to our destination. He told me about the alcoholism that had nearly brought his career to an end. He explained that it was only when he gave up drinking entirely that he put an end to his dependence on alcohol, and I was moved to hear his revelations. Imagine the irritation of my colleagues in first class when they learned of my journey with George Malcolm, a meeting of two Brits who preferred to travel modestly.

In his later years Malcolm was tireless in discussing careers with various young musicians, helping them with practical advice from his home in Wimbledon. One who was especially grateful was a masterly pianist who has made a unique reputation in quite a different keyboard area from the harpsichord, the outstanding pianist András Schiff, whom I came to meet many times at the Salzburg Festival, a piano genius who is astonishingly modest.

Interlude 5: Cambridge

I had indeed met Greville Janner before the call came from Cambridge, through Peter Marchant, and had got on reasonably well with him, but I would not have chosen him as my room-mate. I was in a cleft stick. I could hardly turn the request down, so reluctantly I agreed to share with Greville. As I suspected, it meant that I had to lodge in a room largely taken over by him. In the event our alliance in Room M9 had many benefits. I was an early riser, whereas Greville went to bed late and got up late, all of which worked rather well. It was not quite 'cox and box' but nearly so.

When I arrived in my room at Trinity Hall I was greeted by Greville and, almost at once, there was a knock on the door. It was a man with a formidable moustache, plainly an ex-serviceman, who promptly asked, 'What are you going to *do?*', meaning what games was I going to play. I had not got rid of doing compulsory games at school in order to resume the misery of them at Cambridge, and simply retorted, 'I'm not.' At that the moustache looked at his files and, with the nastiest of sneers, said, 'Westcliff High School', meaning that if I had been a public-school man, as the vast majority of those at Trinity Hall were, I would have responded differently. I never for a moment regretted my decision.

It was thanks to Greville that, instead of joining the Socialist Club, which I had been advised to do, not realising that it was dominated by Communists and fellow-travellers, I joined the Labour Club. We quickly became leading members, particularly as Greville, as son of an MP, Barnet Janner, was very much part of the political world already with ready access to Parliament. It was Greville too who persuaded me to go along to the 'freshers' squash', where, in response to a pep talk by the then president of the Cambridge Union, Denzil Freeth, also from Trinity Hall, much later a junior minister under Harold Macmillan and thereafter a very dear friend, I joined the

Cambridge Union. This cost me seven pounds ten shillings – almost a quarter of my government grant for the term – to become a life member.

Having done that, I was determined to get my precious money's worth and not only used the Union's premises almost daily, not least the library, but also put my name down to speak in the first likely debate. In the event it was almost midnight before I was called, and somehow I managed to make a reasonably amusing speech. I was thrilled when a few days later I received a letter from Denzil Freeth, asking me to make my first 'paper speech' at the Union, against the motion in the first 'undergraduate debate' of the term (i.e. one without a guest speaker) on the subject of the committee system in Parliament – not an easy subject, even after my army studies of the British Constitution.

It was quite a distinguished line-up of principal speakers, as it turned out. Opposite me, proposing the motion, was Tony Lloyd, latterly a distinguished judge as Lord Lloyd of Berwick, and for years chairman of Glyndebourne Festival Opera. As his seconder he had a fellow member of mine from Trinity Hall, then in his second year, Geoffrey Howe. We had little idea that Geoffrey, who inhabited the room immediately below ours with his friend Dick Stone, would go on to have such a distinguished career as Chancellor of the Exchequer and Foreign Secretary, before being demoted to Leader of the House by Margaret Thatcher and subsequently humiliated once too often by her. Though his opposite number, Denis Healey, had wickedly likened his attacks to 'being savaged by a dead sheep', his resignation speech was one of the supreme examples of oratory in the House, when in effect he launched the undermining of Thatcher and within weeks she was out.

After that paper speech I had the privilege of sitting on the front bench in all debates, which was very gratifying for a callow freshman. At the end of term I was also elected on to the committee of the Labour Club and, with Greville (who became Labour Club

Secretary), was a member of what we called 'the Labour caucus'. This was strictly illegal by Union rules, but under the chairmanship of Percy Cradock, the cleverest man I ever knew in Cambridge and the most brilliant speaker, we organised our Labour forces to make sure that we had a fair representation in the Union after the end-of-term elections, when otherwise the Tories would have swamped us. The caucus also ensured that Jack Ashley, later Lord Ashley of Stoke, became president. It was out of loyalty to Jack that, on the Labour side, we refused to wear evening dress, a ban changed after a few years.

We all expected Percy to become a star of the Chancery Bar when he left Cambridge, but in the event he joined the Foreign Service, becoming in due course an expert on China, the first British chargé d'affaires in Peking (now Beijing), later ambassador, and, later still, Margaret Thatcher's favourite adviser on foreign affairs. Percy was a joy to know, for he shared his brilliance in a way that drew you in and didn't leave you feeling inadequate.

One early pleasure during my time in Cambridge was more closely related to my college: discovering that the senior tutor, Charles Crawley, far from being against grammar-school entrants, was only too delighted if anyone was suitable. I got to know him better over the Sunday teas he held at his home in the Madingley Road. There I met his delightful wife, Kitty, with whom I got on famously after we discovered we were both devoted to the Walton–Sitwell *Façade* Entertainment, and were trying to get the full texts of the poems involved at a time when they remained unpublished. We corresponded a number of times when we made new discoveries.

What I did rapidly come to rue was my forced decision to read French and Spanish. I had won what was called the Wootton Isaacson Scholarship for those studying Spanish, but I found it was just like being at school again. I was also a pretty poor modern linguist, with a lack of natural aptitude exacerbated by having been prevented from speaking either French or Spanish during my years at school when the Continent was effectively occupied by Nazi and Fascist forces. To my great delight, I soon I discovered that, under Cambridge rules, one can change subjects between Parts I and II of the Tripos. I was able to drop Modern Languages – despite the slight disapproval of my 'moral tutor', Shaun Wylie, a brilliant mathematician who, as we discovered many years later, had been the leading assistant of Alan Turing at Bletchley Park, where they broke the Germans' 'Enigma' code, a major development of the war, which arguably shortened it by between two and four years.

Law was an obvious choice for me in Part II of the Tripos, when so many of my colleagues including Greville were reading Law, and Trinity Hall had been founded in 1351 for studying Canon Law, and remained very much oriented towards legal studies. I was no better academically at Law than I was at Modern Languages, but I enjoyed it much more, and particularly enjoyed eating dinners at Gray's Inn, which I had been encouraged to join. That was not with the idea of becoming a barrister, which I knew I could never do financially, but because it was a course of study that beckoned.

I was out of my depth at Gray's Inn, but the ritual of eating dinners was fun, particularly at first when the Gray's Hall, which had been bombed, had not yet been restored and we ate our dinners in the Old Library, a much more informal place. At one of the dinners a man who had been a second lieutenant in charge of us in Bad Oeynhausen, whom I fear we did not greatly respect, came up and claimed recognition. I turned and with a shamefully patronising display said, 'Oh, Wright!', knowing I had been at Gray's longer than he had.

I attended lectures reasonably diligently, but that left me free for two daily experiences that were paramount for me during most of my time at Cambridge. At 11 a.m. I would make a habit of going to a coffee bar called The Whim. There a regular group of us would in effect have a coffee party on the lines of a cocktail party. I was almost always the only Labour man among the whole raft of Tories and a few Liberals. It was good too to meet up informally not just with Denzil Freeth but also with Norman St John Stevas and the Liberal Ronald Waterhouse, as well as others who went on to have distinguished careers after Cambridge. Norman would often make a point of straightening my badly tied tie, which I took as a friendly gesture. I just loved the sharp and stimulating conversations.

Another fairly regular attendee at The Whim was Hugh Thomas, later a distinguished historian who, veering between right and left, wrote the definitive book on the Spanish Civil War and one also on Castro's Cuba. He had the reputation of being the wittiest man in Cambridge. He had written a brilliant, sophisticated play, which was staged in one of the small Cambridge theatres. I would cruelly say when he arrived, 'Say something witty, Hugh!' That was enough to silence him for half an hour. He became in due course a life peer.

My other daily experience, at least during my middle year when I was chairman of the Labour Club, was to have lunch in the British Restaurant, a place where, thanks to government subsidy, one could get a good meal of several courses for one and six or two shillings, what in decimal currency would now be seven and a half or ten pence. I went to the British Restaurant because I found it stimulating to be among a group of Communists and fellow-travellers. I learned a lot as the only one believing in social democracy, fending off Marxist arguments. It served me well and, when I went to Iron Curtain countries in later years, I could argue back in Marxist terms, regularly demonstrating that Britain was a more egalitarian country than they were. It certainly strengthened my argument that all my official helpers on any visit were invariably sons of leading Communists. I also cherished the informal meetings I had after lunch, when once or twice a week we would meet in Denzil's rooms at Trinity Hall and have more jolly conversation. Again, I was almost always the only Labour man present, but somehow I was accepted. I was no more successful academically at Law than I had been at French and Spanish, but I still persisted with eating dinners.

Standing out among the many undergraduate speakers in Cambridge Union debates at this time was Douglas Hurd. Like his close friend Tony Lloyd, he was an Etonian who had gone on to Trinity, and it was not until our second year that he began to take part in debates. Yet instantly we recognised that here was someone born to be Union president, and who was clearly destined for a spectacular career. Not only was his command of argument and oratory phenomenal, his tall, imposing figure gave him natural command. Yet there was no suspicion of arrogance in him, and we all were fond of him, delighted in his success.

I had become a committee member at the Union at the end of my first term and progressed to be senior committee member, a role that would normally lead to the automatic sequence of secretary, vice-president and president. Unfortunately, although I was lucky in being given paper speeches every term (meaning that my name appeared on the Order Paper and advertisements for the debate and I was also allowed to speak from notes), which were generally successful, I was not good at gathering votes in the elections for the Union committee at the end of each term, and the usual pattern was duly broken. It is some consolation that my fellow Trinity Hall friend, Geoffrey Howe, followed a similar course. Greville, on the other hand, was a master at rousing support not just from his Jewish friends, but also from organisations such as the Welsh Society, as he had been born in Wales.

I was more successful in the Labour Club, becoming chairman after surprising many people by defeating my then room-mate, Greville Janner, when misguidedly I was persuaded to run against him. It did not make for good relations for a time in the rooms we shared. It might have been some consolation to Greville that I was a hopeless chairman, not least in committees where I had to learn the hard way not to let committee members waste time. The experience was a help when many years later I became Master of the Art Workers' Guild.

My inexperience as a chairman also let me down over the affair of Bertrand Russell, who was president of the Labour Club. He had been misquoted as advocating the use of nuclear weapons, ironic when he became a leading member of the Campaign for Nuclear Disarmament. The report so aggravated many Labour Club members that they wanted to sack Russell as the Club's president. It was only Tom Crump, a more thoughtful member than any of us, who pointed out how Russell had been misquoted, but in eagerness we all ignored his information.

I should have deferred a decision, but I was still a callow chairman and we passed the resolution. So far as I can remember Russell was amused rather than angered, and took the opportunity offered by the Socialist Club to give him a platform. He rightly pointed out that as he had always agreed with government policy, and we did not, we should resign from him rather than the other way about. We were clearly worsted, but managed to persuade Clement Attlee to become our new president.

One great benefit of being on the front bench at the Union was that one was able to meet all the distinguished guests who came to every debate. In the Labour Club too, thanks largely to Greville, the number of Labour ministers who came to Cambridge was enormous. I was able to meet such figures as Harold Nicolson; Compton Mackenzie (founder of *Gramophone* magazine as well as a novelist); James Griffiths, then deputy Labour leader; Barbara Castle; Lord Birkett; Roy Jenkins; Tony Crosland (Labour's future lost leader who died tragically young); and Tom Driberg (just back from North Korea, where he had gone against the instructions of the Party. Another regular visitor to the Union was the then celebrated television star Gilbert Harding. I later suggested to him that I could help him by 'ghosting' his autobiography. Luckily I became a full-time employee of the *Guardian* before there was any question of following that idea up.

I shall never forget my first meeting with Hugh Gaitskell, later my great hero when I was in the Parliamentary Lobby for the *Guardian*. I was to speak with him leading a debate, and impertinently greeted him when picking him up in a cab with the words, 'I might tell you that I do not belong to your wing of the Labour Party.' Others included Kingsley Martin, editor of the *New Statesman*, for me compulsory reading, but best of all was Hugh Dalton, recently ousted from the post of Chancellor of the Exchequer, who gave lunch to a group of us and characteristically had us riveted with his anecdotes of King's in the 1920s.

Such contacts certainly added to the glamour of Cambridge, and I have often said that the great benefit of an Oxbridge education is that one comes to realise there are relatively few in one's generation who are ahead of one in the competitive race of life, a selfish attitude, but probably inevitable. I always remember meeting a college colleague in London accidentally: for the first time it felt as though the capital was just another village.

In my penultimate term I still had no idea what I wanted to do after leaving Cambridge and my day of destiny came when, on 6 February 1952, I went to see the Appointments Board. It was my great good fortune to be interviewed by the Chairman, Mr O. V. Guy, to whom I explained my various activities, including the fact that for two years I had written the reports on Union debates for the *Cambridge Review*, a relatively staid organ designed primarily for senior members. Once I had set all this out, Mr Guy asked what to him must have seemed a perfectly obvious and straightforward question: 'So why not journalism?' It seems extraordinary now, but this was a career I had never even considered at the time.

It was like a revelation on the road to Damascus, in which everything suddenly became clear. Later in the day I met up with John Steane. He warmly encouraged me and I recall we noted that, as a journalist, I might even become a music critic, something I had always thought impossible. It was by writing those Union reports that I found I could write in an attractive way. My mentor was Peter Green, then editor of the *Cambridge Review* and latterly a distinguished author as a history professor in America. Each week he would analyse my report in the most constructive way. If anyone taught me how to write, it was Peter Green. I have always been sad not to have been able to thank him in person, for my letters were never answered.

Chapter Six

Singers

Some of my closest friendships have been with great singers of our age, most notably the three superb exponents of opera and song who appear in the opening sections of this chapter. In the sphere of musical appreciation, vocal artistry has always spurred my opinions most passionately, especially as practised by some of the most extraordinary people I have ever met.

ELISABETH SCHWARZKOPF

'Speak a little louder, Ted – that man in the corner can't quite hear you!' I was having dinner with Walter Legge and Elisabeth Schwarzkopf in a London restaurant and, in my excitement over Walter's reminiscences, my already loud voice got louder still, until Elisabeth restrained me with her ironic remark. I like to think that her teasing reflected an almost parental attitude to me, parallel with Walter's as the mentor to whom I was devoted.

For me Elisabeth Schwarzkopf was one of the very greatest singers of the twentieth century, arguably the greatest of all, thanks to her ravishingly beautiful voice, her supreme control of it and her boundless artistry. It was pure luck that led her to become a singer, rather than a doctor, which was her ambition if she got to university. It was a penalty imposed on her father by the Nazis, who stripped him of his post as a headmaster when they came to power in 1933. As an assistant master he was banned from sending his daughter to university, though she was allowed to study at the Berlin Hochschule für Musik.

There she shone, and became a member of the chorus in the Berlin State Opera. She won a contract as a beginner, a soubrette, and her first role was as one of the Flower Maidens in Wagner's *Parsifal*. Later she sang the role of a boy shepherd, in an opera where she had to sing from the back of the stage, and had to pitch her voice sharper than the rest to cope with the distance between her and the front of the stage, something doubly difficult for her, as the possessor of perfect pitch.

One of her colleagues, the distinguished baritone, Karl Schmitt-Walter, realised her potential after she had sung the formidable coloratura role of Zerbinetta in Strauss's *Ariadne auf Naxos*. She sang the notes, but Schmitt-Walter realised the voice was not properly supported. He suggested she should approach the great soprano Maria Ivogün, to study with her, and with her husband, Germany's leading accompanist, Michael Raucheisen. They carefully looked after her voice, and Ivogün realised that the true individual Schwarzkopf timbre lay in a relatively small range of notes. She expanded that sound, creating in due course the unique voice we have come to recognise.

After Elisabeth had enjoyed a year or so as a soubrette, Ivogün suggested that she should approach the management to become a fully fledged soloist. She did so, but they met her with the devastating news that they could not give her a contract unless she joined the Nazi Party. She went to her father, always her closest adviser, who promptly said that she must go along with their suggestions, as they could at any time prevent her from singing at all, and the main aim was for her to develop as a singer.

In the event Schwarzkopf never did receive her party card and, as the daughter of someone who was disapproved of by the regime, she remained uncertain whether she would be accepted or not. Yet she did receive her contract, which was the important thing for her. It now seems gratuitously unfair that Schwarzkopf should latterly have been criticised for joining the Nazi Party, when the pressures were so complete for her to do so. In fact Schwarzkopf's father refused to let the family have a radio in their flat during the war in case they were accused of listening to foreign broadcasts, another of the restrictions that living in Berlin under the Nazis involved.

One crisis came when on a tour to occupied Paris with the Berlin State Opera she was replaced in her soubrette role in Strauss's *Die Fledermaus* by the mistress of a Nazi leader. She was so furious that she took the bag she was carrying and hit the theatre's cyclorama, severely damaging it. She was accused of sabotage, and her father had to be called from his army post to defend her, which he did. It was another black mark in her record book, as far as the Nazis were concerned.

During the war, when Berlin was being bombed, she would sleep in the deep shelters provided, which in due course led to her developing tuberculosis, in those days much more serious than it is now since the development of antibiotics. She was sent for a whole year to recuperate in a nursing home in occupied Czechoslovakia, where it was thought the high altitude and purity of the air might help to shake off the TB. She thoroughly enjoyed the semi-outdoor life, and after twelve months was indeed cured so far as was possible. She came back not to Berlin but to Vienna where Karl Böhm had invited her to join the company of the Vienna State Opera.

She returned to singing, but was told not to get too close to other artists in the company, for fear of contaminating them with TB. Sadly, this interim period did not last long, before the Vienna State Opera was bombed, and had to close. She and her mother returned to Berlin, where Michael Raucheisen as leading accompanist organised tours of artists to entertain the German forces in Poland. This is the only period in her life when Elisabeth might have been seduced by a Nazi leader, as has sometimes been alleged, but Raucheisen was a stern guardian, and what she remembered most of that period was being able to buy a coat made of horse-leather to fend off the intense cold.

She returned to her lessons with Raucheisen's wife, Maria Ivogün, and it was from this period that a number of recordings have survived of the broadcasts she made with Raucheisen on Berlin Radio. From them it is already apparent what an artist she was becoming, long before she met Walter Legge as mentor.

At the end of the war, the chaos that followed made Elisabeth uncertain of her future, but Karl Böhm once more came to her rescue, inviting her again to go to Vienna. He found accommodation for her and her mother, not in Vienna itself, which was under Russian occupation, but in the upper floor of a chicken run, where she and her mother made themselves as comfortable as they could.

Elisabeth was invited to sing at concerts for the occupying American army, something they greatly valued as they were paid not in money but in care parcels full of hard-to-get groceries. She was invited at one point to go at the last minute to Zurich, where Wilhelm Furtwängler wanted to give her an audition to sing in a performance of Brahms's *Requiem*. She was taken by an American officer in an open jeep at a time when women never wore trousers, and she was frozen on the journey, which was made the more hazardous because she did not have a valid passport. Luckily her American guard got her past every checkpoint, and she was approved warmly at her audition by Furtwängler, marking the beginning of her international career as a soloist.

When in due course she was able to join the revived Vienna State Opera company, thanks again to Karl Böhm, her career quickly blossomed, and she was naturally in the company invited to perform at the Royal Opera House in London. The snag was her German passport. She was required to get naturalised as an Austrian citizen, something that she resisted. Yet again her father advised her that it was a necessary course, and so she was one of the distinguished company that had great success in post-war London.

By this time she had already been signed up by Walter Legge to record for EMI, and she has often told of receiving the invitation from Legge to sign a contract. She insisted that she had an audition, as she said to Walter that she did not want him to 'buy a cat in a sack'. With such a determined candidate he decided to put her through the most stringent testing. Karajan was present, but withdrew, saying that he would kill the girl, but Elisabeth loved the challenge, and it was the beginning of the many hours of instruction that helped to make Schwarzkopf one of the world's greatest singers of *Lieder*.

When she analysed in painful detail the 'takes' of a performance she had just recorded in the studio, Elisabeth would cover her score in pencil marks, noting carefully where she had gone minimally sharp or flat. When she came to record the finished version, she let the music flow, as it always has to, using the preparations as they should be used, not as firm and fast rules, but as useful and indicative guidance.

She continued to perform in public long after she would have wanted to retire, but she did it to please Walter. It was after a recital she gave in Zurich that, on the way home, he said to her, 'My dear, you are a bloody marvel.' It was a compliment such as he never usually gave her. Some forty-eight hours later he was dead, and Elisabeth never sang again in public, much relieved that she had done her duty by her husband.

After Walter's death Elisabeth went to live in the house in Zumikon near Zurich in Switzerland that she and Walter had bought for her parents. There she lived happily, and it was from there that John Steane and I both received invitations to join her in her eightieth birthday celebrations in Stuttgart in 1985, when, after a *Lieder* recital by a singer she had coached, she was awarded the German Order of Merit, something that she had also received some years earlier. She was the first artist to receive that high honour twice over.

The occasion was some compensation to her for the blow she received when a perverse and distorted book was published about her and her association with the Nazi Party. There were plenty of us ready to counter the false accusations, when, as I have pointed out, she suffered under the Nazis in many ways, but it still left its mark on her happiness. The Stuttgart occasion was a delight, even though she disapproved of many points in the performance by the invited *Lieder* singer. She made an elegant speech, and the whole occasion, typically German, could not have gone better.

It was in December 2000 for her eighty-fifth birthday that Elisabeth invited John Steane and me to join her in Switzerland to celebrate with her. She had by this time moved to the village of Schruns just over the border in Austria, but for her birthday she decided to come back to Zumikon. The schedule for the day was unbelievably gruelling. She had booked us in at the tiny two-star hotel in Zumikon.

The day began delightfully when Elisabeth received us in turn in her bedroom, the largest in the hotel, but still very small. She had a hairdresser to do her hair, and in echo of the Marschallin's levee in *Rosenkavalier,* John Steane came along the corridor singing as he always did, echoing the contribution of the tenor in Strauss's opera.

At lunch she was entertained to a reception at the Austrian Embassy in Zurich, but even that was exacting, as the lunch took place on the top floor of a building with no lift, and with her long black skirt impeding her, she had to climb over ninety steps, something that was extraordinarily inconsiderate of the organisers. Yet she did it, and later in the day she agreed to answer questions in a public interview at the university. This she did with her usual flair, even though many of the students at the back were effectively prevented from seeing her, another example of poor organisation.

Finally, she attended a reception, not at the university, but at a library, where there was no room to circulate, and it was awkward eating a buffet supper, yet another example of bad organisation which Elisabeth brushed off with apparently no trouble.

It was on this occasion that she was especially keen that we should go and see the grave of Walter Legge. We found it in a corner of the Zumikon church graveyard, a simple block of marble inscribed with the names of Schwarzkopf's parents and other relations. It might seem a strange resting place for a great British character, but it symbolised the deep love between two individual characters, a unique partnership.

It is one of my happiest memories on one of my last visits to Schruns that we watched the classic film directed by Paul Czinner of *Der Rosenkavalier* with Schwarzkopf as the Marschallin opposite Sena Jurinac as Octavian, with Karajan conducting. Elisabeth commented on her own performance, reluctantly conceding that it was rather good. She then confirmed the story about Jurinac chewing garlic before one of their performances together, as Jurinac herself had described to me some years before, which delighted me. Schwarzkopf told me that they had had to record the sound of the performance first, and then had to synchronise their acting to fit the film, something that was very difficult to do.

When I was Master of the Art Workers' Guild in 2002, I had Janet Baker and Joan Sutherland among my principal speakers, both of whom I interviewed with illustrations. With Schwarzkopf, my third heroine with a DBE, I knew it would be impossible to get her to come over from Switzerland to be interviewed in person, so I went to see her instead, and recorded her comments on her career and many other points of her life, which have given me the material in this section of my memoirs.

On the Sunday before I was due to give my talk on 'Schwarzkopf by Proxy', using the tapes, I rang her up to tell her. Her immediate response was to say she wanted to come over to be present. In one way I was delighted, but in others not, when I was quite certain that she would disagree with what she had said, with 'No, no, that's not what I meant at all!' It would have been wonderful but difficult.

Yet within hours Elisabeth had booked her room at her favourite London hotel, the Connaught, and even booked her flight. I arranged for her to be met at the airport, but then, at the last minute, she rang to say that her doctor had put his foot down, and on no account was she to think of such a trip. It just demonstrates the astonishing energy she had right to the end.

DAME JOAN SUTHERLAND

When you first meet performing artists, it is striking how much you know from their music-making that seems reflected in their personalities. This was the case with Joan Sutherland, after her spectacular leap to international stardom at Covent Garden in February 1959. It was then that I first met Joan, the most unspoilt prima donna you could ever imagine, a great, giving character to whom one instantly warmed.

From that moment it was a joy to follow her in one glory after another, a career that has few if any parallels in history, both in the scale of the achievement and in its span. If anyone had claims to be the Singer of the Century it was surely Joan. And yet here was an artist who, from first to last, retained her sense of wonder, of gratitude, taking nothing for granted; the last person to give herself the sort of airs assumed by far too many leading singers. Joan always remained the great Joan to whom I instantly responded both as a person and as an artist.

I shall never forget the matinee performance at Covent Garden of Mozart's *Magic Flute*, when, with Joan singing Pamina, I first registered the emergence of an unforgettable voice, magnetic both in sound and expression. I was initially disappointed in the early recordings she made, as the engineers seemed unable to convey the full individuality of the Sutherland timbre. After the triumph of February 1959 the Decca engineers quickly found the answer, giving us over the years an astonishing library of great singing, even if one always had to hear Joan in the flesh to appreciate fully the weight and volume of the glorious voice, as well as its unique combination of richness, brilliance and flexibility. No wonder that her early advisers, before Richard Bonynge became her guide, thought she was destined to be a Wagnerian.

My happy memories include many from recording sessions, starting with those for her first double-album recital, *The Art of the Prima Donna*, when she made light of all problems, not least in her dazzling account of the Queen's aria from Meyerbeer's *Les Huguenots*. The sparkling recording she made of Donizetti's *La fille du régiment* – one of her first opposite Luciano Pavarotti – was another great landmark, and so in a different way were the sessions for Puccini's *Turandot*, and the generosity with which she ceded first place to Montserrat Caballé as Liù in their single Act III confrontation. Generosity is a quality that always marked Joan's work, partly because she was the opposite of self-obsessed, seeing herself very clearly, and as I say keeping a sense of wonder.

Make no mistake, Joan Sutherland was a great heroine, but it is no secret that she never expected to be one, being far taller than most sopranos, let alone tenors, and she was always firmly determined to see things in proportion. I remember meeting her unexpectedly once in the Grand Rue in Montreux, near her Swiss home, shopping bag in hand, wearing an ordinary raincoat. I was with an American colleague for the Montreux International Record Award, and her first response was to say, 'Fancy seeing critics in Montreux.'

When I asked her what her plans were, she replied in a jolly, matter-of-fact way, 'Just a few *Sonnambula*s at the Met,' adding that she felt she was 'getting a bit long in the tooth' for that girlish role. To my delight she then did an imitation of herself tripping on as Amin, holding her shopping bag in front of her like a posy. I cannot imagine any other soprano in the world, let alone one of Sutherland's stature, sending herself up in that way. So far from diminishing her, it confirmed her greatness, both as a person and as an artist.

And though over the years no one has filled the role of diva more magnificently than Sutherland, earning her the nickname in Italy of La Stupenda, what dominated as she received ovations at the end of a performance was her natural jollity and exuberance. The cheerful grin as well as reflecting genuine pleasure seemed also to be telling us that this was all a bit of a lark. No other great diva has allowed us, as mere mortals, to share her joy quite so completely.

In all this she was always the first to give credit to her husband, Richard Bonynge, who had had the insight and patience to draw out from her what he instinctively spotted when others thought she was a Wagnerian: that she would achieve new heights in the *bel canto* repertory. Bonynge extended her range without her realising it, as well as demonstrating to her what flexibility she could achieve. Between them both they developed the unique voice of Sutherland, and as an eager learner Joan was ready for that process, just as she was when Franco Zeffirelli among others developed her abilities as an actress. We are fortunate in being able to appreciate the result.

One of my joys was being able to entertain Joan and Richard, especially Richard, at my house in Spitalfields. He decided to buy a service flat not in the fashionable West End of London but in the East at Mile End. This has the advantage of being within easy access of the City airport, with its direct flights from Geneva, and of being just opposite an underground station. That is how Richard and Joan came for meals with me, particularly when they arrived to find an empty fridge. Joan and Richard were the opposite of demanding, and it was always a delight to spend a thoroughly domestic evening, chatting about our memories.

DAME JANET BAKER

The first time I heard Janet Baker sing, I was immediately captivated, not only by the quality of her mezzo-soprano, distinctively rich and varied in tone, but by the intensity with which she sang. It was in Bach's *St John Passion*, a work I knew well, having in my teens sung in the chorus of performances in my home town. It was given in a little country parish church in Surrey as part of the Tilford Bach Festival in 1954, and Janet Baker, at the beginning of her career, had been given this assignment by the soprano Ilse Wolf, who was acting as a mentor for the obviously talented young mezzo.

I also heard her singing the role of one of the witches in Purcell's *Dido and Aeneas*, when I lamented that she was not singing the role of the heroine, Dido. That was something she went on to do soon enough, not least when Professor Anthony Lewis for the specialist L'Oiseau-Lyre label recorded the opera complete. But before that she had made several landmark recordings for the bargain Saga label, one of Schumann's *Frauenliebe und -leben* song-cycle, as well as of Brahms *Lieder*, and also a disc of English song, in both of which she was accompanied by Martin Isepp, son of her long-time singing teacher, Madame Helene Isepp. She was a demanding teacher who did not suit all singers, but proved ideal for Janet Baker.

Unlike Sutherland's voice, which presented problems for recording engineers wanting to capture its full beauty, Janet's mezzo was naturally suited to recording, and I was bowled over by all these early recordings. When her dedicated recording of *Dido* appeared, I even wrote to Benjamin Britten suggesting that he should write something for her. He did not respond to that idea until many years later, when he wrote a beautiful and intense scena, *Phaedra*, to words by the American poet Robert Lowell.

Baker's first recording of *Dido* was a revelation, and I looked forward to hearing her in the recording studio. This I did when, with John Barbirolli conducting, she recorded two song-cycles, Berlioz's *Les nuits d'été* and Ravel's *Schéhérazade*, a magical coupling. Barbirolli was the most sympathetic of accompanists, and Janet responded with heartfelt performances that were also flawless vocally. It was already apparent that, unlike most British singers, she revelled in singing French, not being daunted by the problem of singing on complex nasal consonants, where in German and certainly in Italian, it is on the vowels that the singer must concentrate.

It was the Royal Opera House, Covent Garden that asked me to interview Janet Baker for one of their projects, the first of a whole sequence of public interviews I have done with Janet. She is a marvellous person to interview, always knowing what to say crisply without wasting words. On that first occasion she was wonderfully open, talking about her own career, but less illuminating when it came to comment on other singers' work, when she herself is such an instinctive artist.

She would not on any account let me play any of her own recordings at the interviews, which is why I had to choose a careful selection of other singers of the past. We did our public interviews a number of times, so that flatteringly Janet began to talk about 'our double act', but still with no illustrations from among her own recordings. The change came when we were asked to do an interview for the fiftieth anniversary of the Elgar Society in Worcester. I pointed out that on this occasion it would be absolutely essential to include at least some of her own recordings of Elgar, and she agreed.

It was a wonderful occasion, and my illustrations culminated in the Angel's Farewell at the end of *The Dream of Gerontius*, 'Softly and gently'. It was then that the emotion of the occasion came over at its fullest, and many if not most in the audience were weeping. Janet realised then that her own recordings had just as powerful an impact on audiences as her live performances had. It was then that she agreed that I could not only include her own recordings, but also, on some occasions, concentrate on them in outlining her career, always with moving results.

One of the songs with which I liked to end our 'double act' was 'Love's Philosophy' by Roger Quilter, one of the most uplifting songs I know, to words by the poet Shelley. That song I have always felt could not be more appropriate, when in her private life Janet is Mrs Shelley. The role of Janet's husband, Keith Shelley, cannot be over-emphasised. He gave up his own career to act as Janet's helper and agent, most importantly in her engagements overseas. It is no exaggeration to say that she would never have had her very distinguished international career without Keith at her side, sorting out all the many problems of travel and accommodation, something that on her own she could not have contemplated.

She showed her total professionalism on an occasion when I was scheduled to interview her for a recorded music society called Putney Music. When I rang her at the usual time, I was rather disconcerted to find that she did not answer. Later in the morning I heard from her, when she told me she had been up since 5 a.m. because Keith had had to be rushed to hospital to undergo a serious heart operation. She had stayed there until mid-morning. When she rang, I suggested to her that if she wanted to cancel, I could on my own do a programme about her based on the illustrations we had agreed on. She would have none of it, and insisted that, if she did the interview, it would take her mind off Keith, when obviously she was worried. This she did, giving no sign of any stress in a conversation that was among her finest.

In the United States she had contacts with many of the great conductors of the day, not least George Szell in Cleveland, about whom she tells a fascinating story. Szell was extraordinarily demanding, and set about testing her beforehand. In one of the rehearsals she was astonished to find him giving her the wrong cue for an important entry. She thought it must be a mistake, but in the actual performance he repeated his error, something one would have counted unthinkable with such a perfectionist of a conductor. Janet defied him, and did make her entry correctly despite the cue from the conductor. Ever after that Szell was very appreciative of Janet, even though it was never a really warm relationship.

Other conductors who performed with Janet regularly included Georg Solti in Chicago and London, and she sang Mahler's *Des Knaben Wunderhorn* cycle not just with Barbirolli but with Bernstein too when she performed in Israel, an instructive contrast of styles, as she said. Daniel Barenboim accompanied her both in concert and on disc not just as a conductor but at the piano too in *Lieder* recitals, which were inspired occasions. It was a measure of the admiration that Gerald Moore had for her that he agreed to come out of retirement to accompany her in a number of recordings.

Janet rounded off her operatic career relatively early, choosing her repertory carefully in the three opera houses with which she was most closely associated, first at Covent Garden in Gluck's *Alceste*, then taking the title role in Donizetti's *Mary Stuart* at English National Opera with its deeply moving final aria before the Queen's execution, and finally in a new production of Gluck's *Orfeo* at Glyndebourne by Peter Hall with Raymond Leppard conducting, always a sympathetic partner for her.

Since Janet's retirement and since I moved to my Queen Anne house in Spitalfields, it has been such a joy to welcome her and Keith for lunch, on one occasion with Evelyn Barbirolli as our ideal foursome, occasions I shall always treasure in my memory.

DAME EVA TURNER

My first meeting with Eva Turner took place when we were fellow judges on the panel designed to choose candidates for Sir Robert Mayer's Youth and Music Awards. The others were George (the Earl of) Harewood and Robert Mayer himself, as well as Belinda Norman-Butler, whom I was meeting for the first time. Eva was nothing if not forthright, and she was unduly severe about a young soprano who sang a Handel aria very capably. I looked over Eva's shoulder and there she had written in her large, rounded handwriting, 'She mouths her words too much!' – exactly the quality that always marked Eva's own spoken delivery.

Eva's delivery was most distinctive, for, born and brought up in Oldham in Lancashire, the town where later William Walton was born and brought up, Eva believed in underlining every consonant, particularly the letter 'r', which she rolled at every opportunity, particularly in enunciating Italian words. She was the very first British-born soprano to achieve fully international status (Melba being Australian), and was the first fully to exploit the title role in Puccini's last opera, *Turandot*, making at least two classic recordings of the big aria, *'In Questa Reggia'*. There are also excerpts recorded live of a performance of the opera at Covent Garden in 1937, with her singing opposite Giovanni Martinelli. Walter Legge used to say that, when Eva was singing, her voice penetrated through the back wall of the Royal Opera House, such that you could hear her clearly in Bow Street.

She had a formidable career in the period of the First World War, not just in Italy and Europe but also in South America, notably at the Teatro Colón in Buenos Aires. She used to tell the story of going from the city to sing Rossini's *Requiem* at dawn 'on the plains of Carabobo'. She enunciated that name with such relish that John Steane would provoke her into retelling the story. 'And where was it that you sang, Eva?' 'On the plains of Carabobo,' she would dutifully reply.

Eva was always a joy to meet, and I shall never forget the occasion when, with John Steane, I took her and her lifelong companion Anne to a Buckingham Palace garden party. I had to leave the car in a park halfway up the Mall, and when I rejoined the three others, Eva had already organised her plan. Inside the grounds she insisted on sitting in the diplomatic area, from which we were barred as ordinary members of the public. She bridled indignantly when a flunky came up to get her to move. She was also adamant that we would all have to go and 'sign the book', though no one else from the hundreds present appeared to be doing so. This we duly did before returning her and Anne to their flat in the basement of a house in Notting Hill Gate.

The last time I saw her, I registered that she was present not by seeing her but by hearing her trumpeting voice. She was just a few rows back from me for a Prom at the Royal Albert Hall, and it was a joy to have a chat, however brief. She was so strong that we all thought she would reach her centenary. She outlived her compan-ion Anne, who was younger than her, but we had reckoned without the long murderous staircase leading down to her garden flat. I had always been apprehensive about it and, just after her ninety-ninth birthday, she had a serious fall down the stairs. Even then she lingered for several weeks, such was her strength, but, alas, finally succumbed to pneumonia, one of the great figures of British music lost to us all.

BIRGIT NILSSON

My meeting with Birgit Nilsson in Vienna came through a curious commission I had from the *New York Times*. Some editorial figure wanted a piece on Nilsson's tax affairs, when her dispute with the American tax authorities had prevented her from appearing in the United States for some years. I explained that I was not that sort of investigative journalist, and was certainly not prepared to do a hatchet job on an artist I greatly admired. I would go to Vienna, I said, if they were prepared to accept that stipulation.

I went there and for the best part of an hour I talked with her about artistic matters and her career in general. Then, when I felt I had her sympathy, I asked her about the tax problem. She was very open about it, and explained that a friendly American accountant had come to her aid and sorted it out for her, so she would be able to perform again in America.

I did what I thought was a good and informative piece, and sent it off, only to receive by return one of the rudest letters I have ever had, saying that it was not the sort of article that they were prepared to publish. I was furious, and it was only later that I learned from a friend in the music department of the *New York Times* what really happened. It seems that on the weekend when they were planning to publish my article, the paper's senior music critic, Harold Schonberg, whom I knew well, decided at the last minute that he too wanted to write about Nilsson.

As they could hardly have two pieces on the same subject, my piece was spiked. If this had been explained, I would not have felt slighted, but happily within months I was able to use my piece in the *Guardian* after all. Meanwhile the *New York Times* paid me some half of the original commissioning fee.

What I did retain was a wonderfully illuminating article about Nilsson and her training in Sweden. She was the daughter of a Swedish farmer, arriving at the music college in Stockholm very much as a country girl. Her singing tutor was the Scottish singer and teacher Joseph Hislop, a notoriously difficult figure.

As Nilsson explained, when she arrived for a lesson, he would challenge her about her very loud, sharply focused voice, which was still not fully tutored, and say, 'O listen to the steamer coming into the harbour', which naturally discouraged her. She was also discouraged at every turn by her father. He had the habit, if he attended a performance of hers, of going round in the interval trying to find someone who disliked her performance. Inevitably he would finally find at least one, and then come to her before the rest of her performance, saying how everyone thought how badly she was singing. Need you wonder she had to battle against the odds in developing one of the century's most extraordinary dramatic soprano voices, ideal in Wagner, as her many recordings demonstrate?

She told me how much she preferred the live recordings of her performances that had been issued, notably of *Tristan und Isolde*, to the meticulously prepared recordings she made with Georg Solti under the direction of the Decca recording manager, John Culshaw. None the less, she made some incomparable recordings for Decca not just of the Wagner operas, but of such operas as Strauss's *Salome* and *Elektra*. There is no more chilling an account of the close of *Salome* than Nilsson's, where she boasts of kissing the head of Jochanaan, John the Baptist, on the lips, as she nurses his severed head.

Birgit Nilsson also played an unexpected but significant role in a public interview that Placido Domingo gave at Drury Lane Theatre. Sitting prominently in the royal box overlooking the auditorium was Nilsson, and Domingo gallantly at an appropriate moment said that one of his keenest wishes was to sing in *Tristan und Isolde* opposite Birgit Nilsson. Promptly from the royal box in Nilsson's raucous and penetrating speaking voice came the unforgettable line: 'Well, you'd better hurry up then.' This was yet another wonderful example of her sardonic humour. Soon after that Nilsson retired from opera, giving only the occasional concert appearance.

SENA JURINAC

The only time I met Sena Jurinac came after she had officially retired. She was then concentrating on giving masterclasses, for which she was ideally equipped, having been a member of the Vienna State Opera for most of her career. Her reputation in Britain rested largely on her appearances at Glyndebourne, where for some years she was counted the queen of that institution. She it was who was referred to in the film about Glyndebourne, *On Such a Night*, when an American at Victoria station in London is intrigued at seeing so many people in evening dress in the middle of the afternoon. He hears them talking about the 'new Countess', and is so curious he follows them to Glyndebourne and manages to persuade the management to let him in to the performance.

The 'new Countess' was of course Jurinac, who for the first time was singing the role of the Countess in Mozart's *Le nozze di Figaro*, having till then sung Cherubino, a far lighter role. I myself first saw her when she was making her debut as Donna Anna in *Don Giovanni*, where previously she had been singing the lighter role of Donna Elvira. Like everyone else I fell in love with her singing, and heard her many times after that. It comes as quite a surprise that she appeared at Glyndebourne in only eight seasons, when she had come to symbolise the place, an iconic figure.

When I met her I asked whether she had an explanation why she had made so few recordings. She replied sharply that she was 'never married to a record company'. I took that as a snide reference to Elisabeth Schwarzkopf, who was married to the great recording producer Walter Legge and who promoted her recording career very positively. There was indeed a long-time rivalry that had begun when they were both members of the legendary team at the Vienna State Opera after the war, the others being Irmgard Seefried and Hilde Gueden. In fact her resistance to recording came partly from a reluctance to submit to the restrictions imposed by any record company.

That legendary line-up of Schwarzkopf, Seefried, Gueden and Jurinac was the one that amazed the opera-loving public in Britain when the Vienna State Opera Company came over to Covent Garden after the war. She then sang Dorabella in Mozart's *Così fan tutte*. Jurinac had been born in Zagreb, and always described herself in the Glyndebourne programme as Bosnian, but she was very much a Viennese character, though it was the Glyndebourne production of Strauss's *Der Rosenkavalier* that prompted one of her most celebrated recordings, the film of *Rosenkavalier* made by Paul Czinner, when she appeared as Octavian opposite Schwarzkopf as the Marschallin, with Karajan conducting, a classic line-up.

Jurinac confirmed for me the story I had heard that on one occasion when Jurinac was singing Octavian opposite Schwarzkopf as the Marschallin: she had deliberately chewed garlic, knowing how much Elisabeth hated the smell. It meant that Schwarzkopf had to pretend to be consumed by love for Octavian when she was suffering agonies from the breath of her colleague. Not that Jurinac was by nature a mean singer in any way, for in her personality as in her singing she was a warm and open character.

It was only after she had become well known through Glyndebourne that Jurinac finally appeared at Covent Garden. That was again as Octavian in *Rosenkavalier*, this time with Georg Solti conducting, making his debut at the Royal Opera House. His success led directly to his being asked soon enough after that to become the principal conductor there, ushering in a halcyon period. Jurinac was similarly a great success, Though later in her career she too went on to sing the Marschallin, she was never closely associated with that great role. One's only regret is that she did not leave many more recordings.

ARLEEN AUGER

Arleen Augér was among the warmest-hearted singers I have ever known, her personality matching the purity of her voice. She was born in Los Angeles and brought up in Long Beach, California, halfway between Los Angeles and San Francisco, hardly a place of culture. The exceptional maturity of her voice even by her mid-teens led her to be chosen as a lead singer in amateur productions of Broadway musicals, taking on roles involving characters far older than she was. She had singing lessons, and for five years contented herself singing not just in musicals, but also in churches and other local venues.

In the end, winning a scholarship, she went to study singing in Chicago, and that in turn led to her coming to Europe, where her career really took off. She made her debut at the Vienna State Opera as early as 1967, thanks to the sponsorship of Karl Böhm, ten years before she ever appeared at the Met in New York. The role she sang in Vienna and two years later at the Salzburg Festival was the Queen of Night in Mozart's *Die Zauberflöte*, which she coped with perfectly, as well as with the elaborate high coloratura.

Yet it was quite a different Mozart role with which she first achieved prominence on disc. Karl Böhm chose her as Fiordiligi in his recording for DG of *Così fan tutte*, a classic performance that fully reveals her gifts as an actor, as well as exploiting the beautiful tonal range of her voice. At the time she was a soloist in the long sequence of Bach Cantata recordings conducted by Helmuth Rilling, always singing stylishly and with great purity of tone.

From then on she made a sequence of impressive recordings, the sort of singer chosen not just for her total reliability but for her artistry and the ability to convey the sense of live performance. I was delighted to meet her, but saddened too, when she confessed to having an unhappy marriage. I later heard that she had found a partner with whom she was deeply in love, he similarly having found love after an unhappy union. Her partner was a Dutch businessman, Chairman of the trustees of the Concertgebouw in Amsterdam, a charming person, who was my immediate neighbour at a Concertgebouw centenary celebration lunch.

We arranged to have lunch soon after, and it so happened it was a day when I was due to interview Arleen. When we met, my Concertgebouw friend had no idea that I knew about his partnership with the singer and, when she arrived, he was delighted that my ruse had worked so well. Soon after, I heard that, both having got their divorces, they had married, and looked forward to happiness ever after. It was then that fate intervened, for Arleen was diagnosed with a brain tumour that proved to be malignant and in a tragically short time she died, still in her early fifties. One is deeply grateful for all the wonderful recordings she left as her valuable legacy.

JESSYE NORMAN

I first met Jessye Norman in a BBC Television studio. The Philips company was anxious for me to interview its new rising star for television, and flew me back early from Amsterdam where I had been watching Haitink recording Mahler's Eighth Symphony. In the studio I was introduced to this formidable figure of an African-American woman, tall and magisterial. They put her on a swivel chair and, to her great amusement, she was pitched backwards so that her tummy was higher than her head. She laughed uproariously while they put the error right. I did the interview, but sadly it was pushed out of television news by a political story.

That first visit to Britain demonstrated what a glorious voice Jessye possessed and what a great artist was emerging. It was initially rumoured that she was going to sing 'Rule, Britannia' at the Last Night of the Proms, but in the event it was the solo, 'Hail to the Queen', from Berlioz's *Les Troyens*, a favourite work of the conductor, Colin Davis.

Jessye's sense of fun early in her career came out in an incident I remember when she was taking part in one of the Haydn opera series for Philips conducted by Antal Doráti. The recording was done in a country church high in the hills above Lausanne in Switzerland, and Jessye joined us in a hotel in Lausanne. Responding to a challenge, out of sheer devilment, she stood in the doorway of the hotel restaurant and, to the astonishment of the diners, sang gloriously in her richest tones the opening of Elisabeth's Greeting from Wagner's *Tannhäuser*, 'Dich, teure Halle'. It was not something you would ever have expected of her later in her career, when she became much more serious about her role in music.

That and other incidents reflected a very happy relationship I had with her, for I interviewed Jessye on a series of occasions, sometimes in the small flat she bought as a pied-à-terre near Hyde Park Corner in London. I learned of her extraordinary African-American family in Georgia, the child of an insurance agent who somehow managed to send all his children to university, all of them achieving great success. As she used to say, 'Jessye Norman is not the only star in the Norman family.'

I came greatly to admire her work, not least in *Lieder* recitals, and I remember asking her about those she gave on the enormously broad stage of the Grosses Festspielhaus at the Salzburg Festival. How could she project when she was facing the audience in a wide arc? She explained that very carefully she would face the audience in a range of directions, each time thinking of herself as a sort of lighthouse beaming out in different directions. As to repertory I was particularly admiring of the fact that she would include a group of English songs by such composers as Roger Quilter among those from the more conventional *Lieder* repertory.

Over the years I always asked about her family, and came to regard them with great warmth. The editor of *BBC Music Magazine* said that Jessye wanted to be interviewed in New York for a major article, but I was the only one she was prepared to see, and that for a very limited period over the next few days. I obediently dropped all my other commitments and, as preparatory background, pulled together all the material – quite a lot of it – that I had about the great singer, who by now had achieved an astonishingly dominant status in the music world. She allowed me only half an hour of conversation to get new material, and I returned home as soon as I could.

I realised that I could not simply do a bland profile with no edge to it, so I thought it was a good idea to tell the story of her first arrival, and her enormous sense of fun when faced with the problem of the swivel seat. How different was this young and jolly figure from the almost regal figure that she had become.

I should have known better. Her agent promptly predicted to me that she would never speak to me again, and that is exactly what happened. I was on the Norman *persona non grata* list and have remained there. I had a feeling that in response to my hyperbole when I said, 'We are living in the age of Jessye Norman,' she actually believed it. Certainly, she made herself unpopular with various organisations, not least with the Barbican and the LSO in London, by the dictatorial demands she made for her appearances. Sadly, this coincided with a clear falling off of quality in her still-glorious voice, which began to display signs of unevenness. She also took on inappropriate repertory, at least on record, for example Bizet's *Carmen*. A great pity.

PLACIDO DOMINGO

My first meeting with Placido Domingo came in a recording venue in Barking, east of London, when for RCA Domingo was making his first international recording, preparatory to his debut at the Met in New York. It was predicted that he was going to be the new tenor star, but we little appreciated just how big a star he would become. The programme for the disc was a formidable one, a tremendous challenge for a young singer, for it involved a sequence of arias starting with Handel and covering various operas up to the twentieth century. The orchestra was conducted by Edward Downes, and it quickly became apparent how responsive Domingo was to any suggestion, also how rich his voice was and how impressive his artistry had already become. The result was a superb first disc, and it has always astonished me that the record company has been so reluctant to reissue it in the age of the CD, even at a time when so much old material is being resurrected. It still deserves to be heard again.

From then on Domingo made many recordings, first for RCA, then for many different companies. Always he demonstrated, with a degree of modesty surprising in a major star singer, a ready willingness to take instruction from conductors, and to accept their suggestions. I remember attending sessions for his first recording of Verdi's *Otello*, a work that at first was thought to be too heavyweight for him. He quickly established himself as the finest Otello of his generation, not just musically but in his deeply moving acting on stage.

His readiness to take instruction from a conductor was perfectly illustrated when he was recording the title role in Wagner's *Lohengrin*, a work he had sung early in his career in Hamburg and Israel but not in major opera houses. This recording, made in the Sofiensaal in Vienna, was the last of the cycle of Wagner operas to be recorded for Decca by Georg Solti, a series that had started with his pioneering recording of the *Ring* cycle.

Scheduled to sing opposite him as Elsa was Jessye Norman, but when I arrived in Vienna to attend the sessions, Jessye had still not arrived. She then stipulated that she would allow no one to hear the various 'takes' in the recording. That ban even applied to me, the official reporter chosen by the record company, an illustration of Jessye's insistence on having her own way.

I managed the situation quite well, for I timed my exit from the recording control room when I heard her cab arriving outside the Sofiensaal. I greeted her on the stairs, and said at once how I understood her reluctance to have anyone listening in to her actual recording takes. In fact what I did was to hide in one of the many boxes in the hall, where I could not be seen by the singers on stage.

What was striking was that where Domingo was ready, even eager, to respond to Solti's suggestions for interpretation, Jessye was most reluctant to modify what she had planned beforehand. She sang gloriously as ever, but it was a monumental reading rather than one that brought out the tender, subtler sides of the heroine's character.

Before the sessions, when I was discussing with Domingo his first recording made in Barking, Solti was wildly amused by any Wagner tenor being associated with 'barking' of any kind. It was typical of the happy atmosphere in the control room, with Christopher Raeburn as recording manager, always very skilled, not least in sessions in Vienna.

On another occasion the recording sessions took place during the football World Cup in Mexico City. Solti was so keen that he had arranged for the games to be recorded in his hotel room, even in the middle of the night. In the morning he would discuss the game with others in the studio, equally keen football enthusiasts. Domingo was asked for his opinion, and he then revealed that he had been asked to sing the Mexican National Anthem as a solo at the start of the games, upstaging everyone including Solti. He had been too modest to boast of it earlier.

LUCIANO PAVAROTTI

The first time I met Luciano Pavarotti was early in his career, when with Joan Sutherland in the title role he was recording Donizetti's *La fille du régiment* at Kingsway Hall, then a favourite venue, later destroyed. It was an opera that they had performed together at Covent Garden, and the role of the hero, Tonio, was very well suited to Pavarotti, not least for the spectacular section that involved nine top Cs in quick succession, giving the great tenor the nickname 'King of the High Cs'.

I was due to meet Pavarotti at the Savoy Hotel, where he was staying, and, to my irritation, he kept me waiting for quite a long time. Finally, I was asked to join him in his suite. As I entered, I looked sideways into the bedroom, where there was a nymph-like figure not fully clothed. He saw that I had spotted the lady, and in explanation he boldly said, 'A friend of the family.'

As is well known, Pavarotti never learned to read music, but he had a phenomenal memory and managed to memorise all his roles. He also had exceptionally clear diction, a quality that helped him in all the operatic roles he undertook. In those early days he was grateful for the help that Richard Bonynge and Sutherland gave him, for in many ways they were his early sponsors, notably in the field of recording.

I also remember a session at Kingsway Hall when Pavarotti was singing the tenor role of Macduff in Verdi's *Macbeth* opposite Dietrich Fischer-Dieskau in the title role, an assignment Fischer-Dieskau had taken on at the last minute, when Tito Gobbi let the record company down. In the final scene the confrontation of Macbeth and Macduff involved Pavarotti entering in a tricky passage, on a repeated figure, making it imperative for the tenor to count before starting. Pavarotti found it hard to get it right, and I remember Fischer-Dieskau with typical kindness nudging the young tenor at the crucial moment, getting him to enter correctly.

Later of course, when Pavarotti had achieved a superstar status matched by few others, he became much less easy to deal with, making demands as only temperamental singers can. Just how dominant he became is illustrated by a friend's experience going to a provincial record shop in central England during the age of the LP. He looked for the classical issues that the shop had, but could not find them, until he was told to look in the box marked 'Pavarotti, etc.'.

It was Bert Chappell, an executive employed by Decca, who had the brilliant inspiration of devising the 'Three Tenors' formula. He realised that not only Pavarotti but Domingo and José Carreras too were soccer enthusiasts, as well as the conductor Zubin Mehta. What simpler than to get all three tenors to Rome for the football World Cup and provide them with tickets in return for their taking part in joint performances?

The programme was brilliantly devised too, with each tenor having a solo and all three coming together in trio to sing popular favourites, dividing the contrasting phrases to give each an opportunity to shine. Naturally, the high spot was *'Nessun Dorma'* from Puccini's *Turandot*, which in Pavarotti's performance became the football anthem and a favourite for music-lovers not just in the classical field but much more generally. The result could not have been a bigger success, achieving sales figures rarely if ever attained by a classical issue, both on disc and video. It led to further 'Three Tenors' concerts in various venues, and became for a time a magic formula envied by other companies.

I attended many recording sessions involving Pavarotti over the years, but one of the most memorable was one of the last. It was in Chicago with Georg Solti conducting the Chicago Symphony Orchestra that Pavarotti sought to match his great rival, Placido Domingo, in his most celebrated role, Otello in Verdi's great Shakespearean masterpiece.

Otello was emphatically not a role that Pavarotti should have tackled, as his voice for all its beauty did not have a full heroic power, but on disc much can be concealed, and the sessions found Pavarotti with the enormous handkerchief that had become a signature object for him. He was not the easiest singer to guide, and Solti had quite a problem getting him to perform in an idiomatic way. Yet two performances in Chicago and two in New York were edited to produce a complete recording, which up to a point passed muster, though it confirmed that this was not an appropriate role for the great tenor. Such is musical rivalry.

When Pavarotti died, the tributes on BBC Radio included one by Joan Sutherland, even though she made it plain that she did not want to contribute, so fragile had the relationship become over the years between her and Richard Bonynge and the tenor. She did brilliantly, as one would have expected, but it was a sad close to the life of a unique tenor, who in many ways squandered his talents.

HUGUES CUÉNOD

Hugues Cuénod, of all tenors, had one of the most extraordinary voices. I once asked him how he had been able to continue performing into his seventies and eighties, and his reply was, 'Because I didn't have a voice at all.' In the interwar period he had been one of the Green Carnations in London in Noël Coward's musical *Bitter Sweet*, and later in the 1930s he was one of the team of singers assembled by Nadia Boulanger in Paris to make pioneering recordings of Monteverdi madrigals.

In the 1930s too he was rejected by John Christie as a candidate for Glyndebourne, being considered too old. Ironically, after the war he began his Glyndebourne career, and ultimately became the longest-serving tenor in the company. What he said about not having a voice at all stemmed from the fact that it was a fabricated voice, being built from various notes.

I first got to know Hugi, as we all called him, when I went for the only time in my life to a sauna. Being short-sighted I could see things only as a blur, yet this tall stork-like figure was unmistakable, and I addressed him rather as Stanley had addressed Livingstone, 'Mr Cuénod, I presume?' He turned in alarm, and asked aggressively, 'And who are you?' I explained who I was and that at the Château de Chillon in Switzerland only a month or so earlier, I had presented him with one of the International Record Critic Awards for his contribution to the classic recording – with Janet Baker singing the role of the goddess Diana – of *La Calisto* by Cavalli in Raymond Leppard's controversial realisation.

We became good friends, and for many years I would go and see him, when he came to Glyndebourne, always staying in a simple bread-and-breakfast ménage, Mrs Almond's, in the village of Ringmer near Glyndebourne. I also saw him at his family home in Switzerland in Lully-sur-Morges near Lausanne, where I also met his sister, who could have been his twin. Amazingly, he made his debut at the Met in New York when he was in his eighties, singing the role of the Emperor in Puccini's *Turandot*.

Cuénod's voice had especially impressed Stravinsky, thanks to his having sung in a Vivaldi cantata recording, when he sang in the highest register for a great sequence of phrases. Stravinsky responded by writing the tenor role in his Cantata for him, notably an extraordinary setting of the Lyke-Wake dirge, totally different from the one that Britten included in his *Serenade for Tenor, Horn and Strings*.

Stravinsky also contacted him when he was recording songs by the short-lived pianist Dinu Lipatti, alongside Elisabeth Schwarzkopf. They both received letters from the composer by the same post, asking Schwarzkopf to sing the role of the heroine Anne in the world premiere of his opera *The Rake's Progress* in Venice, while Cuénod was asked to sing the comic role of Sellem, the auctioneer. They both responded eagerly, though Schwarzkopf came to hate the piece, which she said she did not understand, and simply sang it as though it was Mozart. I explained to her that that is exactly how it has to be sung, an opera that, throughout, echoes the style and structure of Mozart operas.

Cuénod amazingly continued active and alert well past his

hundredth birthday, and my only regret was that, as he no longer came to Britain, and I no longer was able to get to Switzerland, we rather lost touch. Yet my memories of Cuénod are among the happiest of my life, an amazing figure who lent his own energy to whomever he came in contact with.

ROBERT TEAR

Robert Tear had one of the longest careers of any tenor in modern times, spanning over forty years. Born in Barry, South Wales, he won a choral scholarship to King's College, Cambridge, singing in the choir for three years, a perfect training. He studied Music at university, but his degree was in English. After Cambridge in 1960 he became a lay vicar at St Paul's Cathedral, also joining the Ambrosian Singers. His operatic debut came when he sang the role of Peter Quint in a production of Britten's *Turn of the Screw*, and that set him off on a course that exploited the striking similarity in his voice to that of Peter Pears, inspirer of so many of Britten's vocal works.

One of his first recordings came in 1967 when he recorded a Schubert song, '*Nachthelle*', with the Elizabethan Singers. Yet his career really took off when he began to perform in Aldeburgh as a valued member of the group centring round Benjamin Britten and Peter Pears. Very soon he was deputising for Pears in some of his roles, even taking over principal roles in the premieres of some works, as for example the church parable, *The Prodigal Son*, in which he sang the title role with Pears as the Abbot, and before that he had been in the group of singers who performed the earlier church parables.

He got into the bad books of Britten and Pears when he turned down the role of Lechmere in the television opera *Owen Wingrave*, which Britten wrote with him in mind, preferring instead the role Tippett had written for him in his opera *The Knot Garden*, Dov, in homosexual partnership with the black character, Mel. Tippett also adapted his *Songs for Dov* with Bob in mind. Tear later came to be less sympathetic to Britten and the Aldeburgh group, when his sense of humour clashed with their habitual serisousness.

It seems that Tear was rehearsing in a performance of Bach's *St Matthew Passion* at the Snape Maltings. At one point he sang with his tongue in his cheek the phrase, 'Then came one of the twelve', with a triplet in the middle, adding 'Hee-haw one of the twelve', referring to Britten's witty folk-song setting, 'Oliver Cromwell Lay Buried and Dead'. Pears was scandalised, shocked by what he thought was nothing short of sacrilege. Bob's sense of humour and readiness to make fun of himself comes out in his autobiography, published under the punning title of *Tear Here*, in which he took the opportunity to do some pointed teasing of Britten and Pears.

Latterly, Tear's versatility led him to sing in Edwardian ballads on the one hand and also in the first performance in Paris of the full three-act version of Berg's *Lulu*, his role being that of the Painter. He also sang the tenor role in Handel's *Messiah* on disc, Basilio in Mozart's *Le nozze di Figaro*, as well as the role of Achilles in Tippett's *King Priam* and incidental roles in rare British choral works. He carried on almost to his death in 2011 singing in various Britten roles, including Aschenbach in Britten's last opera, *Death in Venice*, as well as the *Nocturne*, and most importantly he became a regular choice as Loge in Wagner's *Ring* cycle, a role that allowed his gifts as an actor to have full expression. Altogether he was the complete musician, as few singers are.

IAN BOSTRIDGE

I first registered the tenor Ian Bostridge when I was one of the judges in the Young Concert Artists Trust auditions. A dozen of us were stretched in a line across the auditorium of the Purcell Room, and we heard each candidate in turn, performing from the stage. When Bostridge sang, it was immediately apparent to me that here was artistry of quite a different calibre, for not only did he have a distinctive, highly flexible voice, he used it with great artistry, and his command of the German text and his clarity of diction were exemplary. In short he had everything.

What some of my colleagues pointed out was that he looked odd, tall and gawky, appearing very unhappy. I brushed their objections aside, pointing out that it was not his appearance we were judging but his musicianship, and so indeed we did award him one of the YCAT scholarships. Yet I then took him aside, and gently suggested that he should try to look less miserable when singing.

Since then he has had a spectacularly successful career, rising easily to the top, helped by a recording contract with EMI. What I did not appreciate at my first hearing, was that I must have heard him already as one of the lovers in Britten's *A Midsummer Night's Dream*, an inspired production at the Sydney Opera House, by Baz Luhrmann, which came to the Edinburgh Festival but not to London, and which I have described in my section on the Sydney Opera House and its Festival.

As an academic, an authority on witchcraft and German literature, he had a choice of career, whether to stay an academic or develop as a singer. Happily, he chose music, and in this he has been greatly helped by his friend Julius Drake, one of our finest accompanists, who has constantly encouraged him. Being so acutely intelligent, Ian is a delight to interview with animated views on any subject you care to choose, and I am only sorry that after following his career closely in its early stages I am no longer in touch with him, but content myself with enjoying his discs and writing about them.

IAN PARTRIDGE

Ian Partridge (not to be confused with Ian Bostridge) is one of the most completely professional of tenors, with a distinctive pure voice that he handles with total artistry. It has a rare honeyed quality which makes it a voice ideal for recording, and in his career he has made dozens of recordings of Bach cantatas and of English song, as well as notably outstanding recordings of Schubert and Schumann *Lieder*. His recording of Schubert's *Die schöne Müllerin* has never been surpassed, with his sister, Jennifer, an inspired accompanist. Similarly, his account of Schumann's *Dichterliebe* cycle is masterly.

I was delighted when, for my final year as president of the Federation of Recorded Music Societies, Ian agreed to be my principal guest. Previously, I had always prepared the illustrations for each of my guests myself, but, no longer able to do that easily, I relied on Ian, and he did a perfect job, making it for me a very happy farewell to the Federation, having over the years had such stars as Joan Sutherland, Janet Baker (twice) and others among my favourite artists over the decade or so when I had been president.

SIMON BUTTERISS

No light tenor sparkles more brightly or more consistently than Simon Butteriss, helped by his charismatic personality. My favourite memory of a performance of his came when he was playing the role of the hero's ultra-camp boyfriend, Jack Whorewood, in Sandy Wilson's inspired adaptation of the Ronald Firbank novel *Valmouth*. He had a scene when he played opposite Robert Helpmann as the Archbishop of Clemenza, and Simon outrageously upstaged his senior colleague, who was not at all pleased.

To make matters worse Simon had taken the fancy of a local florist who sent a large floral tribute to him each day, inscribed anonymously but very noticeably in green ink, left prominently in the passageway where the stars' dressing rooms were. Helpmann, who needless to say was in receipt of no equivalent tribute, was seriously jealous. Simon was able to play off the elderly florist in due course, thanking him profusely. That production of *Valmouth* was the finest I have ever seen, confirming my total conviction that the piece is one of the greatest of all British musicals, with Firbank's lapidary prose turned into witty verses for the songs.

Another memorable performance of Simon's came when he sang the role of Don Basilio in the Garsington Opera production of Mozart's *Le nozze di Figaro*. Again Simon turned it into an ultra-camp character but only to bring out the humour, never overdoing it. His versatility also came out when he played the part of the young Laurie Lee in the Greenwich Theatre presentation of *Cider with Rosie*. Here was an actor in his thirties wonderfully convincing as a boy of six. Needless to say, Simon has had a very successful career singing in Gilbert and Sullivan, taking such roles as Bunthorne in *Patience* and Koko in *The Mikado*. He has also starred in numerous other musicals and plays. Such was his precocious versatility that, as a boy chorister in the choir of Westminster Abbey, he even ran away to play the eponymous child in the first West End revival of Terence Rattigan's play *The Winslow Boy*.

Interlude 6: The Guardian

One final benefit from knowing Greville Janner came just before we left Cambridge for the last time in June 1952. He told me that I could get a three-month extension of my grant if I took a cram course for the Bar Finals at a firm in Chancery Lane called Gibson and Weldon. I had passed in my second long vacation the two sections of Part I of the Bar exams that I was not exempted from by my Law degree, and the eating of dinners at Gray's Inn was well advanced, so it was very tempting to round off my Law studies by taking the Bar Finals. This was a delightful extension of my years at Cambridge and I enjoyed those three months enormously. I was able to live at home in Leigh-on-Sea and travel up daily to London to attend my classes.

The first, lasting, benefit from my period at Gibson and Weldon was becoming a lifelong devotee of the *Guardian*. It was on the Tuesday that I first managed to obtain a copy of that newspaper, and it was a revelation. I had read in the *New Statesman* that, for the first time, the *Guardian* was going to start printing news on the front page. Until then, like the other serious broadsheets, it had had advertisements on the front page. This habit, combined with a Gothic-face mast-head, really was most unattractive; so much so, indeed, that I had never seriously read the paper. Suddenly what had seemed stuffy and unattractive was exactly what I had always wanted of my ideal newspaper. Here, I knew instantly, was my paper for life, and my ideal was going to be if I managed to get on the *Guardian* staff, as I dreamed of doing. That was the first joy of my supplementary three months.

The second benefit was that, after Cambridge, it was delightfully relaxing simply to copy down lists of legal rules and exceptions, which Gibson's promised would take me through the Bar Finals if I memorised them. I had already had experience of getting through the two sections of Part I, Roman Law and Criminal Law, from which I was not exempted, by using what were called nutshells, in effect published on the lines of the Gibson notes. It felt as though I could not go wrong.

The third joy of my extra three months was that I got to know another close friend for life, John Addey, one who much later became an expert adviser of firms wanting to take over others. It was a most profitable occupation until the next recession came, bringing with it the abrupt disappearance of takeovers. John was then in deep trouble and, with his luxurious ideas of lifestyle, with Modiglianis on the walls of his grand house in Islington and lavish meals for guests, he fell into bankruptcy, faded away and died tragically prematurely. That was far away from when we first made friends with each other at Gibson's.

I took my Bar Finals in the worst smog London had seen in the twentieth century, and I remember getting to the exam room with difficulty when buses were simply crawling along with their headlights on. I took the exams, and had to wait for the results until the end of 1952. Before that I had had my interview for a job on the *Guardian* with the then editor, A. P. Wadsworth, who came to be my mentor and ultimate hero.

On the advice of the Appointments Board I had written to three different editors: of the *Yorkshire Post*, the *Birmingham Post* and the *Guardian*, sending off my letter to the *Guardian* with a goodbye kiss. From Linton Andrewes, editor of the *Yorkshire Post*, I received a handwritten response that ran to six pages. It was very encouraging but informed me that 'in a busy office like Leeds' they were 'far too busy to deal with a beginner'. From the editor of the *Birmingham Post* I got a brief rejection which was not quite right grammatically.

From Wadsworth I got what initially seemed like a rejection, and I am certain my face fell. My heart definitely did. It was only on a second reading that I realised that, far from being a rejection, it was a promise to investigate further. He wrote, 'I can't say we have anything at the moment. You might send me some of your stuff.' I sent a whole raft of my *Cambridge Review* reports and one or two other pieces I had had published. They evidently impressed Wadsworth enough for him to want to give me an interview, and that is what happened.

I was so innocent of newspaper timing that I promised to get to Manchester for the interview mid-morning. I got up very early and arrived in Manchester soon after 10 a.m. only to discover that the editor did not arrive until three in the afternoon, and would not be free to see me until at least 4 p.m. I had some six hours to wait and, true to its reputation, Manchester offered me pouring rain. I somehow managed to scramble through the day, damp but expectant, and finally got to see Wadsworth in the editor's office at the end of the 'Corridor' in 3 Cross Street.

Happily, I found it a joy talking to Wadsworth, trying to impress without showing off too much. Evidently, he was sufficiently impressed to arrange for me to see the deputy editor, John Anderson, and that was a different matter. John, unlike Wadsworth, was someone who did not respond to anything one said. He would stroll around his office kicking imaginary footballs the while. It was a daunting experience, but at the end Wadsworth called me into his office, having discussed things with Anderson, and said simply, 'I suppose we'd better have you,' the most joyous news I have ever had in my life, cementing my lifelong devotion to the paper.

I managed to catch a train to Bradford and thence to Shipley, where, at 16 Hall Royd, I went to see my beloved paternal grandmother, then in her mid-nineties. She was delighted at my news, something that pleased me all the more when, only a few weeks later, she died. At least her grandson had brought some comfort to her last days.

When I arrived for my first day's work, there was some confusion on what I should be asked to do. I was to be a personal assistant to the editor with an office along the 'Corridor' with its grand, heavy mahogany panelling. In the next office was John Rosselli, who became a great friend, though at first his chilly manner was not encouraging. He was only a year older than me, but he was already an expert on various foreign affairs subjects, writing leading articles every day. On the other side was Mary McManus, who was in charge of the letters and also wrote the television reviews, which had never until that time been regarded as being very important.

My first task of the day was to go through the letters that had just arrived and point to the ones I felt should be used in the paper, and where they could or should be edited. That I enjoyed very much, and very soon Mary and I became great friends. My other task was to go through the obituary file in the library, to weed out the ones that needed to be destroyed, either for having been missed when the subject had died, or, occasionally, because the obituarist had pre-deceased the subject of the obituary.

I discovered one of an architect who designed bathhouses in Salford, who would have been a hundred and thirty if he had some-how endured. Another was by the one-time Bishop of Manchester, William Temple, later a short-lived Archbishop of Canterbury, writing about the historian and political commentator, R. H. Tawney. Temple had long since died, but Tawney was still very much alive. The 'obit' began: 'The role of honour of the Great War is not yet complete. Tawney has died of wounds received on the Somme.' I wanted to keep that obit as a memento, but Wadsworth said it was not worth it and promptly destroyed it.

It was in February 1953, just a month after I arrived, that I went down to London to eat dinners at Gray's Inn, staying for the weekend at my parents' home in Leigh-on-Sea. On the Sunday afternoon I went with my mother to catch the train back to London, only to find that the island of Canvey was completely underwater; the disastrous floods had drowned a number of unfortunate Canvey-dwellers, when the sea wall was breached by the extreme height of the tide.

My one thought was to find some way of getting back to London to eat my scheduled dinner at Gray's. This I did on the service from Southend Victoria to Liverpool Street, and so from there I returned to Manchester. To my extreme embarrassment, the editor wistfully pointed out that they were spending a lot of money getting reporters down to Canvey, when I had been there on top of the disaster. I had not remotely realised that a journalist should not narrowly confine himself to his customary, allotted role when he chanced on an important news story. I learned that lesson the hard way, though the editor was very kind in not blaming me at all, just laughing at my innocence.

Over the following months I did a number of short leaders, including one, I remember, on the *Noël Coward Songbook*, which had just been published. I suggested, reasonably enough, that the songs of Noël Coward were going to last longer than most creations of the period. I also wrote a piece on Norwegian elections. I didn't know much about Norway but I knew quite a bit about elections, so managed to avoid pitfalls.

On the opposite side of the Corridor was a small dark office in which George Wainwright worked. He was already in his nineties, and had in the 1920s been a private secretary to C. P. Scott, the great editor who made the *Manchester Guardian* a respected journal. He had been a friend of Lloyd George, to whom he always insisted on referring as Mr George. George Wainwright had later become the *Guardian*'s librarian, until, not long before I arrived, a full-time professional librarian was appointed, together with an assistant and a substantial staff.

George still refused to give up his role entirely, and would do his best to waylay books that came in. He was marvellous at reminiscing about the old days and, for a time, I would travel with him on the No. 40 bus in the middle of the night, when our duties were over. He was merciless in his criticism of C. P. Scott, whom he described as a 'mean bugger' who would sit by a roaring fire dictating letters, leaving George in the cold on the other side of the room. George also recalled making a characteristic remark, on seeing C. P. Scott back in the 1920s in the middle of the night riding off to his home in Fallowfield on his legendary bicycle from the *Guardian* entrance: 'There he goes and his obituary not written yet.'

I was honoured at that time to be among the select few who were invited to the editor's house in Fallowfield for meals and good conversation. 'Waddy' hardly seemed to realise that it imposed a sort of class distinction on members of the staff, giving the chosen few a sort of privileged officer status. I greatly enjoyed meeting Lilian, Waddy's rather formidable wife (who ran the local chamber concerts) as well as his ailing daughter Janet, who was about the same age as me. On one occasion I was even invited to the editor's country cottage at Over Haddon near Bakewell, getting to know Waddy even better.

My first year on the *Guardian* brought the Coronation of Queen Elizabeth II in June. I remember leaving my lodgings in West Didsbury to walk over to the house of Mary McManus in Fallowfield to watch the television broadcast, a big event. Mary provided food and drink at the appropriate time, and duly in mid-afternoon we broke off to go into the *Guardian* office for our usual duties. It was a joyous occasion, and with us were H. D. 'Nick' Nicholls and his wife.

Nick was a veteran *Guardian* man who had been in his time president of the National Union of Journalists. By rights he should have been pensioned off years earlier, but Waddy was a kindly soul, and gave Nick the job of putting the *Miscellany* column together, a gossip column that simply drew on what other publications had published. It was an easy job for Nick, just sticking likely material together, and it was not until much later that Michael Frayn came on to the *Guardian*, and developed a superbly comic *Miscellany* column, quite different from what had gone before.

Nick would sit at his desk in the office on the other side of Mary's from mine and once his column was finished he would simply snooze away for the rest of the day with his dog equally asleep at his feet under his desk. It was a large, smelly poodle that Waddy loathed so much (being a cat lover) that he never went anywhere near to Nick's office, an arrangement that pleased both of them.

After a year doing my incidental job of looking through the letters and renovating the obit file I was told to go over to the newsroom with duties as a reporter. Initially I disliked the idea, but in fact I enjoyed my time in the reporters' room enormously, even though night duty could be a bore, with part of it consisting of ringing round the police and fire stations every hour. I soon discovered the officials to whom one spoke quickly became annoyed, so I would ring up not hourly but every two hours. On one occasion I was told of a fire in Oldham Street, which I went to see. I was disappointed to discover that it was a miserable little smouldering thing. I decided to ignore it, but, when I made my last call, I was told that the fire was still burning, so I did a paragraph for stop press, and made it sound much more important than it was.

What I enjoyed most was being asked to do a '*Miscellany* Page Lead'. My first was suggested to me by the wonderful news editor, Cockburn by name. In Bury they had the problem that they had run out of space for the portraits of former mayors to be accommodated, so I went round most of the town halls in the area, asking each what they did with portraits of former Mayors and Lord Mayors, with surprising results: some were in the cellars, some had simply been sold, and all of them had given problems to the council officials. It made an amusing piece that drew a positive response from colleagues and readers alike.

I also liked to cover by-elections. I did these with relish and maybe it was my success in this that led Waddy to summon me into his office, in order to offer me a new job. He wanted me to go down to London as 'Our Parliamentary Staff', in effect to be deputy political correspondent and deputy parliamentary correspondent, a job coveted by many. By an unhappy coincidence, however, it so happened that the previous week I had moved into the first flat of my own, and for the first time I felt settled in Manchester. I explained this to Waddy, telling him that I didn't want to move. I did, however, ask to have twenty-four hours to think the idea over.

In my innocence I did not realise it was a plum job that everyone wanted, but I duly came back, and asked, 'Well, can I start a record column as well?' At that, Waddy said, 'I suppose so.' So instead of getting one plum job I got two, which of course was a great joy, for my record column quickly became for me even more important than my job in the Press Gallery.

It was while I was still in Manchester that Waddy called me into his office, and gave me the chance to go on a two-week facilities visit to Italy. I was thrilled at the idea, and jumped at the offer. Heathrow in those days consisted of no more than a few sheds, and to get to Naples we had to start late at night. Next to me was the deputy editor of the *Birmingham Post*, a devout Baptist. I noted that as we were taxiing for take-off he read his Bible furiously, bribing the Almighty, I rightly assumed, not to let the plane crash.

The first half of our tour started in Naples and then moved on to Sicily – with one of our stays in a fabulous hotel in Taormina on the top of the cliff – on to Palermo and up to Rome. What our *Birmingham Post* friend endlessly talked about, being an amateur archaeologist, was our projected visit to the Etruscan tombs some miles north of Rome. I noted that our Italian guides tended to snigger, but thought no more about it. When we entered the first tomb we saw the first examples of Etruscan art with matchstick men in Etruscan red.

Our *Birmingham Post* colleague was so fascinated that he stayed behind when we went into the second tomb. There too were similar matchstick men of a kind that dated from pre-Roman times, but this time they were doing unmentionable things to each other, at which we all gasped, some in horror, others in delight. At that point our deputy editor came in – the Italians had nicknamed him 'Signor Pellegrino', because mineral water was all he drank – and stood in puzzlement: 'I say, what are these two chaps doing?' This had us silently doubled up.

My other big facilities trip came in 1956 when I was already in the Press Gallery, at a time when the Suez crisis had split everyone in both Lobby and Gallery, as well as down in the chamber of the House of Commons itself, into two contesting groups, for and against the attack on Suez sanctioned by Anthony Eden. I was one of a group of journalists who flew out to Kenya for the official opening of the new Embakasi airport (now Jomo Kenyatta International Airport) near Nairobi, a journey that took us two days.

We travelled on an airline called Airwork, and what in retrospect was a delight was the schedule. We started from Heathrow late at night, and dropped down in Rome in the small hours for refuelling. Our next hop was over the Mediterranean, landing in Benghazi amid the dying embers of a bright, vermilion dawn. There was no electricity, and oil flares lit the landing strip. The smell of those combined with camel dung gave us the full flavour of Africa, and we wandered round the airport fascinated. I was with the deputy editor of *Country Life*. As we were returning to the shed, which was the airport terminal, he held up his hand to his ear, and memorably said, 'Hark, the chiffchaff!'

We then flew over the Sahara and landed, because of the looming Suez crisis, not in Egypt to see the tombs at Abu Simbel, but in Wadi Halfa on the Nile in the Sudan. That afternoon we had a boat trip down to a modest Egyptian temple, returning for a relaxed evening meal and a night's sleep in the thatched cottages that were provided. Refreshed, we went on to Khartoum (for refuelling) and finally made it to Nairobi. It has often struck me how much preferable this was to going to Nairobi as we do today in one jump. We did in fact come back on one of the early Boeing 707s in just a single journey.

Kenya at the time was just recovering from the Mau Mau insurgency, and it was good to go to the Kenyan Parliament to talk to the early indigenous MPs such as Oginga Odinga, before travelling upcountry to the so-called 'White Highlands' where we stayed in Eldoret and had dinner in the local whites-only club. They were just beginning to adjust to the idea of African self-government, patronisingly singling out one or two black farmers whom they regarded as being passably efficient.

The big event came when we went to the animal park at Amboseli just under Mount Kenya, seeing lion-cub twins called Ambo and

Seli. We went round in a Land-Rover, but leaping down from the rear rather too enthusiastically I ripped the khaki shorts I had borrowed from my brother and had to be shepherded through central Nairobi with a bare bottom on our way back to our upcountry hotel and more thatched huts.

Soon after I went down to London to join the Parliamentary Press Gallery, we celebrated the eightieth birthday of Winston Churchill, who was still prime minister. I was stationed outside 10 Downing Street one day, to watch the 'presents go in and Sir Winston come out'. Usually my day began soon after 2 p.m. and, unfailingly, I would sit in for Prime Minister's Questions, then a much less rowdy affair than it has been latterly.

In those days these sessions came twice a week, lasting just fifteen minutes each time. It was a joy to observe the last throes of what I called the Churchill–Attlee double act, for though Winston came out with some magnificent paragraphs and witty phrases in his answers, Clement Attlee was just as sharp and a wonderful match for him in his crisp, incisive way.

I specially remember the penultimate Question Time before Winston retired as prime minister in April 1955. His answers to a sequence of often tricky questions designed to trap him were all devastating. On the following Thursday, for his final Question Time, he was plainly less sharp. In retirement he was a frequent attender in the Commons until he withdrew from Parliament altogether.

Attlee soldiered on as Labour leader for just over six more months, before he was succeeded by Hugh Gaitskell, who by then had become my big hero. I had already met him, when I spoke with him at the Cambridge Union, but at that time I had been a rabid Bevanite. Almost immediately, watching him from the Press Gallery, my allegiance totally changed, for where Aneurin Bevan would certainly make very concise speeches in that high-pitched voice of his, Gaitskell consistently articulated exactly the questions and remarks that struck me as perfectly apt.

I even approached him to see if I could prepare a biography, intending it to be very personal rather than formal. He agreed, suggesting a whole sequence of people whom he would like me to interview, notably from his period at Oxford. I duly went through the list, and discovered that everyone was delighted such a brilliant and charming man had become Leader of the Opposition.

Yet not one could remember any interesting personal stories about him whatsoever. Nothing I uncovered seemed to cast the slightest light on his personality or the development of his political ideas. I gradually came to the view that his thoughts so completely chimed with those of his listeners that they immediately attributed them to themselves. I still persisted in my investigations until the time when, in a private meeting of the Lobby, he was asked whether he was going to attend a meeting of the Labour Party Executive at a time of crisis. He said, no, he was going to attend the mayor-making ceremony in Chatham, the constituency he had nursed for Labour in the early 1930s.

I went to him immediately after the meeting, and he confirmed what I had already guessed. The mayor who was being installed was the woman who, with her husband, had fostered him while he was first a candidate. She was a sort of surrogate mother to him, when his parents, rooted in the Indian Civil Service, had in an upper-middle-class way been relatively distant from their son. He had told me how much he felt for his surrogate mother, and was quite clear he had to attend the mayor-making. Here was a man who got his emotional priorities right.

What then was terminally disconcerting for me was that, when I had a long interview with the lady, who by this time had become Mayor of Chatham, she, like everyone else, could not remember a single incident or saying of Gaitskell from the time when he lodged in her house. That warned that it would be impossible for me to produce the sort of book I had in mind, in which I had aspired to explain why Gaitskell was very far from being – in Bevan's hostile words – a 'desiccated calculating machine'. I still believe he was more than that – better than that – but his inner essence was hopelessly elusive and shrouded in mystery, even to those who could claim to be closest to him.

One of my more agreeable chores on Friday afternoons – when both my seniors, Francis Boyd as political correspondent and Harry Boardman as parliamentary correspondent, took the day off – was to go and see Charles Hendrix in the House of Lords. Hendrix was one of the great eccentrics of the Upper House, for that breed was not limited to eccentric peers, of which there were plenty, but also took in many officials of the House as well.

Sir Charles was officially the private secretary to the Leader of the House, at that time Lord Salisbury, nicknamed Bobbity. In fact Sir Charles effectively ran the place, for his friendship with all the leading peers on both sides encouraged him to operate diplomatically, sorting out problems of every description. Even so, in the office he let his eccentricity have free rein, and was known to throw books at his devoted secretary if she displeased him. His passion was for horse-racing, but his betting surprisingly was limited to the smallest possible amounts, such as half a crown (now 12½p), even then a tiny amount.

On my trips to see Sir Charles I was regularly accompanied by my counterpart from *The Times*, and Sir Charles was deeply worried at the time of the Suez crisis in 1956 that we took totally different views – my opposite number in favour of the invasion of Egypt, I violently against. Happily, the crisis blew over finally, leaving memories for me of Anthony Eden as prime minister popping pills when he was answering questions in the House of Commons, something that has latterly been admitted. He had already been a sick man when he became prime minister, and he resigned soon after in favour of Harold Macmillan.

That left another of my heroes, R. A. Butler, again in the cold, a position that was foisted on him once more when the mysterious powers-that-be in the Tory Party favoured Alec Douglas-Home for

PM, as being in their view more reliable. Sir Alec has long been underestimated. I came to admire him, particularly when I followed him, mainly in Scotland on his election campaign in 1964, my last duty before I left the Press Gallery to become full-time *Guardian* music critic, assisting Neville Cardus.

My admiration for Sir Alec did not affect my devotion to R. A. Butler. I remember one private Lobby meeting, when he was answering questions off the record very uninhibitedly – always a delight. At one point he was asked about House of Lords reform. He paused, swinging his keys in his right hand, a typical gesture. 'Lord Salisbury's grandfather had been thinking about Lords reform in 1900,' he pointed out. Then followed another pause and more key-swinging before the pay-off line: 'Things don't change much in that family.' It was his habit to make snide remarks like that, which no doubt were reported back to the butt of each joke, and which effectively prevented him from being chosen as party leader, as he richly deserved to be.

Harold Macmillan, who until that point had been a general failure in a sequence of top posts under Churchill, then to my surprise turned out to be an amazingly successful PM, because he knew how to delegate responsibility to his ministers and remain above the fray. His big failure came when, in a panic, he suddenly sacked a third of his cabinet, including his Foreign Secretary, Selwyn Lloyd, on his 'Night of the Long Knives'. It happened on a Friday, which meant that I alone did the *Guardian* coverage. I hope I did not let the paper down.

My principal personal memory of Macmillan came when the members of the Lobby were invited on a rare occasion to a drinks party with the PM as host. It took place at Admiralty House, when 10 Downing Street was being restored. I, as a very junior member of the Lobby, did not expect to speak to Macmillan, but when I was talking to the very friendly political correspondent of the *Daily Telegraph*, Harry Boyne, Macmillan came up, and started to talk about a visit he had just made to Balmoral to see Her Majesty the Queen. He then told a story he had heard from the then Scottish Secretary, James Stuart, a distant cousin of the Queen.

Stuart mentioned that he had been shot accidentally on the grouse moor, at which the Queen was eager to know the rest of the story. 'What happened then?' she asked. 'I went to the nearby pub and asked for a double scotch,' he said. 'Oh, that is the last thing you should have done, James!' said the Queen. 'That's funny, ma'am, but that's just what the barmaid said!' It was a feeble enough story, but it did allow me (theoretically) to remark, 'The prime minister was telling me a story the Queen told him.' Well, you could hardly get a more formidable name-drop than that. I didn't dare do it without laughing. My other memory of Macmillan came many years later, when, on hearing of Thatcher's privatisation plan, he was reported as saying it reminded him of his Oxford contemporary who had 'sold off the family silver', a very fair analogy, I have always thought.

During my time in the Press Gallery the Parliamentary Liberal Party was reduced to just five MPs, that five including two who won their seats solely because of an arrangement with the Tories in two 'double constituencies', Bolton and Huddersfield, Arthur Holt in Bolton and Donald Wade in Huddersfield, plus two seats in Wales and Jo Grimond, firmly entrenched in his Northern redoubt of Orkney and Shetland. The advantage for me, as the representative of a notionally Liberal newspaper, was that I could visit the Liberal Whips' room just off the Members' Lobby without asking permission, as I would have had to do in the Labour and Conservative Whips' offices.

The remaining Liberals were a very agreeable group, now led by Jo Grimond, whose constituency stretched, as Jo would say, a distance equivalent to that from London to York. I remember one evening when I was being entertained by three of the five in the Reform Club. With us was Jeremy Thorpe, a future MP and leader of the party, and a superb mimic. He said he had recently been walking into Trafalgar Square from Whitehall, when a Mini drew up beside him. Out of it had stepped Robert (Bob) Boothby. 'Goodbye, Pussy!' he said (Thorpe brilliantly mimicking him). 'Goodbye, Pussy!' came the feminine response. Although Boothby was reputedly bisexual, enjoying a friendly relationship with the notorious Krays, gangsters soon to be imprisoned for murder, he was also reputed to have had a long-standing affair with Lady Dorothy Macmillan, wife of the prime minister. Here in Thorpe's story was positive proof.

Sadly Thorpe himself was later disgraced, when his affair with a male prostitute was revealed, even though he was acquitted of seeking to have him murdered. Jeremy was never the same again and has long been stricken with Parkinson's disease.

I would regularly spend election night in Liberal Party Headquarters, which could be sad as the party's representation in Parliament continued to be very low. Jo Grimond was Liberal leader from 1956 until 1967. After he retired, I remember seeing him on a train from Brighton. I had been to a concert, and had to write my notice for the *Guardian* on the train between Brighton and Haywards Heath, where I would get out, find a telephone (this was long before the mixed blessing of mobile telephones) and ring though my notice to the office in time for the next day's paper. The trouble was that Jo, no doubt after a good dinner, was wanting to talk, denying me time for writing my notice. It was a complication that Jo at the time was a director of the Guardian Trust, but in the end I had to grasp the nettle and ask him to leave me in peace, which he did. I just managed to get my writing done in time to dictate in the station at Haywards Heath. Thank goodness, the *Guardian*, in common with other papers, subsequently abandoned the idea of having overnight reviews, which gives us all more time to reflect on what we write.

One of the great parliamentary characters to whom I became close was Tony Benn, or Anthony Wedgwood Benn as he was in those days, who inherited his father's title of Lord Stansgate. Tony desperately wanted to be rid of his peerage, so that he could continue to sit in the Commons, and he repeatedly got himself elected for his old Bristol constituency, only to be disqualified as a peer.

He tried several times over to argue that he could constitutionally divest himself of a peerage, once appearing before the House of Lords judicial committee in a committee room to make his claim. It was a virtuoso performance, with Tony marshalling his facts brilliantly, all without notes. Yet each time after these hearings he failed to have his radical view accepted. He would confide his plans to me, and with enthusiasm I wrote a number of pieces for the *Guardian*, explaining his aims. I almost became Tony's PR, so willing was I to help.

He did of course achieve his aim, when the Tory government, wanting to have Alec Douglas-Home, then the Earl of Home, as the new prime minister, passed legislation to legalise the idea of peers divesting themselves of their titles. Tony promptly took it up, just as Quintin Hogg, Lord Hailsham, did too. Back in the Commons Tony became increasingly unpredictable, which tended to make me less sympathetic, but he was always a joy to meet at a party; a warm and giving character, whatever his quirks of opinion. To his lasting credit, he was among the first to warn that Tony Blair's preference for 'sofa government' was introducing a presidential system by the back door, undermining both Parliament and the Cabinet.

Chapter Seven

Festivals and Other Travels

All music-related life stories tend to the picaresque, and no account of the role of classical music in the world could neglect the great festivals. I was fortunate enough to experience what was really the golden age of some of the most famous festivals and concert venues of the world.

ISRAEL

In June 1967 the outbreak of the Six-Day War between Israel and Egypt and its Arab allies had me thinking that the Israel Festival would be cancelled at the end of the month. I had been invited for the first time, and it was only with a week to go that the organisers in Israel rang me asking whether I was coming, as the Festival was going ahead as planned.

At the last minute it was quite impossible to get a direct flight to Israel, as thousands of Jews were intent on going to see the Wailing Wall in Jerusalem, banned to them for years as being in the Jordanian sector of the city. They suspected that Israel would occupy East Jerusalem for only a short time, and they wanted to pray at the Wailing Wall while they had the chance.

In the end I had to go via Athens, and I was relieved as well as delighted to be met at the airport by my interpreter and guide. He said the only hotel spaces available were in the east, formerly Jordanian, section, and we were to travel there by car from Tel Aviv. It was astonishing to see hundreds of coaches, bumper to bumper, on the road going back to Tel Aviv, bearing pilgrims.

Arriving in the hotel, I took the earliest opportunity to go out and look at the old city, and I wandered round the darkened streets with no sense of danger, as the Palestinians were still cowed by Israel's overwhelming victory in the war and the occupation of the whole of the West Bank and Gaza. My guide came to stay in the same hotel as me, for as he had been a staff sergeant in the British army during the Second World War, later defecting to join Irgun in the fight for independence, he had a taste for bacon for breakfast, totally unavailable in Israel.

Over the following week we visited a formidable range of places including the Church of the Crucifixion in Jerusalem and the Church of the Nativity in Bethlehem; as well as Nazareth, Gaza, Galilee and the Dead Sea near Jericho. Most exciting of all was my visit to Bethlehem. The first surprise was that, contrary to my imagination and the general view, Bethlehem is at the top of a hill, not tucked between hills.

White sheets of surrender were still hanging out from windows like washing, seeking to protect inhabitants during the Israeli assault. In Bethlehem itself the most important visit was to the Church of the Nativity, into which you had to make obeisance as you entered, as the arch at the entrance was very low, requiring you to duck underneath. Orthodox priests were behaving commercially, and the only really moving part of the visit was the chapel supposedly marking the exact spot where Christ was born.

When we came out, we discussed our visit with the extra passenger in our car, the young head of the tourist department in Jerusalem. He was concerned about arranging the details of the Christmas celebrations at the church, when he lamented that it held only 800 people, which limited their scope. We were in Manger Square, which is surrounded by a very high wall, shutting it in. I immediately pointed out that, with closed-circuit television from inside the church, you could get 10,000 or more in the square, all participating in the Christmas service.

The head of tourism was very sceptical, suggesting that the Christians would regard it as some sort of blasphemy, but I rabbited on, not just then but on our way back to Jerusalem, emphasising what a good, practical idea it was. I then thought no more about it until the following Christmas morning. The BBC announcer began the news with the information: 'The bells of Bethlehem ring out this Christmas morning. For the first time on closed-circuit television the service has been witnessed by thousands.'

You can imagine I let out a whoop of excitement, feeling that if I had done one important thing in my life, this was it. The development was indeed the more remarkable in that ordinary television was not available in Israel at the time. Many years later, when the Intifada prevented tourists from visiting Bethlehem, the announcement on the news of the cancellation of the Christmas ceremony referred to the 'traditional closed-circuit television'. That I have become a tradition remains for me something to relish.

My many visits to various holy places in Israel did not prevent me from attending a whole sequence of musical events. I found the concerts of the Israel Philharmonic disappointing, largely because the painfully dry acoustic of their hall in Jerusalem never let you hear the orchestra at its best. It was also a damper that they had to perform each programme five or six times over in various venues including kibbutzim, so that by the end of the sequence the players were tired of the works involved. It showed, even though with repetition they were technically first rate.

On my 1976 visit I much preferred the far less prestigious symphony orchestra in Jerusalem, attached to the radio. It was fascinating to hear about the problems involved for the players during the war of independence, when rehearsals and even concerts would be given with only the players who had managed to attend despite the war. The players felt they enjoyed them all the more. The orchestra's manager, A. Z. Propes, although he had been a terrorist, was a delightful man, born in Russia, masterly in overcoming all the problems facing the orchestra.

The most memorable performance I remember from my visit

took place in the Roman amphitheatre at Caesarea, a wonderful circular auditorium, when very topically after the Six-Day War the work concerned was a Handel oratorio involving the conflict between Egypt and the Children of Israel in biblical times.

Years later I attended festival concerts in Israel celebrating the mastery of Leonard Bernstein. He was always a welcome visitor from the time of the war of independence, when one recital by Lenny in the desert attracted so large a gathering of soldiers that the Egyptians, spotting it from the air, thought an attack was being prepared.

I include these five poems here, written at the time I visited Israel, thinking they might provide further illumination.

Bethlehem 1967
Up, up to the roof of the world: God's birthplace.

Funny, I'd always thought of going down,
Shepherd out of hills, to Bethlehem;
Yet here with fellow Magi I'm spiralling upward.
My host beside me, aquiline in calm,
(A Joshua in business suit) must plan
How Christmas ceremonies can spring
New custom, new wealth of visits from afar.

A hot coming, but this is July, my birthday,
And hotter, we know, last June. Still white flags
Of surrender stand on sills like washing.
No snipers now. They say the market here
In David's City within hours of invasion, sold
Rosaries fixed with the Star of David.
Israeli lads, blonded, got their bargains.

The birthplace. Bend your head, your body too
Through four-foot doorway – forced obeisance,

Darkness, noise, Armenian pedlars in priests'
Raiment. Then down to the Crypt, in steep descent
To the very crib: is still, like Calvary.

Blinded in sunlight, return to the business world –
This Manger Square in December
Will welcome pilgrims, Christians
To gather within embracing walls.
Yet all too few can kneel inside the church:
No room at Christ's own inn.

I face my companion's problem, urge the merits
(No Jew myself) for viewing on closed circuit,
Open for thousands of faithful eyes
To watch the blessing, share the service,
Worshipping with the chosen few inside.

Knowing he has to weigh his tourist needs
Against the call of scripture, my host in caution
Winces at my counsel, sees the danger
Of Christians shocked at Jewish sacrilege.
Nodding politely, he hedges; secretly wonders –
The Wisdom of the Magi?

Comes Christ's birthday. Bells from Bethlehem
Ring out their Christmas cheer, ring out on radio.
This the first year, proclaims the announcer –
New life, new hope – when joy new-born explodes
On screens of light, shining in Manger Square,
Feeding the throng on circuits of television –
Loaves and fishes once before . . .

This doubter's tiny candle pinpricks history.

Gaza

Spit at a tank, and pay the tax-collector:
Here where the Gaza Strip is no one's club.
On shameless walls the 'Votes for Nasser' peel
Like faded veils, expose a naked hate;
While Arab mounties, khaki-clad and booted,
Patrol the streets, their horses baring teeth
More sinister than any Jewish guns.
Israelis, bronzed with a summer jaunt, pop
From toy-town turrets, metal castles; grinning
Invite the kids to clamber from the beach.

But soon the cool will call them home – curfew
To lull a prickly season's soldiering –
Home to their usual in-trays. Even now
The chilling message, shrill, transistorised,
Tells Gaza of its taxman. Get those forms out:
(Arab or Hebrew script it's all the same)
The rich must bribe the piper for the muddle.

And rich there are, riding on candy floss.
Dazzle the world, red, white and green: this building
Splashed to the eaves with paint, proclaims the place
Where enterprise is bubbling 'Seven-Up' –
Pop from the bottle, shekels for the taxman.

Drink to the future, drink to the shrouded beggars:
So many souls you simply stand and shrug.

Nazareth

We didn't get to Galilee: ate hummus instead
From fly-blown plates in Nazareth.
Buzz of a foetid air, where Arabs gnaw

The bones of long-lost causes, chafe at the yawning
Yoke of foemen bureaucrats. The war
Had altered nothing, nothing. They showed us
Where Joseph's shop had stood, but who would credit
Such bare-faced lies tradition rings on tills?
(Saw at your carpentry, my brazen monks;
Rattle your beads, you nuns of Nazareth!)

Our Lord, no Nazarene, was here by luck,
Wasting – far worse than us – His precious hours;
So why revere such holiness: a plea
Simply to pedal wares and take up alms?
At Cana, they say, they have two rival places
(Nothing like competition to foster trade)
Where Christ first made His wine miraculous.
But we didn't get to Galilee; we stayed
Earthbound and sweating over our fly-blown
    hummus,
Praying its worm would spare our feeble guts.

To the Wailing Wall
'Postcards of Moshe Dayan!' The Wailing Wall
Awaits down crooked steps. This narrow track
Was blocked to Jews for two decades: no black
For sorrow flowed at Jeremiah's call.

And here the head-dressed Arab sets his stall;
Trumpets at bright-eyed trippers; flaunts the knack
(Bare-faced) of paying Israel's victory back.
Who turns the ancient tables – Semites all?

Bumper to bumper they bus from Tel-Aviv;
From Boston they fly (no seats for you or me);

Scattered millennial, thought they'd never see
This place of rending raiment. Who's to grieve?

Arab, usurp you neighbour Jacob's line:
Sell him his brother's image. Wailing's fine!

Visit to Calvary
Church of the Holy Sepulchre
Through sets where Figaro might cheat his boss
You climb long steps with butchers smelling strong,
By booths of junkmen, brassy two thousand long,
Where Christ once wept – once laughed – once bore
    a Cross.

But where is Calvary? You simply toss
Your mite, as did the Empress, right or wrong.
A miracle, she said, to trace it: the song
Of angels led her, healed a worldly loss.

Kneel and do worship, unbelieving sinner,
Here at the altarpiece of Christendom.
Grab from the air the touch of faith that brought
All palpitating millions to this inner
Rock. Feel them in absent silence. Come
With present Lord and share what peace they sought.

ZIMBABWE

The invitation I received in the mid-1990s from the irrepressible
Michael Bullivant, founder and organiser of the Bulawayo Music
Festival in Zimbabwe, led to one of the most exciting fortnights I can
ever remember. The arrangement was that I would not be paid for

the five lectures I gave on British music, but instead all my expenses would be paid, including a week of touring up to Victoria Falls, the country's great tourist spot. I also had the opportunity to write a series of articles for the *Guardian*, when I returned.

The artists taking part accepted the same arrangement and included the pianists Piers Lane and (a regular visitor) Leslie Howard, and the violinist Tasmin Little. As well as performing in concerts they gave recitals in several informal venues, notably in schools in various parts of the country. I shall never forget the performance that Tasmin gave one morning in a school of black children, initially very noisy, not knowing what a violin was, let alone ever hearing one. Tasmin wandered up and down the central aisle, delighting the children, explaining the instrument and the music she played, and the children were spellbound.

Michael was the churchwarden of the Cathedral in Bulawayo, a high-profile role; and I stayed with the Reverend Jeffrey Fenwick and his wife Pamela, who ferried me to and fro from each event. In the mid- to late-1970s, Jeffrey had been Dean of the Cathedral in Bulawayo, before becoming a canon residentiary at Worcester, then Dean in Guernsey, ultimately deciding to retire to Bulawayo. That was before the Mugabe regime developed its totalitarian tendencies, though there were already signs that Mugabe was growing dictatorial, particularly in relation to Bulawayo, centre of industry and culture in the country, and a regular rival, not always friendly, to the capital, Harare. My lectures were a success, and were very well attended, although they took place in the middle of the day. Music lovers, not just from Bulawayo but from Harare too, would take a vacation during the festival period, and that allowed them to attend as many events as they wanted.

The recitals went very well too, most of them attracting full houses, with concertos ably accompanied by a symphony orchestra that included good amateurs. I shall never forget the occasion when Tasmin both played her violin and addressed a noisy room of teenage students. As in her visit to school, such was Tasmin's charisma and her liveliness as she moved up and down the room, that the whole rowdy crowd was stilled.

The other unforgettable memory came on our visit to Victoria Falls. Tasmin gave a recital on a barge moored in the Zambezi, a mile or so above the Falls, while we in the audience sat on the steeply sloping bank. We were told that there was a hippo about and, to our surprise, when Tasmin started playing solo Bach, the hippo arrived, seemingly attracted by the music. It was so large that it could easily have overturned the barge, but instead it simply nuzzled the vessel, and finally left, the most amazing audience that Tasmin has ever had. Sadly, once the Zimbabwe currency collapsed, the music festival had to limit itself to a less ambitious programme, but when President Mugabe loses his dictatorial power, I still feel sure Michael Bullivant will resume his splendid project, bringing music to the area.

WEEKENDS AT HOME

Each year the Federation of Recorded Music Societies holds a weekend of music-making, attended by various visitors, notably distinguished guests who are interviewed. It is not strictly a music festival, but it is very similar. Some years ago the Federation chose me as the president, much to my astonishment. The first president had been Adrian Boult, succeeded by his disciple, Vernon Handley, who for years ignored the Federation, not acknowledging his role at all. Coming after such illustrious predecessors, I drew the conclusion that I had been chosen because they knew I could persuade distinguished guests to come to the annual weekend to be interviewed.

So it was, and over the years I have had as my interviewees Janet Baker (twice), Joan Sutherland and her husband Richard Bonynge, Anne Evans, the Wagnerian soprano, the conductor Richard Hickox, the tenor Robert Tear and many others, even though it has become increasingly difficult to come up with new names each year.

When I first became president, we met in a large conference hotel in the centre of Stratford-upon-Avon, by the bridge over the river. One advantage was that I was able to have as my guest Cordula Kempe, widow of the masterly conductor Rudolf Kempe. She lives in a house on the river front, just opposite the Shakespeare Festival Theatre.

Then after a few years the committee found another venue rather less expensive. That was another conference hotel on the outskirts of Daventry in the Midlands, rather more difficult to get to, but just as convenient in other ways. There we meet, though latterly I have not been able to attend the full weekend and, being disabled, have limited myself to a single day trip. None the less, it remains a very worthwhile event.

SYDNEY

It was in the autumn of 1973 that I was invited to the opening of the Sydney Opera House in Australia. It was my first visit and I instantly loved the country, its people, its climate and the feeling that it represented an ethos somewhere between that of Britain and that of the United States, yet at the same time was totally individual. I arrived after a gruelling journey, and was met by the press officer of the Opera House, David Brown, whom I instantly regarded as a good friend.

After a tortuous history of the construction of this icon of a building with its distinctive sails for a roof, the occasion was celebrated with a lavish festival with artists from all over the world. Before that the Australians tended to suffer from what was called a 'cultural cringe', but not so after the opening of the Opera House. Australia became the centre of a distinctive culture second to none, and rightly so.

I was thrilled about everything from the moment when, tired from my journey, I first saw the sails of the roof, 'shining in the midday sun from the north', as I wrote at the time. The patterns on the sails also surprised me, and everything about this unique building delighted me, so perfectly designed for its wonderful site on Bennelong Point just by that other icon of Australia, the Sydney Harbour Bridge. It was typical of the occasion that the first two people I saw, when I went down the steps of my hotel, were Janet Baker and her husband, Keith Shelley. Talk about the global village.

The next seven days were among the most exciting of my life. The Opera House building itself with its elaborate internal fittings, quite apart from the three auditoria and the wonderful terraces on the harbour side looking over to the Harbour Bridge, were breathtaking enough, but the organisers had assembled a wonderful list of performers from all over the world.

Lorin Maazel was there with his Cleveland Orchestra and, in the Opera Theatre housed in the middle-sized sail, Edward Downes was conducting the opening production, which brought the inevitable snag that there were highly inadequate wing-spaces on either side. Yet Prokofiev's epic Tolstoy-based opera, *War and Peace*, was given a rare airing, though I had to complain that one of the incidental scenes had been cut, which made it less effective than the miraculous Colin Graham production for ENO at the London Coliseum.

Australia's own leading conductor was also taking part – Charles Mackerras – and he introduced me to the then very young Mark Elder over lunch. It was a whirl from beginning to end of the week, and I was only sorry that I could not pull in the day trip to Adelaide that had been planned for me, as there was an airport strike. That airport strike also presented problems for my homeward journey, but David Brown dutifully ferried me up to Canberra, before taking me on to Melbourne, where the airport was not on strike. I had a sample of Australian hospitality, when out of the blue I phoned one of David's friends in Melbourne, asking to come round, and to my amazement he organised an impromptu party in my honour, at which I drank too much, arriving at the airport decidedly the worse for wear. Small wonder I was jet-lagged on my arrival back home in London.

When I returned for the tenth-anniversary celebrations of the Opera House, in 1983, I arrived late at the airport, so David had to rush me straight to the Opera House, where I was scheduled to take part in a three-way discussion over oysters and champagne, broadcast live on one of the local radio networks. Happily, adrenalin was pumping hard enough for me to carry it through.

My companions included an Australian woman film-director, Pat Lovell, who had made an important prize-winning film celebrating the Australian countryside, as well as the actor and dancer Robert 'Bobby' Helpmann, who was appearing in a play about Lord Alfred Douglas, Oscar Wilde's 'Bosie'. He played the elderly Bosie, while a handsome young pop star, Mark Lee, played Bosie as a young man. To my amusement, the raddled old Helpmann, ever vain, suggested, 'They [Who? I wondered to myself] do think we are rather alike.'

My other outstanding memory of Australia came on my third visit, for the twentieth anniversary of the Opera House in 1993. I especially wanted to see a much praised production of Benjamin Britten's Shakespeare opera, *A Midsummer Night's Dream*, directed by Baz Luhrmann, yet the only performance David could fit me in to was a matinee for schoolchildren. I was apprehensive that they would be rowdy, but I need not have worried.

This was the first time that I had seen surtitles used for an opera in English, and here they were so intelligently used that the schoolchildren had no difficulty in following the complicated plot. The production then did the rest, because it involved an inspired update to the late 1920s. The only scenery was a central installation like a four-tiered bandstand. The lowest tier held the orchestra wearing bandsmen's uniforms, the next tier the fairies looking like oriental sprites, the third tier the lovers looking like 1920s film-stars and the top tier the two god figures. The rude mechanicals were 1920s soldiers in army uniforms, and they had the freedom of the main stage, not least for the play of Thisbe.

The schoolchildren were mesmerised, following everything intently, and I marvelled at the way that this presentation had in effect got them sympathetic not just to opera, but also to Shakespeare, breaking down any barriers, when everything was so enjoyable for them. The genius of Baz Luhrmann was vividly demonstrated, and I was sad that the production did not get transferred to London, but only to Edinburgh in the UK.

EDINBURGH

Thanks to the idiosyncratic alignment of music critics' duties on the *Guardian*, as chief music critic I never went to the Edinburgh Festival. When Neville Cardus and Philip Hope-Wallace were alive, they naturally wanted to cover the important events, both concerts and opera, while I had the Proms and later the Salzburg Festival. Meanwhile, Gerald Larner, my colleague as Northern music critic, based in Manchester, loved nothing so much as going to Edinburgh, when his girlfriend, later his wife, lived there.

Yet I did attend two concerts of the Edinburgh Festival, both of them very memorable, long before I became a music critic on the paper. The first occasion was when I was doing my National Service in the army, stationed at Buchanan Castle, twenty miles north-west of Glasgow. A trip had been arranged for those of us who wanted to go to an event at the first-ever Festival in 1947, riding in the back of a truck to a concert of the Vienna Philharmonic in the Usher Hall, conducted by Bruno Walter, in his first meeting with the orchestra after the end of the war.

Inevitably, it was a sentimental occasion for conductor and players, and the intensity of the occasion made itself felt from the start. That was augmented still further by the choice of programme:

Schubert's 'Unfinished' Symphony, followed by Mahler's *Das Lied von der Erde*, then a very rare work, which I had heard only in the recording that this same conductor and orchestra had made before the war in 1938, before the *Anschluss* had prevented Walter as a Jew from performing in a Nazi-occupied country.

The performance of the 'Unfinished' was thrilling, and I remember the hair at the back of my neck pricking in the first movement, over the long crescendo of tremolos at the start of the development section. *Das Lied von der Erde* surpassed even that, for the soloists were Peter Pears and the tragically short-lived Kathleen Ferrier, already being regarded as a legendary figure. The *pianissimo* at the end was breathtaking.

My other Edinburgh visit took place a few years later. I was already on the *Guardian* as second political correspondent, doubling as record critic. As an enthusiastic member of the Fleet Street Railway Circle I had arranged with Tom Germaine, PR for the Eastern Region of British Railways, to have a footplate trip from King's Cross to Edinburgh on an inaugural run of a newly named train, *The Talisman*.

The first big excitement came when I saw the streamlined Gresley A4 Pacific backing on to the train. It was *Mallard*, the most famous loco of its class, as it held (and still holds) the world speed record of 126 mph for steam power, made in the 1930s. It was thrilling travelling for the first time on the footplate of a steam locomotive, but what staggered me was the noise, absolutely deafening, literally. It was terribly rocky too as massive steam locomotives had only the most minimal suspension.

None the less, I enjoyed every moment, particularly as we had temporary relief between York and Edinburgh, going to have lunch through the corridor-tender. Coming back to the footplate I was even allowed to operate the hooter, which in boyish enthusiasm I did. When I arrived at Waverley Station in Edinburgh, I phoned Colin Mason, then the *Guardian*'s Northern music critic, as he and I had discussed the possibility of my attending with him the concert of the Hallé Orchestra under John Barbirolli.

It was when the concert started that I realised just how deafened I was. The first item was the overture to Mozart's *Entführung* with all its battery of percussion, and my ears jangled as I have never known either before or since. Relief came in the Mozart piano concerto that followed, with the veteran pianist Clara Haskil as soloist, a magical performance, followed by a Mahler symphony. Yet what I shall remember was the janissary jangle of the *Entführung* overture.

ALDEBURGH

The oddity of my first visit to the Aldeburgh Festival was that I did not see the town of Aldeburgh itself. In my combined role of second political correspondent and record critic, I would occasionally be asked to do concert reviews. This one had as its main item Benjamin Britten conducting Mahler's Fourth Symphony. I misjudged the time needed to reach Blythburgh Church just north of Aldeburgh, but it was a boiling hot day and the doors of the church were open, and I was able to slip in during a pause in the playing. The Mahler was splendid, but I was horribly distracted by my neighbour in the next seat, the guitarist Julian Bream, whom I did not know at the time. He waved his arms about throughout the symphony, but I felt unable to complain to such a leading musician.

My second visit was just as odd, when I stayed with a woman who lived in a house on the Town Steps. Very inconveniently, the bedroom did not lead directly out to the corridor, and you had to cross another bedroom to get to the loo. What I remember most clearly was the impromptu concert that I have already described in my section on Rostropovich, when it was announced that exceptionally Galina Vishnevskaya, Slava's wife, was also going to be allowed to visit Aldeburgh.

It was only on my third visit to the Aldeburgh Festival that I found my true home.

It was with a widow, Jeanne Johnson, very active behind the scenes at the Festival, who entertained guests in her large house on a road leading off the Terrace at the top of the Town Steps. Among those who also came as guests were such figures as the organist and conductor Philip Ledger, who was coaching the Festival's amateur chorus, before being appointed to be choirmaster at King's College, Cambridge, and later going to be Principal of the Royal Scottish Academy of Music in Glasgow.

Vladimir Ashkenazy and his wife also stayed with us at Jeanne Johnson's house. He was not appearing at the Festival, but he came to Aldeburgh so that he could meet up with his friend, the great Russian pianist Sviatoslav Richter, who was also appearing. Richter was guarded night and day by a KGB official, which meant that Ashkenazy, if he was to see him without revealing himself, had to go to Aldeburgh churchyard and climb over the wall at the back of the house where Richter was staying.

This he did, but the oddity was that we as fellow guests never actually saw Ashkenazy, as he arrived home long after we had gone to bed, and did not appear with his wife for breakfast. Jeanne arranged for him to practise on the concert grand of a friend, but it was not strong enough to take the playing of a full professional and it needed serious repairs at the end of the Festival, something that the Festival refused to pay, at least at first, for the pianist was not officially taking part. I cannot remember how they sorted that muddle out.

One of the most memorable concerts I ever attended at the Festival came in the early days, when at the Jubilee Hall Sviatoslav Richter was joining Britten in Schubert piano duets, four hands at one keyboard, the *Grand Duo* and the F minor Fantasy. When years later I met Britten I complimented him on that unforgettable concert, and he told me a fascinating story of the problem he had with Richter, who was not used to sharing a keyboard.

That meant that, as he always did, he spread his arms out with his left elbow over on Britten's end of the keyboard. In the first movement of the *Grand Duo* the second subject brings an expressive theme, which Schubert gives to the right hand of the *secondo* player, Britten's position. It meant that he had to crawl up alongside Richter's arm, barely able to reach the right keys. Even so, the result was typical of Britten in its deep expressiveness. He was always an inspired pianist.

The biggest development in the Festival came when, greatly daring, Britten had the idea of turning the redundant Maltings at Snape near Aldeburgh into a concert hall. Having such a large concert hall altered the character of the Festival entirely, when previously large works had to be accommodated in churches. Plans were drawn up in an amazingly short time and a consortium directed by the firm Ove Arup and Partners, with Derek Sugden, a devoted music-lover, supervising the work.

The hall was ready to be opened by the Queen for the start of the 1967 Festival, and so it was, just in time. It was an extraordinarily moving occasion, as Britten had composed a new ceremonial setting of the National Anthem. The first verse is set as a prayer, *pianissimo* throughout and very slow. Then before the second verse there is a sort of fanfare leading in crescendo to the full-throated setting of the second verse.

We all eagerly wanted to discover what the acoustic of the hall would be like and, as we heard the *pianissimo* first verse, one could begin to feel the beauty of the sound. Then on the crescendo and *fortissimo* chorus the full glory of the warmly enveloping sound of the Maltings was immediately apparent, and I can only admit that it was a moment when tears and a gulp in the throat were impossible to fight.

Britten for that occasion wrote a special overture, *The Building of the House*, with a chorus as optional *obbligato*. In some ways the star of the occasion was Imogen Holst, daughter of the composer Gustav Holst, and an amanuensis and assistant to Britten for some years. At the concert she conducted a few of her father's short choral works, characteristically dancing her way through her conducting. She won a storm of applause, which went on and on, but she refused to take a bow (Britten had told her not to on any account). She did in the end, and we were all exhausted applauding her.

The first year using the Maltings was a special one, but little did we realise that the 1969 Festival would be even more memorable. I was furious that my features editor at the *Guardian*, Christopher Driver, an arrogant man who thought he knew more about music than I did, said to me that he would not let me go to Aldeburgh in that year as I 'enjoyed it too much', which supposedly rendered me ineffective as a critic. My fury was slightly abated when my Northern colleague, Gerald Larner, decided not go to Aldeburgh after all, as he wanted to accept another invitation to go to the Gulbenkian Festival in Portugal instead.

Driver had no option but to get me to go instead at the last minute, at least to the opening weekend. I attended the Saturday afternoon recital, given in the Maltings by the Amadeus Quartet with Clifford Curzon, but I decided against the event in the evening. I retired to my hotel, wrote my piece, and after a meal slept soundly. That meant I missed the extraordinary disaster that took place in the evening, when the Maltings caught fire, and the building was left as a shell. I was deeply ashamed at having missed the fire, but during the day I picked up enough detail to be able to write about it.

I did my best to finesse the story, but decided not to write it up immediately, for I discovered that the band of attendant critics and newsmen were being invited to Britten's home, the Red House, for a press conference, a very rare concession by the painfully shy Britten. That provided me with a most moving portrait of the composer, and added an important personal element to my story, which appeared on the front page of the *Guardian* on the Monday morning. The most poignant moment with Britten came when he pointed to a bare space in his music room, where the press conference was held, and said that

that was where his piano had been, destroyed of course in the fire, along with many of the orchestra's instruments.

More was to follow, when every day there was a fresh news story as well as a review to write, with almost all the scheduled events moved from the Maltings to an array of improvised venues, notably churches. Britten and Pears were determined not to give up, and organised various events in different venues around the county. I especially remember a performance of Mozart's *Idomeneo* conducted by Britten in Blythburgh Church, always a favourite venue, notably of the great Soviet pianist Sviatoslav Richter, which was the more moving for being in that unexpected setting.

Happily, in the following months with all the original team still assembled, the work of restoring the Maltings was done in record time for the opening of the following Festival. A number of minor changes were made as a result of experience, for example to make the stage more solid, as in the original design it had resonated distractingly. Curiously, in the end the fire proved a blessing in many ways, leaving the Aldeburgh Festival with an even finer hall than originally.

Some years after the fire, my friend Jeanne, who had won a diploma in architecture in Brussels when women were still unable to qualify as architects in Britain, decided to buy a medieval house in Great Glemham, some ten miles from Aldeburgh. My architect friend Roderick Gradidge came and gave important advice, providing drawings and pointing out ways of getting round awkward building regulations. In the end the new house was a masterpiece of conservation, which was both beautiful and comfortable to live in. There Jeanne continued to take in guests during Festival time, not so many as before, yet they included the historian Asa Briggs, later Lord Briggs, and his wife, Susan.

One of my most memorable visits to Aldeburgh came in the autumn of 1987, when south-east England was hit by a freak hurricane, blowing at some 125–30 mph. I was due to drive to Aldeburgh the following morning, but realised that that would be impossible, and delayed my journey for twenty-four hours. Even then the obstacles were formidable, and when I arrived at Jeanne's house in Aldeburgh, she was away so I had to collect the key from a neighbour, and found that all electricity had been cut off in the whole area, including at Snape Maltings, where my Swiss tenor friend, Hugues Cuénod, was due to give a masterclass. Instead it took place in the hall of Woodbridge School, where the electricity was still on. I remember coming back to Jeanne's house and cooking myself supper by the light of candles, taking care not to open the deep freeze, so that it would preserve the food stored there.

Over the years it was especially thrilling to attend the first performances of Britten works, notably the operas, including two of the three church parables, given in Orford Parish Church, *The Burning Fiery Furnace* (1966) and *The Prodigal Son* (1968) in which Philip Ledger, dressed like the other players and the singers as a medieval monk, played the keyboard in the crypto-medieval orchestra. I remember how difficult it was to get to the phone in time to get my review through to the *Guardian* in London, writing on my knee and then rushing to a nearby telephone box at a time long time before mobiles were invented.

Most memorable of all was the dress rehearsal and premiere of Britten's last opera, *Death in Venice*, based like the film on Thomas Mann's complex novella. It was written when Britten was already seriously ill with heart trouble, and his insistence on finishing the score before his heart surgery – which sadly did not achieve what was hoped and was further complicated by a stroke – plainly shortened his life. It was Ben's final gift to his lifelong partner, Peter Pears, for the central role of Aschenbach was ideally suited to a singer who had reached his sixties. It was this work that brought Pears his debut at the Met in New York, to great acclaim, justifying in a way Ben's sacrifice.

After *Death in Venice* Ben did write one or two works, including the Third String Quartet, and I remember him wondering whether they were any good in their more bald style. Needless to say, they represented a masterly late flowering.

SALZBURG

My first visit to the Salzburg Festival came courtesy of the London Symphony Orchestra. It was the first British orchestra to be invited to provide a residency at the Festival, with five concerts stretched over four weeks, usually the preserve of the Vienna Philharmonic. Although it was economically ruinous for the orchestra, the publicity and prestige, and the fact that it gave the players a month-long break, compensated.

My arts page editor suggested that I too should go for the full four weeks. It gave me something like a holiday, and there was the compensation that the *Guardian* would not have to pay for my return flight. I had never gone to the Festival before: being conscious of the *Guardian* operating on a tight budget, I felt able to accept invitations for events abroad only when the air flights were provided as a 'freebie'. Needless to say, my concern for the *Guardian* budget was never appreciated.

I have already described the thrill of the rehearsal for the first concert, to be conducted by Karl Böhm, in the section I have written about him. The other concerts were all a success, but I was surprised that at the time André Previn, who as principal conductor of the LSO conducted the last concert, was then little known to the Salzburg audience, something that over the years was fully rectified. His appearances with the Vienna Philharmonic, notably in Mozart piano concertos directing from the keyboard, soon became favourite events in Austria.

In the three years of concerts with the LSO, the conductors ranged wide, with Böhm appearing more than the once, and others including Leonard Bernstein, Lorin Maazel, Claudio Abbado and others. I had no plans to go to the 1978 Festival until I discovered that the Chicago Symphony Orchestra would be visiting the Festival. The conductor was Georg Solti and the principal work in their second concert, on 31 August (along with Tchaikovsky's *Pathétique* Symphony), was to be the Fourth Symphony of Michael Tippett, which he had written specially for Solti and the orchestra.

The Decca Company, which was about to issue the new Tippett work on disc, invited me to go to the Festival, which very gratefully I did, the only time I have attended the end of the Festival rather than one of the early weeks. The Tippett work was a great success, an imaginative survey of human life, starting and ending with breathing sounds, and with the stages of life represented in a sequence of linked movements.

It was great fun being in Salzburg with the Decca team, including the principal recording manager, Ray Minshull, relaxed in a way I had never seen him before. Having been to the Festival four times, I decided that if I stayed in a modest hotel – which my friend Elizabeth Mortimer found for me – I could justify it to the paper. Elizabeth is a British journalist living in Salzburg; she was working in the Festival press office in 1977, and has become a dear friend.

One of the most controversial periods at the Festival, one that I greatly enjoyed, was when the iconoclastic Gerard Mortier was Intendant. The musical establishment of Vienna as well as Salzburg did not take kindly to a figure so little concerned for tradition, though he himself used to claim that he was trying to revive the spirit that dictated the earliest years of the Festival in the 1920s under the great producer Max Reinhardt as Intendant, with Richard Strauss as a leading figure. After one especially vigorous attack in the Austrian press, Mortier answered by buying flowers for a shop that was displaying the hostile review prominently in its window. He gave them real flowers instead of the plastic flowers they already had, saying that the Festival deserved better than plastic.

I came to feel that Salzburg was my other home, and I never missed a year, until I became disabled, and could no longer get to the Festival by air conveniently, even with a friend to help. Reluctantly, I had to give up. But Salzburg over the years was a wonderful place to be in; for many years almost every important figure in the world of music would be there, if they were free, as well as almost all my friends in the principal recording companies. The *Treffpunkt* of Deutsche Grammophon was a compulsory meeting place every morning, always offering entertainment and refreshment. In the end the recession in the record industry forced a more stringent control of funds, which prevented such extravagant publicity, but EMI on a more modest scale continued much longer to provide a more intimate, exclusive *Treffpunkt*, which I greatly enjoyed attending.

I have already mentioned my meetings each year with such friends in music as Walter Legge and Riccardo Muti, and over the years there were many more. Salzburg for a period each summer became the world capital of music, which was a source of great enjoyment for me. Most important of all, of course, was the music-making, and it would be invidious to pick out more than a few salient occasions. Each year the Assumption Day concert by Karajan and the Vienna Philharmonic was a high spot, usually offering a major choral work such as the Brahms or Verdi *Requiem*s. Yet the most memorable Assumption Day concert for me was in 1987, when Karajan offered a programme of Wagner.

Amazingly the works lasted together barely an hour, the *Tannhäuser* Overture, the *Siegfried Idyll* and, after the interval, the Prelude and *Liebestod* from *Tristan und Isolde*. In Karajan's hands this programme emerged as a synthesis of all Wagner's early work as well as the *Ring* and *Tristan*, and one emerged at the end as though one had been to an intense religious service, which on Assumption Day was only appropriate. The soloist in Isolde's *Liebestod* was Jessye Norman, who cannot have been amused when Karajan insisted on her staying through the purely orchestral rehearsals, not just the rehearsal for the *Liebestod*. She paid him back by striding on to the stage each time, when he could only hobble a long way behind her.

Other great occasions included the first European performances of Messiaen's epic opera, *Saint François d'Assise*, in which during the long interval I went to sit quietly by the river, and also the premiere of Luciano Berio's opera *Un re in ascolto* in 1981. The following morning I saw Berio at a reception in the Grosses Festspielhaus and congratulated him. I had earlier met him when he was supervising the recording of various works of his at the Abbey Road studios, adding to my congratulations a flippant remark about the cool reception of the rather stuffy Salzburg audience. Could it be, I suggested, that they found it hard to take seriously a composer who looked like Peter Sellers? Berio took my remark in the spirit intended, and came back brilliantly with 'Don't you mean Woody Allen?' Not many composers would be willing to joke about their own appearance like that.

BAYREUTH

The first time I visited the Bayreuth Festival, it was in the celebration year of 1976, the hundredth year after its foundation by Wagner. As this self-obsessed composer intended, it was the ideal place to sample his music dramas, and so it remains. The year 1976 was when radically the conductor of the *Ring* cycle was Pierre Boulez, and the stage direction was by the young Patrice Chéreau. This was long before the fashion for 'concept productions' became so prevalent, and I for one was horrified when the curtain went up on *Rheingold* to reveal the Rhinemaidens as prostitutes dancing about a hydro-electric scheme on the Rhine.

The productions of each of the music dramas in the tetralogy were just as radical, with Wotan's abode in Act II of *Die Walküre* a Second Empire salon, in which a friend suggested Wotan should have parked his spear in an umbrella stand. Each instalment of the cycle was greeted with vociferous booing, in which I enthusiastically joined, most vigorously at the end of *Rheingold*. Yet the wonder was, when this production was shown on television with every scene in close-up, it was most moving, for Chéreau had concentrated on getting relationships vividly illustrated, his great gift, while the distracting sets were seen only as a background. Having close-up shots of the singers truly helped to bring the production's qualities home.

That first year of 1976 brought the opening of Wahnfried, Wagner's house, as a museum. It had been ruined by a direct hit from a bomb during the war, and the West German government had generously spent a large sum of money on its renovation. Winifred Wagner, the composer's Welsh-born daughter-in-law, wife of Siegfried and a close friend of Hitler, was banned from attending, but watched from her house in the square. The audio cassettes of the Solti *Ring* had just appeared, which meant that I could play them each morning of the performance to prepare myself for the live occasion. I liked to claim that I was the first critic to take his own performance of the *Ring* with him to Bayreuth.

It was not until my second visit that I developed the habit that transformed my enjoyment of the Festival. During the hour-long intervals I would climb the hill behind the Festspielhaus and sit on a conveniently placed seat, drinking a generous draft and studying the act to come, enjoying the view meanwhile. I would then come down from the hill in good time for the next act. Each of the music dramas was designed to end at or near 10 p.m., which left me good time to have a meal in the pub where I stayed.

One of my happiest visits came in 1988, when I celebrated my sixtieth birthday during the *Ring* cycle, specifically with my favourite *Ring* opera, *Siegfried*, on the actual day. As no one else in Bayreuth knew it was my birthday, I decided to be totally selfish. After ritual playing of parts of *Siegfried* on cassette, I visited Wahnfried, and then went round the local Woolworths store, buying myself little presents. Then, after a light lunch, I went up the *Grüner Hügel* for the performance and, as ever, had my meditation and drink in each interval. I cannot remember any birthday I have enjoyed quite so much.

GLYNDEBOURNE

My first visit to Glyndebourne came in 1955. As a determined left-winger I greatly disapproved of any such elitist event, but it took me less than an hour to change my opinion totally. Though inevitably for many in the audience it is more of a social than a musical event, for the real Glyndebourne enthusiast, the Festival is about the enjoyment of music in ideal surroundings, as conceived by John Christie. It was of course a brilliant inspiration of his in 1934 when he founded the Festival, to insist that patrons wore evening dress, and had to take trouble before attending the opera.

That first year I saw Rossini's French opera, *Le Comte Ory*, then a rarity, and loved every moment in a classic production, so full of fun as well as wonderful music-making. The cast under Vittorio Gui was a classic one, recorded by EMI within a month of so of my visit. My visit the following year came on an invitation from John Christie himself, when he asked me to sit in his box for a double-bill of Mozart's *Der Schauspieldirektor* (*The Impresario*) and Strauss's *Ariadne auf Naxos*. Indeed, one quickly gathered that Christie had his own views and refused to depart from them.

A month or so earlier I had heard Joan Sutherland for the first time, and sought to impress on Christie that at Covent Garden she had been an even finer Pamina in *Zauberflöte* than his choice of Pilar Lorengar. He would hear nothing of it, even though that year as Madame Herz in Mozart's *Der Schauspieldirektor* Sutherland was singing like an angel, and deserved to be used in a bigger part.

The oddity of ladies and gentlemen in evening dress boarding a train at Victoria mid-afternoon was something to which the world became accustomed. On my first couple of visits I ate in the restaurant, but quickly abandoned that extravagant course, realising that it was much more fun picnicking on the lawn, where you were not dependent on the vagaries of waiters in the restaurant, so that often you did not finish your meal before the bells were ringing to signal that next act.

The whole of the table on my first visit was filled with American visitors, and one, more dominant than the rest, held sway, boasting, 'This year my theme in Europe is music festivals. Last year it was picture galleries. Tell me, what is your theme?' The poor woman so addressed was totally nonplussed, for plainly she had not thought of having a theme at all, just of enjoying herself. It is capped in my experiences of American tourists only by the memory when I was just leaving the Sistine Chapel, still shattered by the experience. An American, whose feet were plainly agonising her, was saying, 'Churches, churches, churches, it's nothing but churches.' I only hope that Michelangelo's ceiling silenced her doubts.

The number of great performances I have seen at Glyndebourne is far too many to mention, and I have already described some of them in talking about such artists as Janet Baker, Hugues Cuénod and Bernard Haitink. I suppose if I had to choose an occasion surpassing all others, it would have to be Peter Hall's inspired production of Cavalli's once neglected opera *La Calisto*. It was done with Raymond Leppard conducting in a version that he had devised himself, totally inauthentic in its use of a lavish orchestra, and in adding two ravishing arias taken from other operas for the goddess Diana, a role perfectly tailored for Janet Baker.

Peter Hall late on in the rehearsals suggested that Janet should play the role not just of the chaste Diana – obsessed with love of Endimion – but also the role of the predatory Jupiter dressed as Diana but still wearing a sword. One knew from Janet's acting instantly whether she was the lovelorn Diana or the swaggering Jupiter dressed as Diana.

Great events at Glyndebourne over the years have included the fiftieth anniversary performance of *Figaro* in 1984, with fireworks and champagne afterwards, the last performance given in the old opera house, like a glorified village hall, with an acoustic so dry that Philip Hope-Wallace described it as 'like being shut up with a bumble-bee in a matchbox'. None the less it held many nostalgic memories for me, and one wondered what the new opera theatre would be like.

Happily, it was a triumph, and the opening of the new house was another great event; we realised its success was rather on a par with the opening of the Maltings at Snape. George Christie, son of the founder, John, had wonderful luck in his demanding project to build a totally new opera theatre. When he started on the building programme, it was during a period of recession, so consequently all the builders he approached wanted the work and quoted him relatively low figures. Then, when the building was completed, the recession was over, and audiences were only too eager to come to the new Glyndebourne.

During the building work, critics and many others were invited down to Glyndebourne to monitor the progress on the work, a fascinating exercise. Many of us were worried that the fly-tower over the stage was left with its metal exterior showing, where brick cladding would have been more attractive. George Christie then explained that the extra weight of brick made that course impossible. Curiously, what threatened to be an eyesore has come to seem only natural in the finished building. Incidentally, at the time of the opening, Mary Christie, George's wife, in a witty speech said how nice it was at last not to live in a semi-detached, as the original theatre was joined up with the main house, unlike the new one.

One of the great figures of the old Glyndebourne was Helen O'Neill, long-time press officer for the opera house, and a great character, who was brilliant in fending off the many journalists who wanted free tickets without really deserving them. For those who really did write about the place, she could not have been more helpful, providing facilities for those who had tight deadlines to write their reviews, fortunately not a requirement any longer. Helen's successor, Jo Townsend, was a marvellous PR too. Latterly, Jules Crocker, house manager, is also typical of devoted Glyndebourne helpers. Whenever my friend Paul and I have arrived late because of the traffic, she has been an ever helpful angel, much appreciated.

THE PROMS

Quite the most memorable of my early visits to the Proms came when I was still at university, long before I was a critic. With my cousin I went to a programme that included Walton's First Symphony, a favourite work of mine and an integral feature of every Proms season at that time, conducted by the likes of Malcolm Sargent, Basil Cameron and the composer himself. At the end of this performance, Walton took his bows from the box where he was sitting. That happened to be just behind where we were placed in the stalls at the Royal Albert Hall, which encouraged us to go and wait outside the door of his box. A friend of Walton's pushed his way in, and I followed, bearing the miniature score of the symphony, which I asked Walton to sign. I gave him my propelling pencil to use, and ever after that I kept it as a sort of sacred object, not to be touched by anyone else. Needless to say, William was much amused when I told him many years later, having got to know him as a friend.

It would be impossible to pick out particular occasions from all the hundreds of Proms I have attended over the years. I have already mentioned such historic occasions as Rostropovich's performance of the Dvořák Cello Concerto on the day Soviet troops entered Prague in 1968, and such events as the Last Night when I was sitting next to Harry Birtwistle, and they performed his Prom commission, his Saxophone Concerto, *Panic* – even by Birtwistle standards an abrasive work – an occasion that was widely regarded (wrongly, in my view) as a fiasco.

There were many other Last Nights of the Proms that were memorable for me. One of the most striking came when Walton's *Belshazzar's Feast* was on the programme, on 14 September 1974, and William attended, a moment of triumph for him, celebrated with copious champagne. Also the time when Malcolm Sargent, following surgery and only a few weeks from death, addressed the Prom audience for the last time at the Last Night of 1966, a most moving occasion. He confirmed he had been asked to perform at the First Night the following year, but we all sensed that that was most unlikely to happen.

The different conductors who acted as masters of ceremonies have had very varied success, but none was more successful than Andrew Davis, whose virtuoso performance of the traditional Last Night speech was so much more skilled than the many that were simply boring lists of people to thank, mercifully a tradition now in abeyance. The Proms seem to gather strength with the years, and rightly the BBC likes to claim the event as the greatest music festival in the world.

GARSINGTON FESTIVAL

Even against strong competition my favourite among summer music festivals in Britain is the Opera Festival founded in 1989 at his country house near Oxford, Garsington Manor, by Leonard Ingrams and his wife Rosalind. As a wealthy retired banker, Ingrams, who had been financial adviser to the Saudi Arabian government, decided to indulge his passion for opera rather as John Christie did at Glyndebourne in 1934, and there are many likenesses between the Garsington Opera Festival and the vintage Glyndebourne of the 1930s, not least in the freshness of performances by excellent casts of mainly young singers, many of whom have become international stars, having made their first important appearances at Garsington.

With Lady Ottoline Morrell – wife of the industrialist owner Philip Morrell, a onetime Liberal MP – as chatelaine, Garsington Manor in the 1920s became the centre for a cult group of writers, including the Bloomsbury Group on the one hand – Lytton Strachey, E. M. Forster, the artist Duncan Grant and the economist John Maynard Keynes among others – but extending to Bertrand Russell, D. H. Lawrence and Aldous Huxley. Garsington was used to starry gatherings, and Ingrams's founding his opera festival in 1989 nicely fitted that tradition.

From the start Ingrams was inspired in his choice of conductors, using orchestras made up mainly of string-players from the London colleges and key wind-players from fully professional orchestras. A regular contributor has been Elgar Howarth, specialist in twentieth-century works, not least Strauss. David Parry has also been a regular conductor, and a link was established with the Sir Peter Moores Foundation, which has regularly sponsored productions, as have important banks and other institutions, close contacts of Ingrams in his City days.

Ingrams always limited his season to three operas performed over a mere four weeks in June and July. In most of the early years a Mozart opera was included, usually conducted by Steuart Bedford, and frequently there was a Strauss opera too, conducted by Elgar Howarth. One of the most magical moments I remember from Garsington, was when Strauss's rare opera *Daphne* was presented. The final scene has the heroine turned into a tree by Jupiter. At Garsington that took place just as dusk was falling, for unlike Glyndebourne and most other summer festivals, Garsington had no permanent theatre, and instead there was a large covered grandstand-like auditorium, with rows of seats sharply raked looking over the stable block of the original manor, with three arches on a natural stage and access from three sides: through the arches, from the house on the left and from the garden on the right.

In *Figaro,* for example, it was fascinating to see characters arriving through the shrubbery in the garden before they appeared on stage. From the start Ingrams employed top directors and designers, and the most successful productions have generally been those that rely on the main arches, though many have devised scenery to put in front of it. Yet whatever the degree of modernity represented in these productions, they have almost always had great impact, monitored by Ingrams himself.

Sadly, Leonard Ingrams himself died suddenly, just before the 2005 Festival. His widow continued the Festival under the stewardship of Anthony Whitworth-Jones, previously at Glyndebourne, with standards superbly maintained, but in time she stipulated that she no longer wanted to share the house with the opera festival, so another venue had to be sought, as from 2011. I have not yet been able to visit the new home of Garsington Opera – an award-winning, purpose-built Opera Pavilion in a beautiful deer park on the Wormsley estate in the Chiltern Hills, overlooking a lake, close to Paul Getty's famous cricket ground. It sounds magical, but I do find it hard to imagine anywhere remotely as suitable as Garsington itself, with its hilly grounds, its lake surrounded by statues, a place ideally suited to picnicking; though, as at Glyndebourne, there were also a restaurant and champagne bar.

The friendliness of Garsington is another point to emphasise, very different from some rival festivals, and supervising the ideal press arrangements was the brilliant Clare Adams, who has established a tradition very like that of the vintage Glyndebourne. One just hopes that in its new form, with Douglas Boyd providing leadership now, it can succeed in retaining its charm as well as its artistic integrity.

Interlude 7: 'Geordie' Armstrong

During my period in the Press Gallery, as the *Guardian*'s second political correspondent, I was an enthusiastic member of the Press Gallery luncheon club, which invited eminent visitors to speak off the record. The rule was that no reports should be written as a result of the talks, but I had fallen foul of the committee when I once revealed that a Rhodesian leader had visited the club. Although I didn't report what he said as such, the content of my diary paragraph was such that people could guess what it had been.

That was counted an infringement of the rules and I was banned from the club for a period. In the end the committee relented and I was allowed back, but I was then saddled with the most tricky job they could devise. We took it in turns to chair the club meetings, and the committee wanted me to chair the meeting that was to be addressed by the then Home Secretary, Henry Brooke. He was by far the most unpopular and controversial member of the government, having sent to prison two journalists for their refusal to give information about their sources. I had my own reasons for wanting to 'get at' Brooke.

I had first heard about John 'Geordie' Armstrong from my friend Jeff Chandler. He had got to know him when he was in the naval hospital in Haslar near Portsmouth. Geordie had been a sick-berth attendant, and when Jeff read about Geordie being found guilty in a notorious murder trial, he got in touch with him in Wormwood Scrubs. He used to visit him and, after a bit, I went over as well, as even with my limited legal training I felt I might help in his constant attempts to get a review of his case.

I immediately liked Geordie, his Northern plain-spokenness, and I was shocked when I heard the details of his case. His wife had been having trouble sleeping, so Geordie illicitly brought home some sleeping tablets from the pharmacy in the hospital. He urged his wife to be cautious about using them, but she, not being particularly bright, very foolishly gave one to their baby, who was constantly crying in the night. The baby died, and both husband and wife were arraigned on the charge of murder.

The wife, being young and beautiful, made a direct appeal to the jury, while Geordie had no such advantage. Against all probability, Geordie was the one found guilty, while the wife was acquitted. I remember my Law tutor at Cambridge, Cecil Turner, ridiculing the decision, even though he was just observing from the outside. Naturally, Geordie felt he had good grounds to get a review of the case, but one Home Secretary after another had refused, as had the government law officers. That was where I began to take an interest in the case, and decided to help Geordie as far as I could in his attempts to get an appeal. This Press Gallery lunch would afford me an ideal opportunity.

Half my colleagues in the Press Gallery said they would never talk to me again if I insulted Henry, while the other half said they would never talk to me again if I didn't attack him. In the event I solved the dilemma by attacking the Home Office, and you can imagine with what feeling I did so, with Geordie's case in mind. At the lunch I was sitting next to Henry's wife, Barbara Brooke, who would in due course become a member of the House of Lords, to be followed in due course by her husband and then her son, the former cabinet minister Peter Brooke. She understood at once the intensity of the feelings that had prompted my speech. I told her about the case, and she urged me to contact her husband directly, which I did.

It is a tribute to Henry Brooke, generally counted an inefficient Home Secretary, that he tackled Geordie's case with such thoroughness. His private secretary was a record collector, and knew my writing on records in the *Guardian*, very kindly informing me of background details of what was happening in the Home Secretary's office. He emphasised to me that Henry had kept the file for Geordie's case in his office for six months, but then he summoned me to meet him, and explained his thinking.

He felt he could not grant a reprieve, but he promised to do what he could to free Geordie after the shortest time appropriate to murder, then nine years. The time went by, and indeed the timing for Geordie's release did finally come up. In the meantime he had been allowed weekends off, which he spent with Jeff Chandler's family. There he met the social worker who had been charged with the duty of looking after Geordie's surviving daughter. Geordie while still in prison had been given custody of the daughter, over the claims of his estranged and now divorced wife.

Geordie and Helen, the social worker, fell in love, and the next we knew they were going to get married in the nearest church to Wormwood Scrubs. I shall never forget the ceremony, when Jeff and I were the only two on Geordie's side of the church. Helen's family might well have had reservations, for they were solidly middle class in contrast with Geordie, whom one might describe as a blue-collar worker, but they were stoically supportive.

It is good to put a happy ending to the story, for Geordie and Helen were a happy couple over more than forty years. Helen proved to be a wonderful wife, always attentive to Geordie's illnesses. He finally died of emphysema. Over the years I had kept in Christmas-card touch with them, and would occasionally see them when I visited the Aldeburgh Festival, as they lived close by. My happiest memory of all came when, early one morning, I drove over to Wormwood Scrubs to collect Geordie at the very end of his sentence. I collected him as planned, and we went back to my flat and had a champagne breakfast, something which in joy I counted a triumph.

Chapter Eight

The World of Recordings

Even today, in the world of 'streaming', it is through recordings that most of us come to know the great artists of the present as well as the past; and also how we most easily expand our appreciation of the vast musical repertoire that exists. Many of the great characters of the world of the recording are in every respect a match for their colleagues who sing, play or wave batons.

BRIAN COUZENS

The great achievement of Brian Couzens was to found the Chandos label, arguably the greatest of the independents, after the big international companies had curtailed their serious recording programmes. His projects were mostly major orchestral and operatic recordings, including the complete Walton Edition, covering every single note that William Walton composed. He also had an exclusive contract with Richard Hickox, who became one of the most successful recording conductors of all, thanks largely to the freedom he had to conduct the widest range of recordings for Chandos, notably of British music. The Chandos label also had a close relationship with the musical benefactor Peter Moores, over such projects as the Opera in English series.

Brian began his musical career an arranger of other people's music, notably of film music. He became one of the most skilled of orchestrators in the music business, and was much valued for

that. His arrangements covered not only serious classical composers but middle-of-the-road composers with their light music.
That was until he began working for the RCA label, when he
acted as recording manager for a number of their releases, notably
those with Alexander Gibson and the Royal Scottish National
Orchestra.

That led in turn to the founding of the Chandos label in 1978,
when Brian acquired the rights to reissuing many of the recordings he had made for RCA. It must have helped him that he had
had early experience of selling in the family department store in
Southend-on-Sea, as he began to build up an impressive catalogue
of recordings, mostly orchestral, always with the help of sponsors. It
was in that role that he took on the complete recording of William
Walton's music, when the project had been turned down by EMI,
and gave Hickox an exclusive contract when major labels no longer
wished to work with him.

The Chandos label became celebrated for the quality of
sound in its recordings, notable for its warmth and richness, as
Brian has an acute ear, as does his son, Ralph, his aide in monitoring
the recordings. It was an important role taken on by Chandos to
fill in the gaps not only in rare repertory, but also to do so by using
artists who had been undeservedly neglected by the major companies.
These included Neeme Järvi – later contracted by DG – and the
violinist Lydia Mordkovitch, whom Brian 'discovered' on a visit
to Israel.

His sense of enterprise never deserted him. Latterly he has
encouraged Chandos to take on the function of the downloading
of recordings, not just of those issued by Chandos but those of
other companies too, including the multifarious recordings issued
on the budget label Naxos. That has helped Chandos to remain
financially viable, even at a difficult time for the recording
industry, when new technical developments have hit it during a financial squeeze.

TED PERRY

I first got to know Ted (Edward) Perry when he was an assistant in the EMG shop in Newman Street, just off Oxford Street in London. He was by far the most knowledgeable assistant in a record shop that I have ever known, and EMG was the most demanding shop in London, a shop with management so confident of their judgment that they would stock only those recordings they considered to be suitable for their customers. I revered their judgement until I started reviewing, when I quickly realised that while the discs they recommended were all excellent, they missed at least two-thirds of the first-rate issues on relatively trivial grounds.

When I started reviewing, I was not surprised when Ted became the press contact for the Deutsche Grammophon label at a time when it was first being marketed in Britain. He did that job admirably, but after a few years he decided with his then girlfriend, Doreen, who looked after the Philips label, to go to Australia. He soon returned, initially to work for the newly founded Saga label, the brainchild of an eccentric American, Marcel Rodd. That led in turn to Ted founding his own label, which sadly he was cheated out of by his partners.

The big moment came when, with financial help drummed up by Doreen, whom he had since married, he founded the Hyperion label. It seemed at once that he had a magic touch, and Hyperion soon developed a reputation for issuing superfine discs, notably of rare chamber music, which consistently struck a sympathetic note among critics, for most of the music was of material that critics themselves wanted to have in their collections.

Hyperion's success continued through each development in the record industry, notably the introduction of the CD, when the LP issues were quickly issued in the new format. One of their biggest successes came with the issue of a disc with the title *A Feather on the Breath of God*, featuring the singer Emma Kirkby as the soloist. It offered magical performances of medieval choral music by a woman composer, until then very little known, Abbess Hildegard of Bingen. Amazingly, that became one of Hyperion's bestsellers, and such series as their recordings of great Romantic piano concertos attracted a surprisingly wide range of support, along with recordings of early music in period performances, notably of Purcell.

Sadly, Ted died relatively young, and his funeral had a record number of mourners attending the crematorium. He was succeeded by his son, Simon, who might not have the depth of knowledge of his father, but who has continued the success of the Hyperion label, with the help and support of knowledgeable assistants.

NUMA LIBIN

Numa Libin, who called himself Count Labinsky, was an eccentric who had an obsession over the quality of recorded sound. That led him, with the help of the two Reynolds brothers, Gerald and Michael – who had inherited a fortune – to found the Nimbus label. For years he refused to accept the arrival of the CD, but when he did, he had his assistants set up the first manufacturing plant for CDs in Britain, a tremendous achievement for a small company. They relied on the know-how of a scientific boffin, Jonathan Halliday, a delightful, very quiet man and a remarkable genius who devised a new system of encoding a digital message.

Originally Numa met Michael, one of the Reynolds brothers and his future business partner, by chance on a train, and they immediately became good friends. Numa was quickly aware that his friend had enough money to finance the sort of project that he had in mind, and he first made carefully prepared recordings in small premises in Birmingham.

I first heard about this mysterious project from the tenor Hugues Cuénod, who had studied with Ninon Vallin, allegedly the same singing teacher as Numa. I learned soon enough much more about

Nimbus, for within a year or so, thanks to Numa's enterprise and his ability to raise money, the company had moved to a country house at Wyastone Leys in the Wye Valley on the borders of England and Wales, where he helped to set up a close community dedicated to the art of recording.

At Wyastone Leys they had enough room to have their own studio and made recordings, initially using a single-microphone technique, which had some strange balances when orchestras were used. They took a delight in recording great artists who at the time were neglected by the big companies, artists such as Shura Cherkassky, Youra Guller and Vlado Perlemuter among pianists, and the violinist Oscar Shumsky. Numa was soon joined by his assistant Adrian Farmer, who in due course became managing director of the company.

They also recorded the Birmingham-based English Symphony Orchestra under its conductor, William Boughton, and the period performance group, the Hanover Band, founded by Roy Goodman. The recordings they made included the first period-instrument recording of Beethoven's *Missa solemnis*, recorded in the Banqueting Hall on Whitehall in London, an excellent version.

A section of the company was devoted to renovating ancient, historic 78 recordings on the Prima Voce label, notably of singers of whom Numa approved. They drew on the expertise of Norman White, who had a vast collection of ancient vocal 78s. Numa's idea of transferring ancient 78s to CD was to play the originals on the best possible equipment, an EMG horn gramophone, in a room with a sympathetic acoustic, and record the results. In effect this meant that there was a filter of the top frequencies, but amazingly many of the results were astonishingly lifelike with voices in particular often vividly caught, though instruments were less well treated.

Numa had such strong views on the art of singing that he started to make recordings of himself performing, not just simple songs but the greatest and most demanding of all song-cycles, Schubert's

Winterreise, which he recorded both in German and English, using the name Shura Gehrman. I suspect that that could have been his real name. Sadly, Numa did not have the voice quality for such exposure, however carefully nurtured his vocal technique was. Frankly most of his recordings are an embarrassment, however well intentioned the singer. He claimed to having been a pupil of the legendary French singer Ninon Vallin, sometimes adding the equally legendary figure Germaine Lubin for good measure, though every claim made by Numa was suspect.

I remember going to visit them at Wyastone Leys just after Christmas one year, which I had spent at the home of my doctor friend, Michael Heath. Realising that he was a doctor, Numa quietly questioned him closely about the supply of drugs, and Michael quickly realised that he had some sort of addiction. That meant he would disappear for days to a cottage in the grounds.

On that Christmas visit we were exceptionally allowed to visit the inner sanctum, where, in pride of place, there was a beautiful Russian icon, which Numa claimed was a family heirloom. He also claimed it was worth several million pounds, and that he had smuggled it out of Switzerland in a Marks and Spencer bag, which he thought would be less suspect than if he had tried to conceal it more elaborately or inventively. Just what the truth was is anyone's guess.

On one of my visits to Wyastone Leys, I remember saying to Adrian how disappointed I was not to see Numa, but then after lunch he said that Numa was ready to see me. I was taken upstairs to a darkened room where Numa lay on a chaise longue, doing an imitation of Violetta dying in *La traviata*. I gave Numa some hearty words of encouragement, and Adrian then said how moved he had been by what I said, although I had spoken half with my tongue in my cheek.

That was typical of the community at Wyastone Leys, and it says much for Numa's enterprise that, after his death, the company continued successfully in its highly individual way, initially relying on producing CDs for a variety of companies, but regularly pursuing its own individual enterprises too.

MARCEL RODD

The arrival of the LP was a revolutionary development in the record industry, but for some years all the discs were at what was then full price. It was the inspiration of Marcel Rodd, an American living in Britain, to found Classics Club, offering discs for a fraction of what they normally cost. He then set up a record label, Saga, offering discs at similar prices. I was deputed by the *Guardian* to investigate this new phenomenon of bargain LPs, and was at first disconcerted that Classics Club had no published phone number.

I decided that the only course was to go to their published address in North Kensington, which I did. I was warmly welcomed in, as Marcel had just been attempting to get the record critic of the *Observer* to go to his factory and office, which despite its tiny size managed to include a pressing plant to manufacture the discs. When I met Marcel he was full of appreciation, explaining that he had sent a Rolls-Royce 'chauffeured by a peeress of the realm' to fetch the *Observer* critic, but he had refused to come. By contrast he complimented me on my enterprise in finding him and his factory. 'That's journalism!' he kept exclaiming.

I got to know Marcel quite well over the following period. He was a shrewd businessman, who cut his costs to the bone, not least on the pay for his staff. He also wrote a newsletter for members of Classics Club, pretending it was written by a glamorous girl, of whom he had got a series of photos, spicing up the chummy editorials he had written himself.

More particularly, he invented names for the various East European orchestras on his discs and of orchestras whose discs he had pirated, and of some of the artists too. One of his conductors he dubbed 'Havaguess', making it obvious enough that it was a pseudonym. I also met a pianist who in a pub one day heard a disc of a rare piece, which, as he thought, he alone had recorded. He even recognised his own interpretation, and asked the publican what the disc was. To his surprise it was credited to an invented pianist, for Marcel had illegally pirated a disc that was in copyright. What made Marcel Rodd the more engaging was that he was so obviously a bit of a rogue, but in his American way he cared not at all. He once invited me to his snug flat off the Bayswater Road, and that was just as odd as one might have expected, a bachelor flat even though he was married with wife and family.

KLAUS HEYMANN

Klaus Heymann, based in Hong Kong, had the inspiration to realise that a label dedicated to issuing discs at super-bargain prices would be much appreciated, which is how he launched the Naxos label. Originally, Naxos discs were sold exclusively in Woolworths, which meant that no critic took them seriously, and they were not sent out for review. Happily, my cousin, Bill Hall, bought a number from a cycle of the Beethoven piano sonatas played by a Hungarian pianist of whom few had heard, Jenő Jandó.

I quickly realised that these recordings were remarkably fine, offering performances that were refreshingly direct and straightforward. I then used my record column in the *Guardian* to write about Naxos, and I am flattered that Klaus Heymann attributes the early expansion of the company to what I wrote. Very soon Naxos discs were distributed generally, until the catalogue expanded astonishingly wide.

What is particularly remarkable is that Naxos covers not just the central repertory, but also some of the most abstruse areas, and the company has made a point of issuing whole cycles of works – for example, the symphonies of Charles Villiers Stanford, not to mention rare baroque works and works by the little-known contemporaries of Mozart and Beethoven. One began to wonder where the expansion would end, but so far with a company policy of making recordings with relatively little-known artists of high quality and with imaginative ideas for increasing the repertory, the expansion goes on. As the traditional recording companies have reduced their activities, the names working with Naxos have grown bigger and bigger and, increasingly, the company's releases stand shoulder to shoulder with anything else on the market.

Naxos has also made a point of reissuing discs originally published by labels that have become defunct – for example, the English song series originally issued on the Collins label. Another fruitful source of new recordings has been the opera recordings made – usually live – in venues such as the opera house in Stockholm. The wonder is that the documentation with Naxos issues is regularly more comprehensive and helpful than that of the big companies. Although complete texts are rarely provided, the opera summaries are always first rate, and for those who are so minded the complete texts can usually be found online.

PETER ANDRY

If you had asked Peter Andry what his favourite was among all the many hundreds of records he has been responsible for over more than thirty years at EMI, he would have opted for a classic Beecham recording of the 1950s, the coupling of the Mozart Clarinet and Bassoon Concertos with two members of Beecham's 'royal family', Jack Brymer and Gwydion Brooke. Ask Andry what recording he was proudest to have set up, and he would mention first the version of Beethoven's Triple Concerto with the astonishing line-up of three top Soviet artists – Sviatoslav Richter, David Oistrakh and

Mstislav Rostropovich – as soloists alongside Karajan and the Berlin Philharmonic.

It was with that record that Andry lured Karajan back to the EMI label after the company had earlier lost him to DG. In 1965 Andry got the three musicians to Berlin for the three sessions needed, but Karajan failed to turn up for the first one. Even when Karajan arrived for the second session, he first wanted the orchestra to be turned around, giving the engineers ten minutes to do it. Yet the finished result made for a classic recording.

Andry retired from EMI in 1989, having after more than thirty years become president of the International Classical Division, one of the great diplomats of the record industry. His special gift was to chair meetings, and to reach a consensus between different interests. Over much of his time he was chairman of the International Classical Recording Committee, set up to monitor the different projects of the various sections of the company. It was the setting up of that committee under the direction of the company's chairman, Joseph Lockwood, that had directly led to Walter Legge leaving the company, not wanting his wings to be clipped.

Andry was born and brought up in Australia. Among his earliest memories as a child in Melbourne was trying to find out where in the family's wind-up gramophone the man singing was hidden. He later trained as a flautist, at both Melbourne Conservatorium and also Melbourne University, meeting some of the artists with whom he later worked at EMI, among them Menuhin and Klemperer, when he was playing in the Melbourne Symphony Orchestra.

He also wanted to be a conductor, and in 1953 he won a British Council bursary to study in London. He then studied conducting under Walter Goehr and counterpoint under William Lloyd Webber, father of Andrew and Julian. To make some money he played in the orchestra of the International Ballet, and when the company was disbanded, its conductor, Jimmy Walker, suggested that Andry should join him in a new job with the production team at Decca.

That threw Andry into the recording world at the deep end and, in 1956, when the Mozart bicentenary was being celebrated, he went to Vienna as assistant to Victor Olof, the Decca recording manager, to record four Mozart operas in four weeks, an astonishing schedule. They achieved it, and it says much for their efforts that two of the four have long been counted classic versions: *Figaro* under Erich Kleiber and *Don Giovanni* under Josef Krips. That the team in addition produced stereo versions, then still at an experimental stage, also says much for the skill of the Decca engineers.

When Olof left Decca for EMI, Andry went with him, and among his earliest projects was Menuhin's first LP recording of the six Bach partitas and sonatas. He soon had his first contact with Thomas Beecham too, and was an assistant in his recording of Haydn's oratorio *The Seasons*, a performance that glows with Beecham magic. Beecham could be a disconcerting recording artist, as he liked to have a number of projects on hand simultaneously. He could then choose which one to take up at a session, just as the mood took him.

Olof left EMI in 1962 and, under the chairmanship of David Bicknell, Peter Andry became responsible for HMV projects, just as Walter Legge was for the Columbia label. When Legge resigned from EMI in 1964 and tried to disband the Philharmonia Orchestra, which he had founded in 1945, Andry took over several of his projects, including important ones with Klemperer, such as Mozart's *Die Zauberflöte* and Handel's *Messiah*. He went on to record many times with Klemperer, including a version of Wagner's *Fliegende Holländer*, which threatened to come unstuck when the role of Erik was sung by the tenor Ernst Kozub, a flawed artist who had almost undermined the Decca *Ring* cycle with Solti. Yet Andry's calm brought project after project to a successful conclusion.

Andry also had his problems with Karajan, not least over the first stereo recording of Wagner's *Die Meistersinger*, for Karajan left the recording of the overture to the very end, having refused earlier to specify dates for the session involved. It was when the East German associate company, VEB, threatened to get Karl Böhm instead, that Karajan agreed and, as with so many Karajan projects, flying by the seat of his pants produced vivid results.

When Andry retired from EMI, he then had an astonishingly difficult job to do for the newly founded Warner Classics company, a subsidiary of the film company. His task was to bring together and co-ordinate the work of the Warner Company in Britain, Erato in France and Nonesuch in the United States. Against the odds he did this very successfully, even though troubles in the record industry have presented extra problems since. It made a fitting finale to his career.

JOHN CULSHAW

John Culshaw came to be regarded as the counterpart at Decca of Walter Legge at EMI. His great achievement was to mastermind the historic recording of Wagner's *Ring* cycle by Georg Solti. At the time it was claimed to be the first stereo *Ring* cycle but, as we now know, the same Decca engineers had in 1951 recorded a *Ring* cycle live at Bayreuth, which has widely been acclaimed as even finer than Solti's, the one under Josef Keilberth now finally issued on the admirable Testament label.

The Solti *Ring* by contrast was recorded in the studio, the favour-ite venue of Decca, the Sofiensaal in Vienna. Culshaw's direction was superb, and generally, unlike Legge, he wanted above all to present brilliant recordings in brilliant sound. He also had the gift of holding together a first-rate engineering team, though the Decca team had been substantially created before Culshaw took over as the senior Decca recording manager.

As an engaging writer himself, he has left a vivid account of his frequent struggles with parsimonious management to bring his vision about. His successor, Ray Minshull, has suggested that this account is not always strictly accurate, but that hardly detracts from

Culshaw's achievement, not just in presenting Solti's *Ring* cycle, but also in supervising many other projects, not least the many recordings of Benjamin Britten, which became a central monument of the Decca catalogue.

Culshaw had learned the art of managing recording sessions when he was working for the newly formed Capitol label, where he produced some outstanding recordings. He then came over to Decca, and his career took off. That was a vintage period for the company and, with the help of the Decca press officer, Jack Boyce, who had a genius for getting publicity for each project, his achievements were consistently highlighted, helped by the highly readable books he published periodically. It was sad for Decca, but a fine achievement for the BBC, when he turned from the record world, and began his career in similarly promoting music programmes on television, in which he was helped by the contacts he had made while at Decca, notably with the circle around Benjamin Britten and Aldeburgh. Sadly, he died prematurely.

RAY MINSHULL

Ray Minshull was senior recording producer for Decca for a far longer period than John Culshaw, but it was always his moan that he never had any credit for that achievement, which included a formidable list of opera recordings, for which he generally delegated responsibility to the operatic specialist in his team, Christopher Raeburn.

Unlike Culshaw, Minshull was relatively diffident in pushing the claims of his recordings, which included a series of coups with such artists as the pianist Vladimir Ashkenazy and the conductor Charles Dutoit, who made a dazzling series of recordings with his Montreal Symphony Orchestra in a venue, St Eustache, some distance out of the city, which had taken the Decca engineers, notably James Lock, several years to find.

Minshull was very gifted in achieving his aims with the minimum of fuss, whether it was in struggles over budgets with the management or in handling temperamental artists. It is in good measure due to Minshull that such artists as Solti, Ashkenazy and Joan Sutherland remained totally loyal to Decca, when most artists moved from one label to another. It is sad that he himself felt so bitterly that he was not appreciated, but the verdict of posterity should certainly develop in his favour.

CHRISTOPHER RAEBURN

Christopher Raeburn was the most meticulous recording manager I ever saw at work. It was he who was responsible for supervising most of the recordings that Georg Solti made for Decca over the latter half of his career, notably the operas. Raeburn's whole career was spent in Decca and, with such engineers as James (Jimmy) Lock, he helped to create the brilliant Decca sound. As a musicologist himself, he would prepare each recording in the finest detail, and I remember when Solti was recording Strauss's epic opera *Die Frau ohne Schatten* in the Vienna Konzerthaus, he did what I always thought more recording managers should do, namely listened to the rival recording from EMI in company with Lock, to ensure that each section was going to outshine that formidable competition. So often I felt that recording producers took too little account of the competition.

Chris joined Decca in the days when John Culshaw was in charge of the label, and he progressed over the years, so that he developed close relationships with a number of artists such as Vladimir Ashkenazy, with whom he recorded the complete Beethoven and Mozart piano concertos. Yet with his special interest in singers and voices, opera was what he cared about most. He was responsible for Solti's opera recordings, from his first recording of Strauss's *Der Rosenkavalier* with Régine Crespin onwards, and one of the most spectacular recordings he made was of Puccini's *Turandot* with Zubin

Mehta conducting, with Pavarotti as Calaf as well as Joan Sutherland as the icy princess opposite Montserrat Caballé as Liù.

Such a concentration of stars meant that rivalry between some of them could lead to problems, but Raeburn was always the perfect diplomat, sorting things out. I remember when he was recording Wagner's *Lohengrin* in Vienna with Placido Domingo in the title role opposite Jessye Norman as Elsa, and the tensions were great, as Norman resented even the slightest criticism, while Domingo relished it, and responded to every suggestion made by Raeburn.

Chris was especially proud of having sponsored the early careers of various singers, notably of Cecilia Bartoli, who was just a shy teenager when she made her first recordings and needed encouragement, before she rapidly developed into a very positive, even wilful, artist. Chris would guide such a singer without ever getting in the way. He was also very diplomatic with even the most difficult conductors, and was recording manager for several of Karajan's Decca recordings, including Verdi's *Aida*, with its spectacular sound. Although he was never the senior producer at Decca, he was a pillar of the company's operatic programme, thanks to the skill of the senior producer, Ray Minshull, in handling his team of recording managers.

ANDREW RAEBURN

Chris Raeburn's younger brother, Andrew, was one of the most talented recording producers, working mainly for the small Argo company, until the conductor Erich Leinsdorf spotted his potential, and persuaded him to go to Boston as his personal assistant, not least on recordings – a role he performed brilliantly.

Sadly, he never returned from America to work in Britain, though he paid regular visits, generally staying with his cousin, the great film director John Schlesinger, director in Hollywood of the iconic film *Midnight Cowboy*. In the United States and Canada, Andrew had a whole sequence of jobs, and thanks to him I was invited to give lectures and take part generally in a piano festival that Andrew was organising in Calgary, Alberta. That October happened to be the coldest in living memory but Calgary was cleverly designed with a whole ring of buildings linked on the first floor: that meant that you did not always have to go out in the cold.

The festival itself was held at the local university, which could be reached on foot – a bracing walk before the events of the day. My main lecture, I remember, was on the contrast between Artur Schnabel and my own favourite, Wilhelm Kempff, in the concertos and sonatas of Beethoven. I am not sure how many of those present were convinced by my arguments, but it was a most stimulating occasion, involving concerts and recitals as well as lectures and discussions. Sadly, that was the last time I saw Andrew, but we spoke fairly regularly on the phone, and I treasure the many happy memories I have of him.

HARLEY USILL

Harley was a pioneer in setting up a small record company, which achieved spectacular results within sharply defined limits. He it was who sponsored on his Argo label recordings of King's College Choir in Cambridge, which were markedly more successful than anything we had heard before. They included recordings of the celebrated service of nine lessons and carols at Christmas.

Needless to say, there were those in the industry who wanted to get into this lucrative market, and EMI then proceeded to record at King's, and with the help of the recording producer Christopher Bishop and with talented engineers made a long sequence of recordings at King's, not just with David Willcocks, but also with his successors Philip Ledger and more recent choirmasters.

Meanwhile Harley Usill turned instead to recording the other Cambridge choir at St John's, which, under George Guest, was achieving results rivalling those of King's or any other collegiate church or cathedral. I well remember a session at St John's when they recorded Britten's *A Ceremony of Carols*. I was charmed when one of the youngest choristers asked George Guest whether he would like them to sing at that point 'with a touch of Continental tone', newly popular thanks to the example of George Malcolm at Westminster Cathedral.

Another speciality of Argo, thanks to Harley Usill, was speech recording, initially of poets such as T. S. Eliot but then monumentally in Shakespeare's plays with members of the Royal Shakespeare Company taking part anonymously. It seemed a dangerous venture, but in fact proved a great success when university libraries everywhere bought copies of each play. The series also proved popular throughout the world, helping to teach English to students of all nationalities, as the productions of each play were relatively slow moving, with words always exceptionally clear.

Argo also became known for its recordings of train noises on the Transacord label, founded at an earlier date. It was at the end of the period of steam locomotion, and noises of steam locomotives were recorded both on the footplate of the loco as well as from the line side, often very atmospherically. Harley was able at times to add apt musical accompaniment from discs in the Argo catalogue.

In the end the variable economics of the record industry forced Harley to seek the help of the Decca company under Edward Lewis. Happily, the arrangement left Harley fairly autonomous within the Decca group, working from his old office in South Kensington, and issuing new discs without too much interference from Decca House.

HAROLD LAWRENCE

Harold Lawrence was an inspired record producer for Mercury and other American record labels. He so impressed the management of the LSO, when working with them, that they asked him to come to

London permanently to be the orchestra's general manager. Harold was too kind-hearted a character to be good at handling a band of players who could often be difficult, but none the less, with his strong and characterful wife, Mary, he left an indelible impression on the music world of London before returning to his home in Oakland near San Francisco.

Harold was in charge of a number of LSO tours to the Salzburg Festival and other venues, but in the end he was pushed out. Before that Mary had set herself a major project. She wanted to find a rehearsal venue for one or more of the independent London orchestras. She made a thorough search, not least of newly redundant churches being sold off by the Church of England. The one she lighted upon was in a backwater of South London, Trinity Church, set in Trinity Church Square close to Tower Bridge, nicely cut off from major traffic noise. Despite mountainous difficulties Mary finally succeeded in her efforts, and everyone connected with the project would be warned when the phone rang, and the message came: 'Mary Lawrence here.' Finally, her persistence paid off, and the LSO got a lease on this Regency period church, which in due course was named Henry Wood Hall, after the founder of the Proms.

That finally happened long after Harold and Mary had returned to the United States, but many of us remember the struggle there was not just to get the lease but also to obtain the planning permission required to adapt a church that was a listed building. That meant it could not be changed without the relevant authorities approving of the plans. Yet in the end all the problems were sorted out, and the money obtained to do the necessary renovations and adaptations, with superb results. It meant that the LSO and the LPO not only had a venue for rehearsing, but could let it out for recording sessions, for its acoustic proved very suitable for that purpose. Concerts were also held there, with a fair degree of profit obtained for the always cash-strapped orchestras. Happily many of us remember the ground work that Mary Lawrence had tirelessly put in.

PETER ALWARD

Peter Alward spent the whole of his career in the record industry working for EMI. It was his mother who noticed an advertisement for a job at EMI when after university Peter was wondering what to do. He applied and, after being interviewed by the alcoholic boss of the Cataloguing Division, was duly hired. Happily, that was in a room next to the International Classical Promotions section, and so he got to know John Whittle, the Head of the Department, and his assistant, Douglas Pudney.

Peter mentioned to them that if ever there was a chance of a job in that department, he would love to be considered. In due course such a job did come up, which then meant that for some time he was the dogsbody in the department, going to record shops and the like, and simply making himself useful. It was only when one evening at Covent Garden he met up with Peter Andry, president of the International Classical Division, that he had the chance to ask to be considered for a job.

One great asset Peter has is that with a German mother he is bilingual, which meant that Andry saw how useful he could be in relating to the German half of the company, Electrola. For a time he was based in Cologne, later in Munich, as well as in London, building up useful connections, for Peter has always been gifted in making contacts, a useful quality in such an international company as EMI.

On another level he became very friendly with Herbert von Karajan, who liked the idea of an Englishman fluent in German. That was so, even though Karajan at the time was making most of his recordings for the rival company of Deutsche Grammophon. There is the story of a DG executive in Salzburg waiting for the great man to arrive, and then who should appear first out of the car, not Karajan but Peter Alward, representative of the rival company.

Peter has always defended Karajan from any charge of anti-Semitism. As he says, being half Jewish himself, he would have had no patience at all with such an attitude, and would have been acutely conscious of anything even hinting at it. The fact is, his contacts with Karajan were a great help to his company. Similarly, the conductor Wolfgang Sawallisch invited Peter to join him for dinner with his friend the then Archbishop of Salzburg, Cardinal Ratzinger, later translated to be Pope Benedict XVI. That was because Ratzinger was a great music-lover, and Peter was able to discuss music and recordings with him, as he wanted.

Peter decided to retire early from EMI, having become vice-president of the International Classical Division, though his decision was widely regretted. Since then he has had the enviable role of being a freewheeling operator in the music world, something that as a man still relatively young he greatly enjoys.

STEWART BROWN

Stewart Brown trained to be a professional clarinettist, but sad events in his family, when his father and brother died in quick succession, forced him to take control of the family building firm instead. Still hankering after some connection with his career as a musician, he decided to promote a disc of historic recordings by his favourite clarinettist of the past, Frederick Thurston, who was sadly under-represented in recordings.

He issued it on his own Testament label, and having promoted one disc he went on to many more. One of the first to make a big impact was the pioneer recording of Elgar's oratorio *The Dream of Gerontius*, with Malcolm Sargent conducting the Liverpool Philharmonic and Huddersfield Choral Society. It was issued in 1945 just as the war was ending, and had been out of the catalogue for many years.

Stewart coupled it with another historic recording, the first really complete account of Elgar's *Sea Pictures,* with Gladys Ripley as soloist, another issue originally on EMI. Stewart obtained permission to reissue it in a two-CD package, and the quality of the transfers, made by EMI technicians, alerted us to the arrival of an important label dedicated to issuing transfers of the highest quality of historic recordings.

Backed by the family firm, he became ever more adventurous, and his catalogue of issues expanded impressively, not least when he secured rights to issue for the first time what in effect was the very first recording of Wagner's *Ring* cycle made in stereo. When Decca issued the *Ring* conducted by Georg Solti, it was advertised as the first version in stereo, but in fact it was the second.

An almost identical team of Decca engineers had recorded the *Ring* live at the 1951 Bayreuth Festival, the first season after the war. The legendary engineer 'Wilkie' Wilkinson was in charge, and secured astonishingly fine and vivid sound, in some ways even finer than the spectacular studio recordings for the Solti *Ring*, with the conductor Josef Keilberth directing a performance of the highest-voltage electricity. This had been recorded by Decca, but put on the shelf when John Culshaw masterminded the Solti *Ring*.

That was an understandable decision, but one that deprived the public from ever hearing what in many ways is the greatest *Ring* cycle recording ever. There had also been copyright problems when it was recorded, for some singers were contracted to record companies other than EMI.

Boldly, Stewart Brown cut through all the problems, and gave to the world in vivid sound this historic live recording. It was an instant success, but it is some measure of the problems that Stewart had to face, that in Germany the members of the latest Bayreuth Festival Orchestra – many of whom had not been born at the time of the recording – tried to claim copyright in it, and wanted royalties from Stewart.

It was a formidable – and expensive – task fighting the case in the often perverse German courts, but Stewart fortunately managed to win through in the end: it is symptomatic of the thorny challenges that adventurous record company executives have to face when reissuing ancient historic recordings on disc. Stewart followed the *Ring* recording with a whole series taken from broadcasts of opera, notably in Germany, as well as BBC broadcasts of fine performances, often with artists who had not made studio recordings of the same works, making the Testament label one of the most important issuing historic reissues, a great achievement. In all this he has been loyally supported by his wife, Sarah, daughter of the great contralto Monica Sinclair.

MIKE DUTTON

When a record company executive loses his job, it is rarely a beneficial development for the individual involved, but it was for Mike Dutton, after he was pushed out most unfairly from EMI, having done masterly transfers of all of Elgar's electrical recordings of his own music. Mike then immediately founded his own label, and has prospered ever since, going from strength to strength in promoting not only superb transfers but also completely new recordings on the Dutton Epoch label, notably of rare British works.

Mike is full of adventurous ideas, and has been responsible for some of the best CD transfers ever made, helped by his subtle ear, very concerned for balance of high and low, loud and soft, experimenting with each recording so as to produce the finest possible sound. He has also found a profitable market doing CD transfers of dance bands from the 1930s, a source of welcome nostalgia for many collectors.

Mike got into the business of sound recording in a severely practical way. In the 1970s he provided music for his school's theatrical productions, mainly of operettas, and in helping the staging he learned to use not just the projectors and primitive video recorders but other equipment too. He was employed in a shop where he was able to learn about electronics, then worked for Rediffusion as a TV engineer, though the apprenticeship scheme was quickly dropped. He also went to work in a Dixons shop in Wembley as a salesman. A friend there told him of a studio in Willesden that was looking for a tea-boy, Morgan Studios. They asked him whether he was mad, and whether he liked music, quite apart from making tea. They liked his enthusiasm and gave him the job.

There were four studios owned by the firm, which meant that Mike would switch from one to another. As he says, 'I remember hearing Sir John Betjeman, the arranger Jim Parker and the New Philharmonia in Morgan One. Then you'd have Bonnie Tyler singing 'Lost in France' in another studio and a heavy metal band in another, so I got experience of this huge range of music. We'd be doing a rhythm section in the morning, strings and brass in the afternoon, and then vocals and mixing. It meant that records were turned around very quickly.'

As he says, it was a fantastic training ground. His senior colleague was a fine teacher too, teaching Mike all he needed to know about recording orchestras live: 'How to mike the drums, the woodwind, the strings, how to control everything. Never trust anyone to do it for you.' He became involved with Andrew Lloyd Webber, which meant that he produced a lot of show records, including *Cats*. He worked for five years in the theatre on productions of shows, but still felt he wanted to get into what really fascinated him, sound recording.

A friend who had been in Morgan Studios then invited him to be an assistant lining up tape machines and the like. He was attached to the Pye Company, then called PRT, and found an enormous library of early Pye discs. That was the beginning of Mike's devotion to transferring early LPs to CD, and he got some excellent results with Barbirolli's recordings with the Hallé on that label, including some of the first bargain issues of historic recordings, among them Holst's *The Planets* and Vaughan Williams's *London* and Eighth Symphonies.

When Pye went bankrupt, its classical catalogue was sold to EMI. Mike was entrusted with sorting out the catalogue, and listing what was there. That is how he 'wiggled his way' into EMI, an important development in his career. EMI decided to carry on the work of transferring Pye LPs to CD on the Phoenix label, which meant that Mike carried on what he had already started with PRT. He did not like the cartridge that EMI favoured, and managed to do some transfers with an Ortofon moving-coil pickup, which brought a marked improvement, and it was then that Mike took over the important job of transferring Elgar's own recordings to CD, with great success, until the management decided he had spent too much money on the project, costing things out in a strange way. He lost his job, and founded his own label, Dutton Laboratories.

That was in 1973, and he decided from the start to concentrate on remastering 78s, following on his work for EMI. He acquired rights to the Cedar process of 'de-noising' without losing the top frequencies, and after buying a new turntable, did some remastering on such recordings as the Barbirolli *Planets* (again), the Moeran Symphony conducted by Leslie Heward and several Beecham discs of overtures. Nowadays with a limit on the number of classical reissues he can sell at around 500, he finds one of the most fruitful areas for expansion is in the middle repertory, such things as Mantovani records and Decca's Phase Four series, but he still does bring out some classical reissues.

Since he founded the Dutton Epoch label, making completely new recordings of mainly rare British works, two of the most important issues so far have been of Elgar works never previously recorded. He recorded the cantata *The Spirit of England* as Elgar originally conceived it, with three soloists instead of two. Elgar did sanction the idea of having only two soloists, with the soprano and mezzo songs sung by the same singer, which naturally promoters have preferred on the grounds of cost, but Dutton has three soloists, as first conceived.

He also recorded a reconstruction of Elgar's Piano Concerto, made from the composer's sketches by the pianist David Owen Norris, who also played the solo in the recording with the BBC

Concert Orchestra under David Lloyd-Jones. It may not be a great work, certainly no match for the inspired reconstruction of Elgar's Third Symphony made by Anthony Payne, but to add to the value of the disc it also contains, among other items, a first recording of a *Lament*, which commemorated the death of Queen Alexandra, widow of Edward VII.

SIR PETER MOORES

Peter Moores is among the most generous benefactors of the arts, particularly music, in Britain. He has contributed some £35 million to various projects, which cover a very wide range. Having inherited a fortune from his father, the founder of the football pools firm of Littlewoods, he has used his wealth in an extraordinarily constructive way over many years. The family quarrels over the various areas of the Littlewoods fortune have completely passed him by, as he effectively sealed off his side of the inheritance to pursue his own individual projects.

Not only has he helped young singers whom he admires in their early years, when they need it most – he can instance Joan Sutherland and Geraint Evans among many others – he has latterly financed a great range of recordings. His own special interest is opera in English, which has led him to sponsor a series of over fifty recordings, mainly complete operas, with outstanding British casts, when the regular record companies tend to avoid such projects, conscious of the need to get as wide an international market as possible, promoting opera recordings in the original languages. That has allowed him to build casts that include a number of the performers who have received the award he regularly gives to young singers, and though none has yet matched the eminence of Joan Sutherland, they make an impressive list.

His other special project is the *Opera Rara* series, founded and brilliantly developed by his lifelong friend, Patrick Schmid, whose knowledge of rare operatic repertory, particularly from the early nineteenth century, was astonishing. Sadly Patrick died prematurely, having suffered from Parkinson's disease in a particularly virulent form. Not that Patrick's death deterred Peter, who continued the series in his friend's memory with brilliant results, and with documentation second to none in its scholarly detail.

Another side of Peter's work as benefactor was his purchase of a country house and estate, Compton Verney, for which he bought art treasures, as well as furnishing it lavishly, making it a place for the public to enjoy, a project that is an ongoing expense for him. Just what he will devise next is anyone's guess, but with outstanding assistants in his London office, as well as in his own country estate in Lancashire, he is unlikely ever to rest on his laurels.

ANNA INSTONE AND JULIAN HERBAGE

One of the great figures of the BBC was Anna Instone, head of Recorded Music Programmes. With her husband, the scholarly Julian Herbage, she produced *Music Magazine*, very much a traditional BBC programme, which for years was heard not on the specialist Third Programme, but on what was then called the Home Service, latterly Radio 4. In those days before 'ad-libbing' became the rule, we would set up the programme on a Saturday morning, and have a preliminary run-through. We would then return early on Sunday morning for a second run-through, after which Anna would allow her 'boys' time to have coffee in the canteen seven or eight floors above, before finally we would do our broadcast live. By more recent standards this was over-preparation, but it was very much the rule.

In rehearsal Anna would repeatedly correct me with: 'You're getting on your soapbox again!' I felt it was rather unfair when others were manifestly less fluent. That was until I realised that she was taking the trouble to make me a good broadcaster, for which I was eternally grateful.

Anna, surprisingly given that we thought of her as such a *grande dame*, had been a very adventurous figure in her younger days at the end of the 1920s. Her father had founded Instone Airlines, which in due course became a constituent part of Imperial Airways, one of the predecessors of British Airways. She got in the papers, it seems, by one day flying over to Brussels for lunch, going on to Paris for *thé dansant*, before returning to London (via Croydon airport) for dancing at the Savoy in the evening – a thing of wonder at the time.

As a renowned musicologist, Julian Herbage had prepared an edition of Handel's *Messiah*, which Adrian Boult favoured in his recordings. His soprano in his last one was Joan Sutherland, who used cadenzas for her arias prepared by her husband, Richard Bonynge, a specialist in early nineteenth-century opera, rather different from those by Handel. When Herbage in the control room heard what he regarded as anachronistic cadenzas, he rushed down to the main hall, only to find each time that he was too late, for Sir Adrian, always a quick worker, had already started the music again. Each time Herbage had to retreat in frustration, but a year or so later, when Sutherland's contributions to the set were issued separately, he dubbed the resulting disc 'famous mad scenes from the *Messiah*', one of the few instances when Herbage was credited with a joke.

Even before Anna asked me to broadcast on *Music Magazine*, John Lade chose me as one of the first contributors to *Record Review*, which has latterly evolved into *CD Review*. My very first broadcast was a comparison between the rival versions of Puccini's *Madama Butterfly*, of which in those days of mono recording there were only three, with Renata Tebaldi, Maria Callas and Victoria de los Angeles as the rival divas. I emphatically chose Victoria de los Angeles, ravishingly beautiful and tender. Before long after that John came to regard me as a stalwart of the programme, as year after year I would contribute repeatedly.

Most memorably I did a comparison of the rival versions of Tchaikovsky's *Pathétique* Symphony, No. 6. In my script, as usual broadcast live, I had the phrase 'Kletzki's fluctuations', but unfortunately I fluffed the first word, and to make matters worse, I stopped after the first syllable and became the first broadcaster to use that four-letter word on Radio 3. Believe it or not, we received not a single complaint, so obviously was it a natural 'fluff'.

VALENTINE BRITTEN

Valentine Britten, like Anna Instone, was a traditional BBC executive in the Reithian mould. She was head of the BBC Music Library, with her office across the road as a sign of superiority. One mark of her traditionalist approach was that she always wore a hat, even when working in her own office. The first time I went to see Valentine I was advised that it was always a good idea to praise her hat, which was very easy, as indeed they were always striking in a tasteful way.

Valentine and I immediately became good friends, and we loved to have a gossip about various colleagues, discreetly of course. A conversation with Valentine was always tremendous fun, though I got the idea that with her underlings she was nowhere near so relaxed. One happy memory involved a recital that John Lade was giving at a 'recording conference' on the clavichord. Just as John was effortfully about to start playing, Valentine whispered to me that the clavichord case looked like 'a coffin for a smoked salmon', not the wittiest remark but one that was a delight at a solemn moment. Sadly, Valentine, like everyone in the BBC, had to retire at the age of sixty. As a devout Catholic she arranged to go and look after the shop attached to Prinknash Abbey. It seems the monks were less appreciative of her than the BBC had been; the last I heard of her was that she had quickly resigned.

HANS KELLER

Hans Keller was the most formidable producer in the BBC Music Department. He was lucky to escape from Nazi-occupied Vienna soon after *Kristallnacht*, arriving in England when still in his late teens. Though he had no academic qualifications – Jews were prevented from going to university – he was one of the most scholarly figures I have ever known, and one who was naturally combative. In Radio 3 producers' conferences, he would regularly pursue arcane and involved arguments, above all with his fellow Jew and noted academic Lionel Salter.

I was fond of them both, and felt flattered that they seemed to approve of my work, both in print and in broadcasts. One of Hans' remarkable qualities was that his enthusiasms knew no bounds. He would argue and give lectures as readily on Gershwin, whom he greatly revered, as on Mozart or Britten, and besides music another of his great enthusiasms was soccer, on which he wrote in similarly scholarly language. That led to his becoming known as Hans Killer, a regular figure in *Private Eye*, a wonderful compliment. In due course he would be credited with talking about the 'twelve-tone football jersey'.

No one was more amusing, and at the same time challenging, in discussions over a beer in one of the pubs near Broadcasting House, something I greatly enjoyed whenever I had the time. Hans was very happily married to a talented artist, Milein Cosman, who specialised in line drawings of musicians at work, notably conductors. They made the perfect Hampstead couple.

Sadly, soon after he retired from the BBC Hans contracted motor neurone disease, the cruellest of blows. I last saw him when Milein brought him to view a TV film about Mahler that Leonard

Bernstein presented. Hans greatly approved, and when I next saw Lenny, he was delighted to have such an endorsement about his ideas on Mahler and his Jewishness.

It was at around that time that I received the last of the many postcards Hans sent me. He had heard one of my World Service broadcasts in the middle of the night, being an insomniac. It was on the Musikverein, the great hall of the Vienna Philharmonic. I had incorrectly pronounced the word, accenting the first syllable, where Hans rightly printed out the word for me with the accent on the second syllable, 'sik'. It was a sign of my regard for Hans that I felt flattered he thought it worthwhile to correct me.

IVAN MARCH

It was when I was still working for the *Guardian* in the Parliamentary Lobby that I received a letter out of the blue from Ivan March, founder and proprietor of the Long-Playing Record Library in Blackpool. He was proposing to start a *Stereo Record Guide*, covering what was new in a rapidly expanding field. He had read my weekly reviews in the *Guardian* and knew I would be an apt collaborator for him.

After one or two hiccups the first *Stereo Record Guide* appeared under Ivan's own LPRL imprint. He was endlessly inventive and also presented a series of three March Festivals at the Norbreck Hydro just north of Blackpool, and very successful they were, with many different figures in the record industry brought together for a series of lectures, demonstrations and reminiscences, which were widely enjoyed. Sadly, after three years the record companies withdrew their support, and the March Festival was no more.

Meanwhile the *Stereo Record Guide* was flourishing, as was as a guide to bargain issues, which had become increasingly important. It was then that the big Penguin publishing company took a hand:

after one or two *Bargain Guides* from LPRL they decided to publish the *Stereo Record Guide*, which became the *Penguin Guide*. That has continued to the present day under different guises, the best guide to CDs and videos in various formats, despite significant competition. Ivan and I were joined initially by Denis Stevens for a few years, and later by Robert Layton, making a lasting trio with never any argument between us. Now in the age of e-books we still hope to continue, helped latterly by Paul Westcott.

TONY POLLARD

No one in the record industry has had a keener sense of duty than Tony (A. C.) Pollard, onetime publisher and proprietor of *Gramophone* magazine, until it was sold to Michael Heseltine's Haymarket Publications. The wonder is that Tony has no claims to being a musician, though his knowledge of the industry is second to none, as is his assessment of artists and discs. Tony inherited the firm from his father, who was the accountant to Compton Mackenzie, who founded the *Gramophone* in 1922, but sold it during one of his periods of financial instability.

Tony's background was in army service (hence his sense of duty) and it was not an easy transition for him into the record world. Yet he did it triumphantly well and everyone he came across has always respected his knowledge and flair. I have myself always been loyal to *Gramophone*, despite temptations from rival organisations. I was glad to help Tony when, after much thought, he decided to found the *Gramophone* Awards. I had had fair experience of the vagaries of voting in relation to discs as a founder member of the International Record Award (IRCA), started in Montreux, and, drawing on that experience, supported Tony in devising a scheme that attempted from the outset to eliminate most of the potential problems for such an undertaking.

We also retained the freedom to modify the structure year by year from practical experience, a process that still continues. So far as I am aware, neither Tony Pollard nor his son Chris, who took over from him, has had any direct contact with the Awards since they sold the firm, but they remain shrewd observers. I count it one of my proudest accolades that in 1993, a year before receiving my OBE, I was given a *Gramophone* Award myself, 'for special achievement'. I hope I deserved it.

Envoi

At the beginning of this book I referred to the notable speech that Benjamin Britten gave when accepting the first Aspen Award in 1964. In that address, Britten vigorously lamented the fact that the ready availability of recordings meant that even such a masterpiece as Bach's *St Matthew Passion,* written originally to be performed only on one specific day in the calendar, namely the culmination of the year for the Christian Church, could now be heard at a whim and, consequently, at the most inappropriate times, even during one's daily chores.

That, he felt with some justice, was an insult to Bach and his original intentions:

> It is one of the unhappiest results of the march of science and commerce that this unique work, at the turn of a switch, is at the mercy of any loud roomful of cocktail drinkers – to be listened to or switched off at will, without ceremony or occasion.

Since that time, recordings have proliferated many times over, to such an extent that almost any extant performance can now be discovered in some recorded form, almost anywhere. It isn't just recorded music that has burgeoned, but publishing and writing of every kind has too, whether in newspapers, books or online, on a scale never previously conceived. The dangers have grown proportionately, which makes Britten's warning ever more relevant. Yet there is an upside to all this, and it is up to the individual to use all the new opportunities wisely and constructively.

I am therefore optimistic enough to feel that this is the message for the future: as the new forms of communication, whether in music or publishing, become ever more ingrained and potent in all our lives, they can offer a magnificent enrichment of human existence, a message of hope rather than of pessimism. I sincerely hope so.

Acknowledgements

My thanks to: Elizabeth Francis-Jones, for all her help in compiling this memoir; Michael McManus, for his help in editing the text; David Pearce, for his photographs; and Jeffrey Spedding, for his paintings (www.jeffreyspedding.moonfruit.com).

Index